The On-Demand Brand

10 Rules for Digital Marketing Success in an Anytime, Everywhere World

RICK MATHIESON

AMACOM AMERICAN MANAGEMENT ASSOCIATION
New York • Atlanta • Brussels • Chicago • Mexico City • San Francisco
Shanghai • Tokyo • Toronto • Washington, D.C.

Bulk discounts available. For details visit:
www.amacombooks.org/go/specialsales
Or contact special sales:
Phone: 800-250-5308
Email: specialsls@amanet.org
View all the AMACOM titles at: www.amacombooks.org

This publication is designed to provide accurate and authoritative information in regard to the subject matter covered. It is sold with the understanding that the publisher is not engaged in rendering legal, accounting, or other professional service. If legal advice or other expert assistance is required, the services of a competent professional person should be sought.

All brand names and trademarks used herein are the property of their respective owners.

The BURGER KING® trademarks and advertisements are used with permission from Burger King Corporation.

Library of Congress Cataloging-in-Publication Data

Mathieson, Rick.
The on-demand brand : 10 rules for digital marketing success in an anytime, everywhere world / Rick Mathieson.
    p. cm.
Includes bibliographical references and index.
ISBN-13: 978-0-8144-1572-6
ISBN-10: 0-8144-1572-5
1. Branding (Marketing) 2. Internet marketing. I. Title.
HF5415.1255.M38 2010
658.8'27—dc22

                                                                    2009040693

About AMA
American Management Association (www.amanet.org) is a world leader in talent development, advancing the skills of individuals to drive business success. Our mission is to support the goals of individuals and organizations through a complete range of products and services, including classroom and virtual seminars, webcasts, webinars, podcasts, conferences, corporate and government solutions, business books and research. AMA's approach to improving performance combines experiential learning—learning through doing—with opportunities for ongoing professional growth at every step of one's career journey.

Printing number
10 9 8 7 6 5 4 3 2 1

For J & K, as Always

CONTENTS

Introduction IX

RULE #1 Insight Comes Before Inspiration 1

Q&A: The Klauberg Manifesto. 21

RULE #2 Don't Repurpose, Reimagine 31

Q&A: Alex Bogusky Tells All. 51

RULE #3 Don't Just Join the Conversation—Spark It 59

Q&A: Virtually Amazing: Sibley Verbeck on
Building Brands in Second Life 2.0 81

RULE #4: There's No Business Without Show Business 89

Q&A: Adrian Si: Rewriting the Rules of
Branded Entertainment. 107

RULE #5: Want Control? Give It Away 113

Q&A: "Obama Girl" Makes Good: Ben Relles's Racy Videos
and the Democratization of Digital Media 127

RULE #6: It's Good to Play Games with Your Customers 135

Q&A: Mike Benson and the ABCs of Advergames. 151

RULE #7: Products Are the New Services 157

Q&A: Agent Provocateur: Goodby's Derek Robson
   on Reinventing the Ad Agency........................... 169

RULE #8: Mobile Is Where It's At 179

Q&A: BMW and Beyond: "Activating" Traditional
   Media through the Power of Mobile 199

RULE #9: Always Keep Surprises In-Store 207

Q&A: The Future of the In-Store Experience,
   from the Father of Social Retailing® 221

RULE #10: Use Smart Ads Wisely 231

Q&A: The Social Net—Privacy 2.0 251

Additional Resources.. 261

Notes 263

Acknowledgments 273

Index 275

About the Author 281

Call it the digital generation.

The websites are so twentieth-century generation.

The iPhone toting, Facebook-hopping, videogame-fragging, Twitter–tapping, I-want-what-I-want, when-where-and-how-I want-it generation.

By whatever name, today's marketers are desperate to connect with an ever-elusive, increasingly ad-resistant consumer republic.

And they're quickly discovering that the most powerful way to accomplish that is through blockbuster digital experiences that say goodbye to "new media," and hello to "now media."

Enter: The On-Demand Brand

INTRODUCTION

You can always blame it on Burger King.

It was, after all, nearly three decades ago that the "Home of the Whopper" first introduced a simple, seemingly innocuous notion into popular culture that would have profound and unexpected repercussions well into the twenty-first century.

As those around in the 1970s can tell you, consumers everywhere were told that, yes, they could "hold the pickles," or "hold the lettuce."

With a song and a smile, TV commercials featuring dancing cashiers reassured a previously unrecognized nation of anxious fast foodies that "Special orders don't upset us. All we ask is that you let us serve it your way. Have it your way—at Burger King."

Have it your way. A simple, refreshing, underheralded introduction to "mass customization," the technological capability to personalize any order, on demand.

Fast-forward to the present day, and you can see the workings of what has irresistibly and incontrovertibly become an on-demand economy. The medium that introduced us to that old-time fast food campaign couldn't be more different. Where once there were three broadcast television networks, there are now literally hundreds of TV channels, seemingly niche-programmed down to subsets of subsets of consumer tastes.

History buffs, homosexuals, gardeners, and gearheads all have their own TV networks. Programming is no longer a one-time-period-fits-all affair. Indeed, it is no longer a one-device-fits-all affair, either.

In what the television industry often refers to as 360-degree programming—the practice of making content available for consumption via any number of consumer devices—you can watch the latest episode of NBC-TV's *The Office* or MTV's *The City* either live or time-shifted on your TV screen, your computer screen, the screen of your mobile phone, your car's built-in entertainment center, or the monitor on the airline seatback. On your schedule. At your convenience. Always.

What's more, this content is no longer bound to what you view and hear, but how you interact with it, mold it, make it your own.

Today, you can take part in extended realities of your favorite shows—online games and experiences that expand upon the program's plotlines and characters so you can delve into backstories or divine the next major plot twist.

You can react to, or spoof, what you see on the Boob Tube via YouTube—creating and uploading your own video satires in record time.

You can comment on or even shape storylines by lobbying online among the show's community of interest—those who are passionately involved with the show and even those who produce or distribute it—via forums, blogs, and more.

You can even live *within* your favorite TV programs, through 3-D virtual worlds where you can hang out with characters and fans in environments replicated from the shows.

This media revolution has not occurred in a vacuum, of course. It has been enabled by technological advances that have come to define every facet of modern life.

Back in the antediluvian days of Burger King's "Have It Your Way" campaign, consumers who knew their bank tellers on a first-name basis looked on skeptically at the rollout of ominous, monolithic machines known as ATMs.

Today, these same consumers routinely and cavalierly check balances, make purchases, and place trades from home via their laptop computers or while on the go, via their iPhones and BlackBerrys.

The trip to the bookstore is often usurped by a quick click to Amazon.com. Business trips and vacations are arranged in moments, with nary a thought of calling one's travel agent (remember those?). And high-ticket items, from automobiles to real estate, are regularly searched, categorized, compared, and even purchased on the fly.

In just about every corner of society, "just a moment" isn't good enough anymore. Waiting for anything—cash, food, our favorite products and experience, dished up just the way we like them—simply will not stand.

Clearly, this revolution is having a seismic impact on every facet of how we work, learn, and play. But in an age of immediate, malleable, and very social real-time media, its most profound effects are on those seemingly least prepared for this changing world: marketers.

GOODBYE "NEW MEDIA," HELLO "NOW MEDIA"

Indeed, a generation of consumers weaned on Facebook, iPhones, TiVo, Twitter, chat rooms, and instant messaging has grown accustomed to living seamlessly and simultaneously on- and offline, accessing the people, content, services, and experiences they want—when, where, and how they want them—using whatever devices they have at hand.

In short, "now" is the new "new."

I've long referred to this phenomenon as "the Burger King Syndrome," the notion that in an increasingly fragmented, tech-driven media universe, the only rule that matters is as simple and powerful as those television commercials of yore: Have it your way—or no way at all.

Over the last few years, what was once a world of quaintly interactive Flash- and HTML-based "new media" web experiences has morphed into a digital universe that's highly personalizable, uniquely sharable, and eminently social—characterized by new applications and services that are driven by the so-called "Web 2.0" effect. Now, the web is no longer merely about content retrieval. It's about real-time content creation, participation, collaboration, and exhibition.

Amazon shoppers long ago moved from just buying books and videos to dissecting them—arguing their merits and debating their value with others—threatening to unseat professional movie, television, and music critics along the way. Likewise, those trips to iTunes are not complete without reading shopper reviews of everything from *The First Avenger: Captain America* to the latest album from Coldplay.

This "social web" is growing fast.

According to the Pew Internet & American Life Project, 35 percent of the adult Internet population in the United States actively uses social networking sites. Once logged on, updates to their personal "profile pages" are instantly broadcast to their far-flung family and friends' computers and mobile phones.[1]

Most are updates of the most banal variety—"I just had a burrito and I'm thinking about taking a nap"—or involve updates and results from a myriad of supremely irritating quizzes and games, from "What Does Jesus Think of You" to "FarmVille."

At this writing, over 1 billion people participate in social networking worldwide, with a growth rate of about 25 percent per year, according to comScore.[2] The growth rate in Europe is 35 percent; in the Middle East, it's 66 percent.

And then there's microblogging.

Nearly 8 million people[3] regularly use applications like Twitter, with which they send and receive "tweets," very short updates for "followers" about what the "twitterer" is doing at any given moment—homework, coming home from a date, or picking their noses—in 140 characters or less. Never mind that 60 percent of people stop using Twitter within a month of signing up,[4] at this writing anyway, it's a hyperbolic wonder.

For whatever reason, television news and talk show personalities seem especially enamored with sending an endless stream of updates to feed the cult of personality—a notion that went into overdrive when Oprah Winfrey began twittering, and when actor Ashton Kutcher became the first person to top 1 million Twitter followers, or "tweeps."

The content of these celebri-tweets tend to range from the solipsistic to the soporific. A missive from David Gregory, host of NBC's *Meet the Press*, for instance, might share with followers that he just finished rehearsing this week's show, and that he's thinking about having a bagel before airtime. A typical tweet from Oprah: "Worked out an hour. And now going to read the Sunday papers and have a skinny cow or 2!"

None of this is to say Twitter hasn't become an important tool for journalists, editors, writers, and others in the media industry who use it to stay on top of, or follow, news as it breaks—as evidenced by developments many first heard about via Twitter—from the death of pop star Michael Jackson to unrest over disputed presidential elections in Iran to the earthquake in Haiti.

Which brings us to that original form of microblogging—text messaging—which everyone from political activists to party-going teenagers to celebrity stalkers uses to organize collective actions ranging from staging protests to throwing raves.

Today, over 100 million Americans send and receive text messages on any given day—including 65 percent of all mobile subscribers under the age of thirty.[5] Indeed, if tweeting is the purview of celebrities, texting is the lingua franca of teen lifestyles. According to research firm comScore, just 11 percent of Twitter's users are between the ages of twelve and seventeen.[6] By contrast, over 83 percent of teens use text messaging.[7]

In the mobile space, this on-demand connectivity is taking new forms every day. Looking for instant access to new recipes? The latest sports scores? A digital musical instrument you can play with others around the world in real time? How about the best Mexican restaurant within a three-block radius, at least according to some 142 patrons who've recently eaten there? Today, it's safe to say that, yes, there's a mobile app for that.

And all of this is just for starters.

Thanks to an explosion of broadband accessibility in recent years, nearly 62 percent of all Internet users in the United States—some

184 million people—consume the kind of free or ad-supported online video to be found at Blip.tv, YouTube, or Hulu, or subscription-based services like Time-Warner Cable's TV Everywhere service. According to Pew, nearly 57 percent[8] of these viewers routinely send links to videos they've watched to others, creating a network multiplier effect that frequently produces viral hits. Just ask Susan Boyle, who rocketed to international fame after her spinster-turned-superstar appearance on *Britain's Got Talent*. Within nine days her performance of "I Dreamed A Dream" was viewed over 100 million times online.

Of course, some like to do more than just watch. According to Pew, nearly 15 percent of online consumers actually post their own "user-generated" videos to sites like YouTube, where they can be instantly shared with the 79 million people who have so far viewed some 3 billion videos there.

Meanwhile, nearly 4 million online Americans[9] regularly log onto virtual worlds like PlayStation Home, Second Life, There, and Vivaty. Once there, they select and customize "avatars"—cartoon representations of themselves—and proceed to make friends, buy real estate, open businesses, join clubs, attend art exhibitions, go swimming, or even fly—at whim or with the help of a handy jetpack—while jacked into virtual versions of their real-world selves from anywhere on Earth.

Today, these worlds increasingly work in reverse—in adventure games like JOYity, in which users run around real-world cities, from London to Helsinki to San Francisco, with an "augmented reality" game overlaying the physical world, and visible only by viewing the cityscape through a smart phone's camera screen.

Factor the $4.8 billion we spend on online games, from World of Warcraft to Tap-Tap Revenge,[10] the $11 billion a year we spend on console games like Guitar Hero, and the endless hours we spend on multiplayer casual games like Lexulous, and it's clear that instant, social gratification is here to stay.

In short, something cool, and truly profound, is happening in the on-demand economy. But for Madison Avenue, keeping up is hard to do.

IT'S *NOW*—OR NEVER

Whether your target audience is eighteen years old or eighty, traditional TV spots and even expansive online initiatives are no longer even remotely enough.

Websites? Bores-ville. Ad banners? Artifacts of a bygone era. Email blasts? What's email?

Today, your audience is simply and relentlessly rejecting media—and brand marketers—that fail to fit into their increasingly interconnected, digital lifestyles.

"You've got a youth market that's grown up in an almost completely digital world, and that is multitasking with more media," says Patrick Quinn, president and CEO of PQ Media. In addition to their consumption of TV and radio, today's consumers are playing more video games, communicating on their mobile phones more often, and involved in more activities outside the home.

"As a result, they have very different behaviors than the generation of consumers before them."

Unfortunately, many marketers and their ad agencies find it hard to negotiate this ever-shifting media landscape.

"There are a lot of advertising people who want to hang onto the past, want to hang onto thirty-second television commercials and full-color magazine ads, and I think it's very hard to catch up," says Tom Bedecarré, founder and CEO of hot digital agency AKQA. "It's hard to get used to the idea that you [need to] have software engineers and technology people as part of the creative team if you want to connect with what people are doing from their PCs, or their TVs, or their mobile phones."

Indeed, many are flummoxed by this reality.

"For a lot of advertising agencies, their perspective about interactive has been, 'Oh, well, we'll call it a "web film" and we'll run it online,'" says John Butler, cofounder and creative director for San Francisco–based ad agency Butler, Shine, Stern & Partners. "That's not what it's about. Building brands in the digital age comes down to a single word, and that word is 'experience.'"

So what are marketers to do? How do you create the kind of experiences needed to engage consumers in an increasingly fragmented media universe? How do you identify and capitalize on the right mix of digital channels and interactions that will build awareness and demand for your offerings—before your audience hits the snooze button?

While the pace of change accelerates, many marketers feel themselves falling behind. At one time or another, most have suffered the stress of having to maintain the pretense that they're hip to all things digital. And all are guilty, at least once, of fruitless attempts to capitalize on what's "cool" long after consumers have moved on.

Many just don't understand that it's not (merely) about tracking the latest technologies and trends. They lack the tools—the philosophical framework—to create the kind of experiences consumers want and demand in the digital era.

This book is designed to change all that.

Building the On-Demand Brand

This book is based on conversations I've had with hundreds of today's top marketers over the last few years, as well as on briefings I've conducted for executives from companies such as FedEx, Virgin America, Bloomingdales, MasterCard, Hard Rock Café, American Express, Yahoo, House of Blues, Allstate, Novartis, HP, and many others.

It is also as an extension of my blog, GENERATION WOW (genwow.com), which explores many issues facing marketers in the digital era, and includes frequent interviews with industry thought leaders on their own approaches to postmodern marketing.

This is not a book about technology. In an anytime, everywhere world, technologies change by the nanosecond—as do consumer tastes. And, as you'll see, it's impossible (and perhaps unnecessary) to keep up with every hot new digital happening.

Nor is this book about the hippest online companies. Though several will be discussed, just as in the first cycle of dotcom boom and bust, many Web 2.0 companies will no doubt fail in years (maybe months) to come—if they haven't already by the time you read these words.

Instead, this book is about an approach, a way of assessing consumer insights and then harnessing innovation to best capitalize on the major consumer digital trends of the next decade—the ones we recognize and deal with today, as well as the ones we haven't yet imagined.

This approach involves a core set of ten rules or principles for building on-demand brand experiences.

Some of these rules involve overall strategies, while others address the best ways to capitalize on specific tactics, channels, or platforms. As you'll see, the subjects of these rules are hardly discreet silos; rather, they represent a spectrum of approaches that, either on their own or combined with others, can make powerful contributions to integrated marketing communications initiatives.

While some of these rules seem rather contrarian—you won't find much in the way of breathless cheerleading here—I think you'll find most represent commonsense principles that we all know we should follow, but too often don't.

It's also important to note that these rules apply in both good times and bad.

With luck, you are reading these words in the comfort of a robust economy. But as I write them, the nation and the world are still dealing with the repercussions of the worst economic downturn in generations. These rules are meant to help you connect with consumers in powerful new ways, whether your efforts are aimed at general brand building or even the hardest of hard-sell tactics and promotions—which, ultimately, are still brand experiences—regardless of economic conditions. But be warned: Whatever your objective, these rules will be rendered useless if your brand doesn't produce compelling products that people want to buy—at prices they want to buy them for—and if you don't service those customers well.

Each chapter will look at one of the rules in depth, and how it has been applied in some of the most successful digital initiatives of the last decade—and what we can learn from them. I hope to deflate some of the hype around digital marketing in the process.

As you'll see, from Toyota and MasterCard, to Warner Brothers and McDonald's, to Coca-Cola and Kellogg's, many of today's top marketers are already moving beyond the first wave of viral video, social networking, user-generated content, and mobile marketing campaigns, and are now thinking much bigger, bolder, and far more bodaciously.

You'll discover how:

• Showtime, MasterCard, and NBC have literally redefined "viral video" with highly personalizable video content that astonishes those who experience it, while supercharging awareness and demand for their offerings.

• Burger King, Coca-Cola, Toyota, and AXE have hit pay dirt with "advergames"—and other forms of branded video games—that have directly and dramatically boosted sales of their products.

• Fanta, GE, Doritos, Papa John's, and Ray-Ban are leveraging the power of augmented reality to combine the virtual world and the physical world to create blockbuster branded experiences as never before possible.

• HP, Travelocity, and Yahoo are using a new generation of "smart advertising" technologies to target consumers based on age, gender, geographic location, online activities, past purchase behavior, and much, much more.

• BMW, Sears, Pizza Hut, and MLB use new mobile strategies and apps to redefine the notion of instant interaction between brand and consumer—while substantially improving the effectiveness of their print, broadcast, outdoor, and direct mail advertising.

- Jeep, Starbucks, Budweiser, and others use their own MySpace and Facebook pages to make friends and to promote their brands as lifestyles in and of themselves.

- Adidas, Lexus, and Chantix have recognized that products aren't just products anymore; they're services—delivered digitally and on-demand.

Along the way, we'll take time out for exclusive Q&A-style interviews with some of today's top marketers and industry luminaries—including Laura Klauberg, senior vice president, global media for Unilever; Alex Bogusky, cochairman of Crispin, Porter + Bogusky; Adrian Si, head of interactive marketing for Toyota's Scion brand; Mike Benson, executive vice president of marketing for ABC Entertainment; Derek Robson, managing partner of Goodby, Silverstein & Partners; and many others.

Each of them will share some of the lessons to be learned from their most successful digital initiatives, and some of the surprising ways they keep their organizations ahead of the pack.

As these industry innovators will demonstrate, "Have It Your Way" long ago transcended its fast food origins to become the promise and imperative of every company, in every category, that hopes to serve today's brand-fickle, want-it-now consumer.

"We have created an on-demand society that wants to control what they engage with," says Jeff Arbour, vice president of New Zealand–based digital agency Hyperfactory.

"Brands need to invest in direct sales efforts, but many of those messages are going to get lost in the other five thousand advertisements that a consumer is bombarded with on a daily basis," he says,

"Thus the importance of creating branded experiences that induce an emotional connection."

Indeed, by 2012, marketers are expected to spend over $61 billion a year on digital platforms to create that connection[11]—and to generate breathtaking competitive advantage through the power of *now*.

One thing is clear: If you want to be *in demand*, you've got to be *on demand*—or else.

THE ON-DEMAND LEXICON:
(Some terms you'll want to know as you read this book)

advergames/branded games   Video games (often, but not always, free) designed to promote a product or brand. These games, whether played online or offline on consoles like Wii and Xbox, can be quite engaging, can reinforce the brand—and, in the best games, can drive sales—through repeated use and their viral and often social nature.

alternate reality game (ARG)   Interactive games that apply new elements on top of the real world or the fictional worlds of popular films or TV shows, usually involving multiple media platforms—print, web, mobile, and so on—to tell a larger narrative. Often this is in the form of puzzles or scavenger hunts that lead users to the next step in the adventure.

augmented reality (AR)   Sometimes called "mixed reality." Experiences that combine the real world with computer-generated content, often in the form of 3-D holograms that seem to float in front of the user when viewed on the screens of computers and mobile devices.

branded apps/widgets   Onscreen utilities delivered via web or mobile interface. These applications might deliver product promotions, sales countdowns, or other content provided by a brand to its customers.

branded online entertainment   If "infotainment" is news presented in an entertaining fashion, branded entertainment can be seen as "advertainment"—content (videos, games, contests, etc.) designed to directly or indirectly promote a product or brand in a highly entertaining way.

consumer-created/user-generated content Content that is ostensibly produced by everyday consumers instead of professionals. For example, it's not uncommon for brands to invite consumers to create commercials or other content for their products as part of promotional contests.

crowd sourcing The act of allowing crowds, in this case consumers, collaborate on a project. In marketing this can mean creating content, selecting which commercials a marketer might use, or even helping to choose the ad agaency that will perform work for a brand.

hyper-targeting Also referred to as "smart advertising, "addressable advertising," or "behavioral targeting," this is advertising that relies on data mining to present the most compelling offer to a website, mobile, or TV user, based—if the data is available—on his or her age, gender, income, location, online behavior, past purchase history, and more.

in-game advertising Advertising that appears within third-party video games, and is typically targeted to the types of people who play a specific title, in the same way television advertising is targeted to the types of people who watch specific TV shows. Not to be confused with advergames or branded games, which are games overtly designed from the ground up to promote a specific brand or product.

mobile marketing Commercial messages and experiences delivered via, or activated by, mobile devices. This can include advertising experienced while surfing mobile websites. It can also include any offline advertisement—print, broadcast, outdoor, direct mail, point of sale, or other—in which consumers can respond to an offer, access product information, or initiate a transaction.

multiplatform/transmedia A holistic approach to communication that propagates brand-consistent content, strategies, or tactics beyond a single medium, reaching across any mix of platforms—television, radio, print, direct, outdoor, mobile, web, game consoles, etc.—or channels therein: social networking, gaming, blogging, virtual or augmented reality, user-generated video, texting, and so on.

short code   Abbreviated telephone numbers, typically four to five digits long, that can be used to address text or multimedia messages. Short codes are increasingly used as a response mechanism in many forms of advertising, alongside 800 numbers and URLs, whereby the respondent can receive information and other content back from the advertiser via mobile device.

smart code   In various forms—including QR Codes, Memory Spots, ShotCodes, and others—these 2-D barcodes are featured in print, broadcast, direct mail, outdoor advertising, and even on products, to act as links to digital content. Consumers scan the code using a mobile phone and instantly connect to web-based information, product demos, and more.

social networking   Quite simply, online communities of people who share interests and activities through one or more kinds of interfaces, including website, chat room, forum, email, instant messaging, text messaging, blogs, 3-D virtual world, or any mix thereof.

social retailing®   In-store experiences that extend out to the digital world, enabling shoppers to connect with friends outside the physical store for instant feedback and conversation via touch screens or other solutions that link in-store interfaces with Internet-based social networks, email, mobile, and more.

viral video   Video content—often humorous—that leverages formal or informal social networks to spread in a fashion similar to a viral epidemic, from one person to multiple people, who in turn spread it to many more people, exponentially.

virtual world   A computer-simulated environment, frequently featuring a 3-D graphical user interface, in which members of a social network play games or otherwise interact via "avatars"—cartoon representations of themselves.

Insight Comes Before Inspiration

LAURA KLAUBERG COULD safely count herself as one of the world's most influential forces in digital media—except for that whole embarrassing incident on Facebook.

Klauberg, Unilever's powerful senior vice president of global media, has long played an instrumental role in shaping the personal care giant's strategies for capitalizing on integrated, 360-degree consumer advertising campaigns spanning both traditional and nontraditional media outlets.

Think of such initiatives as *In the Motherhood*, a web-based TV series from Suave Shampoo featuring Leah Remini and Jenny McCarthy that enabled the site's devoted fan base to vote on upcoming story developments.

Don't forget Dove beauty brand's massive television, web, outdoor, and mobile initiatives for the much ballyhooed "Campaign for Real Beauty," which encourages women around the world to eschew big media's conventions of beauty.

On the other end of the spectrum, think AXE Deodorant's brow-raising viral videos and racy games such as AXE Shower Gel's Dirty Rolling game—in which players get points for directing a young couple as they get, well, interactive, rolling across all manner of things (a lawn, shrubs, ice cream cones, other people). The idea: Get the couple as "dirty" as possible, before they end up showering together.

In Klauberg's view, digital media is fundamentally transforming the way brands interact with, and engage, consumers—especially young ones.

And she has inspiration: her daughters—ages eighteen, twenty-one, and twenty-three—who provide a living laboratory for how young people interact with digital media.

Not that the lab is always peaceful. There was, after all, the time the girls were mortified when Klauberg set up her own Facebook profile page and then "friended" them in an effort to immerse herself in the online social networking scene.

"I caused a riot among about two hundred kids," Klauberg deadpans. "Within literally hours, there were posts on everyone's pages about keeping me out."

Klauberg says that the whole experience helped open her eyes to the way today's generation interacts with media.

"That's really their world. They do everything on-demand, on their terms."

Klauberg's not alone. Around the world, brands and their ad agency partners are struggling with how to best reach out and connect with this generation. Their approaches vary widely. Some are well thought out. Others, decidedly less so.

ON-DEMAND, OR DIGITAL DU JOUR?

It seems that in every advertising agency across the land, if you've heard it once, you've heard it a million times.

Let's do "x"—insert your own trendy marketing buzzword here—from branded entertainment, to "user-generated content," to augmented reality, to advergames and more. Not because it has any relevance to their clients' target consumers—who don't, despite what you may think, necessarily want to seek out ways to engage with your brand.

Rather, it's because "x" is the sexy digital watchword of the day, and every agency needs to be doing it—whatever "it" is—before the agency's (or at least its creative staff's) coolness credentials are questioned.

And if you think it's bad at agencies, it can be worse among the ranks of brand marketers—especially the larger and more established brands.

Who hasn't heard this uttered at least once from a high-level executive's mouth: "We need a mobile (or social media, or viral video, or some other 'x') strategy."

Never mind that these are channels, not strategies, and that it's akin to someone proclaiming, "We need a TV commercial strategy," or "We need a brochure strategy."

I was recently in a meeting in which a top executive at a major consumer products brand exclaimed, "We need to get into online video." When asked why, and I'm not kidding here, he replied, "Because it's cool and everyone's doing it."

He certainly could be right on both counts—the trend and the need.

But as I've learned in talking with some of today's most innovative marketers, the most successful digital initiatives typically don't start with the idea for a cool new digital experience, or a me-too approach to major trends. Instead, they start with consumer insights culled from painstaking research into who your customers are, what they're all about, how they interact with consumer technologies, and what they want from the brands they know and trust.

For a case in point, look no further than Klauberg's Unilever, and its Dove beauty brand's "Campaign for Real Beauty."

By now, most marketers are familiar with this award-winning campaign. But many may not know its origins.

For those not in the know, the effort is an integrated tour de force; an expansive print, television, outdoor, web, and mobile initiative that encourages women around the world to ignore big media's beauty stereotypes—as counterintuitive a message as has ever come from a beauty goods brand.

Mind you, Dove would have no doubt been successful with a standard-issue TV campaign featuring conventionally beautiful women pitching the brand's Calming Night Bar, Smooth & Soft Anti-Frizz Cream, or its Energy Glow Lotion.

But Dove took a different approach.

Instead, Dove marketers and ad agency Ogilvy & Mather and research firm Strategy One worked with researchers at Harvard University and the London School of Economics to conduct a ten-country study of more than 3,200 girls and women ages eighteen to sixty-four in order to better understand women's views about what beauty means today—and to measure satisfaction with their own beauty.

Instead of finding a sisterhood of preening narcissists, the study found that a mere 2 percent of women would describe themselves as beautiful. In fact, only 4 percent of eighteen- to twenty-nine-year-olds would do so.

What's more, women of all ages say marketing pitches featuring supermodels make them feel worse about their looks, and forever pressured to strive for "the eye-popping features and stunning proportions of a few hand-picked beauty icons."

The marketers used these insights to tap into a broader dynamic emerging within the zeitgeist: a growing desire for "empowerment" and "authenticity." Not the "truthiness" sort, mind you, but rather the "live-your-best-life" variety personified by brands like *Real Simple* magazine and Oprah Winfrey.

They also tapped into coinciding research showing how teens and women use digital media, from the Internet to mobile phones.

The Pew Internet & American Life project, for instance, has found that young women have become the most prolific drivers of many social media channels. Nearly 70 percent of American girls between the ages of fifteen and seventeen have built and routinely update profile pages on websites like MySpace and Facebook. Some 35 percent of girls have their own blogs, compared to 20 percent of boys. And 32 percent of girls have their own websites, compared to 22 percent of their male counterparts.[1] While the breakdown of gender participation in these kinds of activities approaches parity in adulthood, women are more likely to use them as a means of fostering and maintaining nurturing, empowering emotional connections with others.

In a kind of perfect symbiosis, Dove's resulting multiplatform marketing campaign seamlessly hocked products like Intensive Firming Cream and Exfoliating Body Wash while encouraging women to define their own beauty and reject popular culture's ever-narrower definition of attractiveness.

ONE BEAUTY OF A CAMPAIGN

Indeed, although later studies revealed women actually feel better about brands that use the young-and-thin aesthetic, even as they feel worse about themselves, Dove has stuck to its positioning, deploying a number of innovative digital marketing strategies to engage its target consumer.

In Times Square, digital billboards featuring everyday women in underwear—the models more Rubenesque than anorexic—asked passersby to participate in text voting on whether the featured woman was a) wrinkled or b) wonderful; a) fat or b) fabulous; and a) oversized or b) outstanding.

Contests asked consumers to create TV commercials for airing during the Oscars. And the groundbreaking viral videos Evolution and Onslaught showed how harmful media images can be on our sense of beauty.

In Evolution's case, a video uses time-lapse imagery to show an average-looking woman transformed into a beautiful billboard model, thanks to an army of makeup artists, stylists, and the miracles of

FIGURE 1–1. *Unilever is a master at shaping digital experiences for distinctly different audiences, from the video Onslaught for Dove's "Campaign for Real Beauty," to Dirty Rolling, a titillating viral game for AXE deodorant.*

Photoshop. The tagline proclaimed: "No wonder our perception of beauty is so distorted."

The spot ran during the Super Bowl and was shown a handful of other times on TV. But it became a viral phenomenon online, drawing nearly 6 million hits on YouTube alone.[2]

Onslaught, on the other hand, featured a freckle-faced little girl hit with a barrage of beauty-industry imagery, from emaciated models to bikini-clad provocateurs to Botox needles (see Figure 1–1).

Highly interactive online video experiences drive home the point in other ways. In Amy, a boy stands outside a girl's house for hours, calling her name in hopes that she'll come out and visit. Copy reads, "Amy can name 12 things wrong with her appearance. He can't name one." Users are able to customize the name the boy calls out, and then send the customized video to encourage girls they know to see themselves as others do—not as flawed, but beautiful just they way they are.

It is also, as I recently told *Broadcasting & Cable* magazine, an enormous paradox, designed to "equate the idea of rejecting society's conventions of beauty by buying products from the beauty industry."[3]

A bit more playful, *Waking Up Hannah*—dubbed as the world's first interactive romantic comedy—is an online video experience that enables visitors to choose from three different story lines and then watch as the title character gets ready for a blind date.

The site enables visitors to do things like help Hannah get ready for the evening (you can choose which Dove products Hannah will use), click on her mobile phone to view her text messages and pictures, and hear ongoing commentary.

There's even the occasional glam: One component of the campaign involves a cross-promotion with the hit CW TV series *Gossip Girl*. In this case, a "Dove Go Fresh" website featuring videos, blogs, and games about four Upper East Siders—an aspiring designer, an "It" girl, a filmmaker, and an Ivy Leaguer—who share their real stories about growing up, surviving, and succeeding in New York City.

The centerpiece of the entire effort: Dove's "Campaign for Real Beauty" website, which features educational downloads for parents, teachers, and teens on how to foster feelings of self-worth and self-acceptance.

Visitors can also contribute to a special "self-esteem" fund—an impressive effort designed to promote positive body image among girls and women worldwide. Dove even donates a portion of sales from select products. In fact, by 2010, educational programs sponsored by the fund had touched the lives of 5 million young people in forty countries throughout Europe, North America, Asia, and the Middle East.[4]

Which is admirable, yes. But this is far more than just the perfect match of cause and commerce.

Following the launch of the "Campaign for Real Beauty," market share for Dove's firming products, for instance, grew from 7 percent to 13.5 percent in its six biggest markets (the UK, France, Germany, Italy, the Netherlands, and Spain),[5] far exceeding the marketers' expectations.

In fact, global sales for Dove products increased over 10 percent in the first two years of the campaign, according to statistics from Information Resources Incorporated. That puts Dove sales at well over $600 million per year.[6]

It was also the first campaign to ever win both the television and cyber Grand Prix awards at the Cannes Lions International Advertising Festival.

In short: This campaign demonstrates that success is not about understanding technology, it's about understanding your customers—and then capitalizing on that insight across the digital platforms that make sense for your audience, in the ways that will resonate most.

To that end, let's look at key tenets for following Rule #1.

KNOW THY CUSTOMER—AND THY CHANNELS

If you don't know who your customers are, what they like, and how they use—and want to use—digital media, you're just shooting in the dark. But armed with customer insights, the sky's the limit. And Dove's parent, Unilever, is not the only company to realize this.

Toyota has practically made it an art form—from product design all the way to market implementation.

When it launched its youth-targeting Scion brand, the company researched and refined its target audience, building an exquisitely-detailed profile of a young, eighteen- to twenty-four-year-old male that Jeffrey Rayport, chairman of Marketspace LLC, describes as "a tuner, one of those guys who has a forehead tattoo, a tongue-stud, lives in Southern California, buys used cars, customizes them with fuzzy dice and mag wheels, and expresses himself and his entire identity through the World of Warcraft scenes that are airbrushed on the doors of the car."[7]

The company then did something amazing in its simplicity. It created a car to fit this profile—essentially a stripped-down Corolla with an intentionally unrefined chassis that is purposefully marketed as "incomplete"—meant to be cocreated with the customer as he pimps his ride with Scion-branded and third-party accessories and options.

The brand then went out and found its creative "dude demographic" where he lives. With very little television ad spend, Scion has infiltrated car shows and sponsored streetcar design competitions. In fact, according to Rayport, Scion has discovered in its ongoing research that its customers spend as much money in the first three years of ownership customizing their cars as an expression of themselves, and their identities, as they did buying the car in the first place.

Scion has also quietly, yet radically, redefined the way to market cars online to an audience that not only disdains advertising, but also avoids most media channels through which an advertiser would typically market its products.

There is, for instance, Scion Broadband, an online entertainment portal that showcases short films, Japanese anime, live music events, and short episodic TV-style shows, along with video demos of those cool new Scion models.

There's the partnership with gamer site Kongregate to help aspiring game developers learn how to create new shoot-'em-up video games.

And there are myriad virtual world initiatives, including Scion City in Second Life, Club Scion in Whyville, and Scion experiences within Gaia.

In Gaia, for instance, users can buy and customize Scion automobiles using the world's virtual currency. They can buy, sell, and trade items like rims, paint, decals, and spoilers to customize their rides. Within the offering's first hour of launch, Gaians acquired over 28,000 Scions, a figure that grew to 600,000 within six months.[8]

We'll learn more about Scion and its efforts later on in the book. Suffice to say, it has all met remarkable success—helping to sell 175,000 cars in its first four years, and making it one of the most successful car launches in North American history.

For Procter & Gamble, this kind of innovation-through-insight is standard operating procedure.

To better understand and address the needs of parents, P&G—a notoriously staid, conservative corporation—recently teamed up with Google, the antithesis of corporate sterility, for a staff-swapping program whereby P&G marketers would spend time working at Google, and vice versa. The idea: Gain insights on the way its customers use technology, and spur new ideas.

That may sound more unconventional than it is. P&G, the world's largest advertiser with $8.9 billion in annual ad spend, has a long history of revolutionizing new media. It was P&G, and its first nationally advertised brand, Ivory Soap, that wrote and produced the first radio and television "soap" opera, *Guiding Light*.

As part of its staff-sharing project, Google helped Procter & Gamble understand how women use the Internet and in particular, the influence of so-called "Mommy Bloggers"—blogs like CityMoma, Mommy Needs Coffee, This Full House, and a host of others that collectively attract over 21 million moms seeking advice and camaraderie every week. For example, it turned out that 85 percent of people who read blogs in the BlogHer blog network report that they've purchased a product based upon a blog recommendation.[9]

At Google's prompting, P&G invited mommy bloggers to a Pampers press conference, where they toured the facilities, met executives, and got a primer on diaper design—all of which they promptly covered in their blogs.

It was a real eyeopener to Pampers marketers. As spokesman Bryan McCleary tells the *Wall Street Journal*, "This is a very different type of communication than what Procter & Gamble is used to." He adds that P&G marketing teams have discovered that bloggers don't really cotton to P&G's marketing messages. Instead, "What they like are exciting stories . . . and those things actually can become word-of-mouth advertising, if done in the right way."[10]

None of this is to say P&G (or its archrival Unilever) have scored wins every time. As the *Journal* reports, P&G was embarrassingly slow to recognize the importance of these mommy bloggers in earlier online promotions geared to women, and only began its outreach after Google pointed out how influential they can be.

And Unilever faced a backlash when it was pointed out that the company was encouraging women to look past beauty stereotypes with its "Campaign for Real Beauty" on the one hand, while creating racy, arguably sexist games and ads for its AXE brand on the other.

The AXE Vice website, for instance, features a "special correspondent" who investigates an "alarming new trend in society: squeaky-clean nice girls who turn into lust-crazed vixens" when they come in contact with men wearing AXE Vice.

Both infractions—failing to recognize the ascendency of mommy bloggers, and sending seemingly contradictory messages to women—are actually quite forgivable. P&G only recently realized the Internet could be a powerful tool for promoting consumer packaged goods like diapers.

And in Unilever's case, the company has multiple brands speaking to multiple audiences—and is a case study of the power of knowing your customer. After all, what resonates with adult women won't resonate with young men—and vice versa.

As I told *B&C* magazine: "Dove is trying to express its understanding of today's woman and become an empowering agent for them. But AXE has a different job to do."

THOU SHALT COMMIT MULTI-PLAT-FORNICATION

With customer insights in hand, it's time to innovate through the channels or platforms that make the most sense for your audience.

MTV, for instance, is a master at using multiple platforms to reach its audience, having long ago set out to achieve what MTV president Van Toffler calls "multi-plat-fornication"—his mischievous term for making MTV as ubiquitous on mobile phones, PCs, iPods, and gaming consoles as it is on cable television.

Of course, this is as much about defense as offense for MTV, which has found it ever harder to remain relevant to its target twelve to twenty-four, tech-savvy demographic. Just as its television programming needed to move away from its "all music, all the time" origins in the face of stiff cable and online competition, it quickly learned that multiplatform strategies don't just mean simply streaming MTV programming to every screen available. Instead, it's about strategically capitalizing on each medium's unique strengths.

During a recent MTV Video Music Awards broadcast, for instance, not only was the show simulcast on the web and mobile phones, but viewers could also help choose the Best New Artist award minutes before it was presented, by sending their choices via text message. They could also follow "tweet trackers" for the latest on artists like Kanye West and Lada Gaga as they appeared on the telecast.

And in recent years, the awards show has even been recreated in real time within Second Life—in one case with a painstaking 3-D reconstruction of the ultra-exclusive Hardwood, Pink, and Sky Villa fantasy suites in the Palms Casino & Resort in Las Vegas, where most of the televised performances were taking place, so fans could actually attend the event from anywhere in the world.

Similar strategies are being deployed for many of the network's popular reality TV serials. Viewers can go behind the scenes of popular television shows like *The City* or *Nitro Circus* via a web-based, on-demand channel at MTV.com, where they can sign up for text alerts, download ringtones, and more. They can live within 3-D virtual worlds based on several of its shows at VirtualMTV. And they can play games like The Real World/Road Rules Challenge on the PC, MTV Cribs on their mobile phones, or MTV's Guitar Hero–esque Rock Band on their Sony PlayStation or Xbox 360 gaming consoles.

"MTV had to evolve with its audience," Toffler says. "If MTV stayed the way it was in 1981, playing A Flock of Seagulls videos 90 times a day, I'm not sure it would be as relevant as it is today."[11]

Meanwhile, no other brand has stayed relevant for as long as Coca-Cola, which is, perhaps, the ultimate multiplatform player.

Coke's been on TV, radio, and in print for nearly 100 years. Online, it has redefined what a "sparkling cola beverage" can be.

Like most consumer brands these days, Coke has its own Facebook page. Unlike so many others, Coke actually has a lot of Facebook fans—over 3,526,697 in fact, many of whom come together to declare their love for the Real Thing, and to debate everything from "Coke v. Pepsi"; the merits of drinking from a can or bottle; and what foods go well with an ice-cold Coke.

Coca-Cola even has its own virtual world, called CC Metro, where members can engage in activities centered on music, gaming, sports, entertainment—including a hoverboard skate park and a theater presenting Coca-Cola videos. There's even a "music mixer" tool that will let users develop their own tracks. And users can chat with one another via text or voice-over Internet Protocol.

And when Coke aficionados aren't in front of a computer, the brand is accessible via mobile devices through offerings such as the Spin the Coke iPhone game—which is dubbed as a way to "break the ice or to give that someone special a not so subtle hint," and "The Magic Coke Bottle," which is a kind of magic eight ball for the iPhone era.

MINI USA, for one, aims to be just as ambitious in its own efforts to reach its irreverent, "funtech"-loving audience. With a twist, that is.

John Butler, the gregarious cofounder and creative director at MINI agency Butler, Shine, Stern & Partners, tells me the strategy for this car brand isn't to convince people they want to buy a MINI, but rather to get MINI drivers to do all the selling.

"Here's a group of consumers who are rabidly passionate, and they're evangelists for the brand," he says. "So we said, 'Let's advertise to people who already own the car.'

"If you can make them feel like they're part of this elite little club, they're going to go out there and they're going to spread the word. They're going to sell the vehicles for you."

As a result, a print campaign in major consumer publications may reach 10 million people, but only the 150,000 MINI owners who receive special 3-D glasses in the mail can even see the coded messages hidden in the ads.

Everyone else is told to go to a dealer to pick up their own pair of 3-D glasses—starting at just $19,999.

FIGURE 1–2. *Using RFID technology, MINI's Motorby Billboards call out to MINI owners by name.*

Online, they can participate in training courses like "MINI PowerParking" and other online games involving various obstacle courses at the Greater Gotham Motoring School. Users can even earn certificates and go to local dealers to pick up special patches for their driving jackets.

And for the ultimate in brand reinforcement, digital billboards in the real world call out to MINI owners in Miami, Chicago, San Francisco, and New York. The billboards connect wirelessly with special radio frequency identification (RFID) tags built into MINI car key fobs, and then display a fun, personalized message—"Motor on, Jill!," "Hi Jim, Nice Convertible!"—to drivers as they pass by (see Figure 1–2).

Only a few people have ever experienced the signs' personalized experience, but the attention the effort has earned has generated over 90 million media impressions across MINI owner group forums, auto blogs, *Newsweek, The Today Show,* and more.

In other words, with insights on your customers, there's no telling what platforms your innovations will take you next.

HONOR TRADITIONAL AS THE SIZZLE TO DIGITAL'S STEAK

With all this innovation, there is a temptation in our industry to get swept up by the hyperbole surrounding digital and proclaim the ascendency of interactive platforms as replacements for traditional channels like television, radio, and print. But that's simply ridiculous.

According to Nielsen figures, despite what they may claim, the average American now watches 142 hours of television per month—up about 5 hours over the last few years—compared to about 27 hours per month spent using the Internet. What's more, 31 percent of Internet use occurs while we're in front of a TV set.[12] And nowadays, we're watching more TV content online. In other words, we're toggling between various forms of media, rather than foregoing some forms, as many believe.

And make no mistake: Television still reins supreme—in ways that could never have been predicted.

According to the *New York Times*, 99 percent of all the video consumed in the United States still occurs via a TV set. And even audience drop-off may not be a bad thing.

"In the law of unintended consequences, the networks' audience erosion has become both a challenge and an opportunity," says John Rash, director of media analysis at advertising agency Campbell Mithun in Minneapolis. "They don't have as big an audience to sell, but their remaining share is that much more dominant over the fragmented media landscape."[13]

Factor in exposure to radio, direct mail, outdoor, print advertising, and so on, and digital's role is put into a little more perspective. But that doesn't mean the role of traditional isn't changing.

As the examples thus far illustrate, many of today's most powerful integrated campaigns use traditional advertising to build awareness and then point consumers to deeper, richer, more meaningful experiences online, or via mobile and other digital platforms.

Take AMF Pension, a Swedish insurance company that has effectively used traditional advertising to generate a significant amount of engagement through digital channels in an effort to encourage young people to start thinking about retirement planning.

One recent campaign started with a TV spot that used makeup and special effects to portray famous young Swedes as senior citizens. And outdoor posters featuring the faces of these notables changed from young to old depending on the viewing angle.

The call to action: an invitation to young people to visit a website where they can upload pictures of themselves, which are then digitally manipulated to show them what they might look like when they're seventy.

Consumers could also take camera phone pictures of themselves and send them to a mobile short code. Within three minutes, they'd

FIGURE 1–3. *Print and broadcast ads showed famous young Swedes as senior citizens, and invited consumers to use the web and mobile phones to upload pictures of themselves for a glimpse of what they themselves might look like at seventy.*

receive the picture back, modified to show them their future, septua-genarian selves (see Figure 1–3).

Along the way, consumers could click through to more information about AMF and its products, as well as to tips for financial planning.

Result: 322,946 pictures were submitted online, and awareness of the company rose 33 percent. In fact, an estimated 15 percent of the target audience in Sweden interacted with the AMF brand at some point during the campaign.[14]

Many brands have used this kind of facial recognition technology to engage fans. You can upload images of yourself to "Simpsonize" yourself to look like a character from the Fox TV show, turn yourself into a Vulcan as part of promotions for the *Star Trek* movie franchise, and turn yourself into a cyborg as part of the *Terminator* series.

Likewise, Volkswagen North America uses its TV commercials and print ads featuring Brooke Shields to target new parents who might be interested in the VW Routan minivan. The call to action points consumers to a website where they can learn all about the Routan's family-friendly features, build a custom Routan and get a cost estimate, and find local dealers.

There's even a viral component where you can upload pictures of yourself or friends as "mom" and "dad" to see what the "junior" might look like—often to humorous effect (see Figure 1–4).

As the site says: "Make a baby without actually 'making a baby' . . . Use this tool to have a Routan baby with a loved one, or a person you hardly even know. Just find the right mate, and make a baby so adorable you just can't help but love."

Or recoil from, as the case may be.

Called "The Routan Babymaker 3000," the app is a hoot. But given the so-called "moms" and "dads" of either gender uploaded for the amusement—and consternation—of fellow officemates, it may as well have been called "The Trouble Maker."

Not that I'd know from personal experience or anything.

FIGURE 1–4. *Facial recognition technologies help consumers create humorous mashups to imagine new possibilities, like this one for VW.*

THOU SHALT NOT PUT BUZZ BEFORE BUSINESS

Obviously these initiatives are highly experimental—if it were as easy as creating any old viral video, advergame, or some other digital diversion to generate enough buzz to bring in business for our brands, we'd all be rich.

For many lifestyle brands, this kind of experimentation is enough—especially in categories where an aura of hipness is a prerequisite for sales success. Indeed, all of the examples above went beyond mere sizzle and reinforced overall brand messaging and positioning and helped move the sales needle considerably.

But while there is obviously a lot of fun and games in all this fun and games, it's important that we approach digital initiatives with specific objectives in mind.

Amid economic realities that have hit the U.S. auto industry especially hard in recent years, Mark-Hans Richer, Harley-Davidson's chief marketing officer and former head of marketing for GM's

Pontiac brand, was among the first to condemn what many feel is the ad industry's current obsession with splash over sales.

"This is a new golden age for marketers," Mr. Richer recently told attendees of a conference hosted by industry trade publication *Madison & Vine*, which covers the intersection of marketing's Madison Avenue and the entertainment world's Hollywood and Vine. "The shackles are off, and the possibilities are literally endless. If we aren't conducting radical experiments, trying new ways to engage our targets and adding value to them, then we're not doing our jobs."[15]

But, he adds, "It's not about chasing the buzz; it's about chasing the biz."

That's especially true in tough economic environments where even the government has had to step in with "cash for clunkers" programs to try to fuel new auto sales.

"The word for crisis is in fact two symbols in Chinese—'danger' and 'opportunity,'" says Nick Brien, CEO of media-buying holding firm Mediabrands and former CEO of advertising titan Universal-McCann.

"When our clients are talking about cutting, we have to make sure that if they're going to cut budgets, they don't cut innovation," he says. "[In a tough economic environment] it's going to be much more about marketing from the original French word 'marcher'—to sell."[16]

The marketers who get this formula right—by fueling innovation through substantive consumer insights—will score big in the on-demand era.

Those who don't will have to settle for some fun—but ultimately fruitless—experiments.

Q&A

The Klauberg Manifesto

Laura Klauberg, senior vice president of global media at Unilever

SHE'S THE QUEEN of All Media—and she's seriously into digital.

Laura Klauberg, Unilever's powerful senior vice president of global media, has been a major driver in many of the company's most successful digital initiatives, from "In the Motherhood" for Suave, to "The AXE Effect" for AXE deodorant, to the Cannes Lions Grand Prix–winning "Campaign for Real Beauty" for Dove.

Klauberg is the first woman, and first American, to head media for Unilever's global marketing operations, where she personally controls the world's second largest media budget—a full $4.7 billion a year. Which means her opinion matters—a lot.

It was Klauberg, after all, who recently sparked heartburn throughout the U.S. television industry when she appeared to question the wisdom of allocating TV ad budgets months in advance, during the so-called "upfront" season, when media buyers make commitments to secure advertising time in the following fall's TV schedule—arguing that a rapidly changing media market demands more nimble maneuvering.

In Klauberg's view, digital media is fundamentally transforming the way both brands and consumers use media. Simply "going digital" means very little. To truly capitalize on the power of on-demand experience requires what she calls a "big brand idea" driven by consumer insight.

Rick Mathieson: Unilever is one of the world's largest and most important advertisers—especially in television. How is that starting to change?

Laura Klauberg: Historically if you looked at the way we spent our communication dollars, even as recently as five years ago, you would see a pretty traditional-looking mix, which was largely television driven. And we have also always been a pretty significant spender in print, and in magazines specifically. Those two mediums used to constitute 90 percent of our overall communication mix.

But if you look at it today, it's significantly changed. TV still dominates our spend, but we've dramatically diversified our communication mix, where print still is important, television's still important, but the whole digital space is growing significantly and more than doubles every year in terms of the total dollars that we're investing.

RM: What have you learned so far as you have started to invest more heavily in digital?

LK: The first lesson—and this lesson I think pertains to any medium—is to stress the brand idea. If you have a big brand idea, whether you're talking about television, or you're talking about print, or you're talking about digital, it makes a significant difference. Particularly in the digital space because it provides an opportunity to engage consumers in unprecedented ways—in ways that just running a thirty-second television ad or a static print ad didn't in the past.

But if it doesn't start at the core with a really engaging brand idea, no one's going to bother to interact with or engage with you.

RM: Obviously some of the most innovative work Unilever's done has been for the Dove brand, with the "Campaign for Real Beauty." Why, even after all these years, has this multiplatform initiative been so powerful in the marketplace?

LK: It goes back to the essence of what Dove is about; it's about redefining beauty stereotypes.

What we've learned on a global basis is that women feel passionate about that subject. And any time you find a group of consumers that feels passionate about something, they want to speak out on it.

I think that whole brand platform has really lent itself to the digital space because we've afforded women an opportunity—whether it's posting a message on a message board or it's [asking consumers to create] a Dove commercial, as in the case of Dove Cream Oil, where we got far more entries than we had ever anticipated.

When women feel strongly about something, and you give them a platform to speak out, or to create something, or to engage with one another, they'll jump on it. That's why they'll send a video to all their friends. They'll post the *Evolution* video on their Facebook page or their MySpace profile and write on the Dove message board on our site. They'll go and create a piece of advertising that is their view of what the brand is about.

If we had just been talking about how we clean better than soap, I don't think we would've had that response. The Dove idea really resonates emotionally with women.

RM: From the outside looking in, this seems like a leap of faith: a major beauty industry brand encouraging women to eschew beauty industry stereotypes.

LK: It goes back to consumer insights. It's about really understanding what the consumer is saying, how she feels. There was a strong insight that women felt very, very strongly about that issue. They've been told for years you need to be ninety pounds and be beautiful and look like Barbie.

And the reality is we had done a global study a number of years ago where we learned that 2 percent of women around the world felt beautiful. That was a real "ah-ha" moment for us. I think moving to that campaign idea wasn't an easy one. It took a lot of risk and a lot of courage. But in the end, everyone held hands and said we think this was the right thing to do with the brand.

That's in part because it was actually consistent with the heritage of Dove. Dove had always used real women in their advertising. They basically had used a testimonial format for years. You always had real women talking about their lives, their skin, their families, in a very authentic away.

So I think it was very consistent with the heritage of the brand, but it took it to a whole new level. And you've seen what the response has been.

RM: How do initiatives like this provide a guidepost to the different ways in which people consume and interact with brand messages?

LK: What we're seeing is that traditional thirty-second advertising is not the only way to communicate any longer.

And I think that whether we won an award or we didn't win an award, that made a statement within the advertising community—particularly among those communities that tended to historically think in terms of thirty-second TV ads—that the world has really changed.

The experience that we had with *Evolution* was a real wake-up call to anyone who was not a believer that other types of mediums, other formats, other ways to engage consumers are incredibly powerful, incredibly impactful.

RM: Of course, "Campaign for Real Beauty" isn't the only groundbreaking initiative from Unilever.

LK: We did something called *In the Motherhood*, which was a series of online webisodes sponsored by Suave. The Suave brand really appeals to the average mom who puts her family and everything in her life before herself and before her own personal needs. For *In the Motherhood*, we actually asked consumers to contribute ideas for scripts.

Professional scriptwriters would polish up the consumers' ideas, and then we produced those into short videos that were aired online.

The results were pretty astounding. We had over five million consumers come to the site. The reason why it was so engaging is that it was content and a subject that women felt deeply about, which led them to really engage and to really interact.

We think it's actually a very, very big idea—bigger than just doing online webisodes. We think the whole campaign has real legs.

That's an example of having, at the core, an idea that resonates [with your target], whether it's women, or it's eighteen-year-old guys in the case of AXE, or it's thirty-year-old guys in the case of Degree [deodorant].

We have found that with most of the campaigns that we've done, whether it ties into the Oscars in the case of Dove, or whether there's a tie-in with the show *24* on Fox, which we did with Degree, identifying those things in the culture that are highly relevant to consumers, yet have a natural affinity with our brands, is how we have found lots of success in terms of building consumer engagement.

RM: You recently caused more than a few television executives to go apoplectic when you appeared to question the wisdom of allocating TV advertising budgets months in advance during the so-called upfront season. Are you thinking about foregoing the upfronts?

LK: Television still is a very significant piece of our mix. So we're not pulling out of the upfront.

But what we have done is, we have tried to develop a channel-agnostic approach, which starts with the big brand idea.

And [that comes from] knowing what we know about who we're trying to reach, how they consume media, how they engage, how they interact, what's the best way for us to get that message to consumers.

And in some cases it may be 100 percent digital program. In the case of AXE, where I'm trying to reach an eighteen-year-old guy, well, most eighteen-year-old guys aren't heavy television consumers. So how do I reach them?

If I have a very broad target—and I really need mass reach—TV may be the primary medium, but there may be many other ways in which to reach the consumer.

RM: What's your advice to marketers hoping to create a culture of digital innovation throughout a large marketing operation like yours?

LK: One of the things that we've actually done here at Unilever, which I think has been great, is that we've challenged all of our marketing people to embrace the new consumer technologies.

It's one thing to hear about it, read about it. But unless you yourself are doing it, and working with it—particularly if you have a brand that's used by somewhat younger consumers—it's very difficult to develop a multiplatform marketing campaign when you yourself don't really fully understand or use the technology.

Just as an example: I don't know how many times in my career I've worked with marketing people that said they never watch TV. Or 'I never read a magazine.' But yet they're in marketing.

I've heard that over the years, many, many times from colleagues who weren't heavy television viewers.

If you look at a lot of the things that we've done in the last few years, a lot of it has been integration with content—finding the right marriage between content and our brand. And if you don't know what the content is, it's very difficult to be able to identify what those opportunities might be.

If you never watched the show *24*, you would never know that it was a perfect fit with the Degree brand, which is about managing stress. 'Protection for when you need it most.' Well, you can't think of a better character than Jack Bauer. But if you've never turned on Fox and watched *24* you'd never know.

So it's about really being in tune with the culture, and then finding the points where there might be a great intersection of a brand and what's important to consumers.

We've also done some fun things internally. We have a program called "Translators." It's somewhat of a mentoring program but it works in reverse.

We pair young new marketing people, people that are just out of school, with senior executives. And they spend an hour or so once a month basically engaging in technology.

So as an example, [back when the iPhone first came out] I had a session with one of the junior people here. And he sent me an email three days before and said these are some options on what we can do in our session. So I said I love them all, but make sure you bring your iPhone.

He did bring his iPhone, and we did an hour demo. And of course I wanted one the second he left my office.

We're doing things like that because what you'll find is that, in our business in general, but particularly with people that have been around for fifteen or twenty years, they're not as savvy when it comes to understanding some of the new technologies. It's sometimes like, "What's 'social networking?'" or "'Community,' what is that?"

We all have Facebook profiles. I have the benefit of having three daughters who are right in the bull's-eye there.

Obviously, I live with them, so I probably am more attuned to what's happening—partially because of my role, partially because of the life I live with them. So I'm very, very much aware of how they consume media.

They don't sit in front of the television for hours. It's just not the way they grew up, and I'm not convinced that's what they'll do when they're thirty.

I also think you have to be willing to take some risk. You have to be willing to let go of your brand a bit.

When we decided to do Dove Cream Oil and invite consumers to make a TV commercial, you have to be willing to see what kind of ads consumers are going to make on your behalf.

You really do have to give up an element of control and not be afraid to do so.

On *Evolution*, there must've been a dozen parodies that were on the Internet.

One was called *Slobolution*, which basically ripped off the entire approach. They even used our music. They took this nice-looking guy and in two minutes he was smoking and drinking beers and eating cheeseburgers and turned into this fat slobby-looking guy at the end.

So it's a shift in mindset. We don't control—we can't control—what's out there, and we have to start getting comfortable with that.

RM: You mentioned your teenage daughters. Tell me what else you've learned from them and how they've impacted the way you view digital.

LK: It's interesting. They live on Facebook and it's their whole way of living and breathing and communicating. It's kind of their life. And that for me has been absolutely astounding.

Here's a funny story. I went and set up a Facebook profile, and I 'friended' them. And I caused a riot among about 200 kids. Within literally hours, there were posts on everybody's pages about keeping me out. And so I sat there alone for about three months. Then we got a bunch of people in the office to do it. So now I have many more friends than I did before.

It was an interesting experience because that's really their world. They do everything on-demand, on their terms.

They'll watch a fair amount of TV shows that they like, but they watch them time shifted, or they watch the DVD.

But 'appointment viewing' for them is very rare. They don't line up on Thursday nights to watch *Grey's Anatomy*. They'll watch *Grey's Anatomy* and they like *Grey's Anatomy*, but they tend to watch it when they want to watch it, as opposed to when the network runs the show.

Every week you read about another magazine going out of business or just migrating to a digital version. Teens still consume print magazines, predominantly in the fashion arena. But their world is really a digital world. And that's how they consume music. That's how they consume news. That's how they maintain a relationship with their friends. It's a very, very different world than the world I grew up in.

So it really has had a pretty big impact on me, in terms of the way I think about the way we've communicated historically and the great need to rethink how we market our brands.

RM: Was your interaction with your kids an inspiration for your own transformation, switching from brand marketing, which you did for many years, to media a few years back?

LK: I don't know if that was really the impetus. I would say just having been in this business for years, I've seen a sea change occurring. I think there's been more change in the last two years than there was the prior twenty.

I think what's exciting about it from a marketer's standpoint is I like to say, 'If you can imagine it you can probably do it.' There really are no set rules.

If you just look at some of the most creative, innovative work that we've done as marketers in the last two years or so, the sky's the limit.

So I'm finding this a very, very exciting time to work in this space, being a kind of mix of entertainment, brands, and collaboration with consumers. It's just a whole new way to communicate. And it causes us, as marketers, to really rethink how we go to market.

I think it's a very exciting time.

Don't Repurpose, Reimagine

MAYBE JUSTIN TIMBERLAKE deserved the quick kick to the crotch.

The young pop star—whose impossibly high-pitched voice momentarily spiked an octave higher—had just been propelled through the air and flown into a mailbox, his legs splayed in a flinch-inspiring moment that made for a hugely entertaining TV commercial for Pepsi-Cola.

Needless to say, the spot had something for everyone. Teenage girls got to swoon over the guy who once boasted he's single-handedly "bringing sexy back"—I hadn't realized it'd gone anywhere before scrambling to take part in a Pepsi sweepstakes for tickets to his next concert.

And detractors got to enjoy the Schadenfreude of Timberlake's ill-fated flight—initiated, apparently, by women willing him closer through the sheer power of sipping Pepsi.

I guess you had to see it. And you probably did.

Moments after its airing during the Super Bowl, the spot was available seemingly everywhere online, including, of course, YouTube—with Pepsi marketers hoping for a viral sensation.

It certainly was—for a few days or so, its expiration date shorter than the fizz in a forgotten can of Pepsi Max.

As successful as the effort was—we're talking about what was certainly one of the most memorable commercials of its year—one could argue that its digital follow-through suffered from a lack of imagination.

Sure, one screen is no longer enough. Today, you've got to formulate multiplatform strategies to connect with your audiences wherever they live.

But to far too many marketers, that seems to just mean posting television spots or movie trailers on YouTube and on corporate websites in hopes they go viral—or launching a "user-generated video" contest in hopes consumers will evangelize the brand on their own.

For Pepsi, which has inarguably revolutionized digital experiences on behalf of its customers, what was merely a chance to replay a popular TV spot with a pop star, could have been so much more—a game, a personalizable message, a social networking event, or something all together different that could have given it life far beyond Super Bowl Sunday.

In a medium where the possibilities are endless, television is the jumping-off point to experiences that should be much more interactive and engaging. You've got to invent new ways to help your customers engage with your brand and make it their own.

Case in point: HBO's Voyeur Project.

The View from Here

The subscription cable television network could always advertise its shows on other television networks—and it often does.

But in an effort to highlight its longtime "It's not TV, it's HBO" positioning, the cable network recently looked beyond the television screen to build a truly groundbreaking experience.

Working with film directors Jake Scott and Chris Nelson, along with BBDO and interactive agency Big Spaceship, the network filmed a massive drama played out across eight groups of characters in a stage designed to look like a cutaway of an apartment building on Broome and Ludlow streets in New York City. The dramas were then projected on the sides of the real building at that location, creating the illusion that the walls had been cut away for anyone within eyeshot to see.

Street teams hit the avenues of New York, inviting residents to take part in what was billed as a truly unique event, directing them to the venue.

Meanwhile, content related to the drama's characters was placed on a dedicated microsite and on various other sites, including MySpace. And photos and video clips were posted on YouTube, Flickr, and other social networks—as well as on HBO channels and in mobile phone promotions.

At HBOVoyeur.com, viewers could pick up virtual binoculars and zoom in on certain characters for more intimate viewing in a Hitchcock-meets-the-digital-age twist.

In just four weeks, HBOVoyeur.com received 1.2 million hits, with the average visit time reaching nine minutes.[1]

Needless to say, the impact was tremendous, tying perfectly to HBO's value proposition as a leader in storytelling, and allowing consumers to interact with the brand in a memorable way. This was not repurposing content—it was reimagining it for new mediums.

"It's in the HBO DNA to continually strive for marketing innovation and breakthrough creative ideas," says Courteney Monroe, executive vice president of consumer marketing for HBO. "We wanted to do something really, really different, and create more of a multiplatform content experience to reinforce certain attributes about our brand."

The effort was so successful that by 2010, the successor to Voyeur, called "Imagine," had likewise made waves—this time in the form of a giant four-sided video cube appearing in various U.S. cities. The

FIGURE 2–1. HBO: Venturing Beyond Voyeur: HBO's "Imagine" campaign built on the success of the Voyeur Project by bringing giant four-sided video cube to U.S. cities. The idea: to show four sides of the same scene simultaneously, each side changing the perspective about what's really happening as part of a multichannel initiative to drive home HBO's "it's more than you imagined" brand positioning.

cube was designed to show four sides of the same scene simultaneously, each side changing the perspective about what's really happening—with the idea that it's only when you've seen all four sides that you get the full picture.

The effort, from BBDO and noted director Noam Murrow (*Smart People*), was designed to build buzz for an ambitious online initiative involving a microsite where viewers could unlock thirty-seven different video sequences as they progress through each one. Once unlocked, viewers were treated to the scenes presented in a whole new way, tying its various parts into a single, complete—and perspective-changing—narrative (see Figure 2–1).

"We like to think of ourselves as a network that defies people's expectations; we change their perspectives and we challenge the status quo," Monroe tells me. With both campaigns, the idea was to create something so engaging that it would "get people talking about the brand the same way they talk about our programming" and would drive home that "HBO is the best place to go for storytelling—the stories themselves are unique, and the way we tell them is unique, too."

Interestingly, the campaigns were as much about brand reinforcement as for demand generation. According to Monroe, a subscription service like HBO must remind viewers how innovative HBO programming can be, and why it's worth the monthly expenditure. It seems to be paying off. Despite a severe economic downturn, in the three years encompassing both "Voyeur" and "Imagine," subscribership grew substantially at HBO, to an all-time high of 27 million households.

MONKEY SHINES

It's important to note that this kind of approach doesn't just work for entertainment brands.

CareerBuilder.com, for example, has a long history of extending popular TV commercials into experiences that make the most of the digital realm.

Its popular chimpanzee TV campaign, featuring office-trapped Homo sapiens beset by bonobos, held resonance for anyone who's ever had the sinking suspicion they work with a bunch of monkeys.

Instead of (just) posting the spots online, the company has created branded applications like Monk-e-Mail, which lets you type up an email that will then be performed aloud by the text-recognizing, talking chimp that delivers your message.

Not only has the app been used by over 12 million unique visitors[2] who have sent nearly 100 million Monk-e-mails[3] but as a whole the campaign has helped CareerBuilder.com surpass Monster.com to become the number one job search site—insulting countless friends, family, and coworkers along the way.

Newer efforts, like the Anonymous Tip Giver, enable you to send anonymous email messages to annoying coworkers and others.

The messages feature office-bound characters from CareerBuilder TV ads—including a talking crocodile, a demonic executive, and a man whose shirt inexplicably has holes cut out over his nipples—and lets users write or record their own messages, or choose from prefab tips such as:

- "Next time you're like, giving a presentation like, to the boss, you should like, say 'like' less."

- "One out of ten people think your barking ringtone is funny. That one person is you."

- "Gum is the perfect segue between a tuna sandwich and a job interview."

Vox Populi

The United Nations' recent "Voices" campaign, meanwhile, used entirely different digital platforms to spread its message.

The campaign, launched in Australia, includes outdoor posters, print, and online elements that feature pictures of people in need. Consumers are invited to use their camera phones to snap a picture of the poster and then send the image to a short code. The system then instantly sends a prerecorded audio message from the person pictured in the poster back to the consumer, giving these people a voice on some of the issues they face.

Consumers are then prompted to visit a UN website where they can leave their own comments and thoughts about the interaction (see Figure 2–2).

"The voices of this campaign tell an Australian story that is completely outside the experience of most people," says former Saatchi & Saatchi CEO Simone Bartley. "It's easy to tune out, to ignore the fact that many Australians face a life in which they suffer abuse, poverty or neglect."[4]

The point here is simple: Digital quite simply is not for repurposing content that exists in other channels. It's about reimagining content to create blockbuster experiences that cannot be attained through any other medium.

Here are some rules for keeping Rule #2.

IF YOU CAN DREAM IT, YOU CAN DO IT

There's literally nothing you can't do in digital—it's the ultimate sandbox.

Just ask Carmen Electra.

In the weeks before the debut of her movie *Meet the Spartans*, a spoof of the hit Leonidas-in-a-loincloth epic *300*, 20th Century Fox set out to develop personalizable, "video-synchronized" promotional emails and mobile phone calls.

At the center of the effort: Carmen Has a Crush on You, a website where users are invited to send a personalized message from Ms. Electra.

Users are asked a series of questions about themselves and the

FIGURE 2–2. *The United Nations "Voices" campaign invites consumers to snap a camera phone image of posters featuring people to receive prerecorded messages from them about the challenges they face.*

email recipient, and can upload pictures of themselves or the recipient.

The resulting video message is a sight to behold. We enter as Ms. Electra is being "interviewed" about her film for a segment on an *Extra*-style celebrity news program.

Along the way, Electra becomes sidetracked with talk about a new love interest, and is cajoled by the reporter to tell viewers more. With amazing seamlessness, Electra names the user by name, even flashing a tattoo of the user's face on her hip, created using the image the user has uploaded.

Users have the ability to personalize Carmen's story by changing the subject of her love interest to someone they know. Users can then enter the phone number or email address of friends they designate, and then send a link to the video to their recipients. Even after all this time, the effort still stands up as one of the most gobsmacking examples of personalizable video.

Cable network A&E has been just as inventive. In addition to running the usual TV promotions for its ghost-hunter reality show *Paranormal States*, it has used outdoor billboards to transmit eerie messages to passersby, in a fashion that sounds as if it's coming from inside the person's own head.

The billboards make use of "targeted audio," which directs sound much as a laser beam directs light, transmitting audio in such a way that it can create a "sound bubble" around people directly in its path. You might hear spooky voices promoting the show, while the person standing next you doesn't hear a thing.

Look for other brands to start using these technologies—most notably in supermarkets, where you'll be greeted to offers only you can hear, seemingly from inside your own head.

Of course, as I recently wrote in *ADWEEK*, targeted audio presents some vexing issues to marketers. "On the one hand, the promise of speaking directly to consumers at the point of purchase is tempting, perhaps all trumping," I write. "On the other hand, the prospect of invading minds to sell Hamburger Helper is enough to make anyone want to hurl."

From all accounts, nobody was ticked off by *Paranormal State*'s use of targeted audio. But several people reported getting the willies—which, to be clear, was exactly the desired effect.

General Electric, on the other hand, uses "augmented reality" to show off its new "smart grid" technologies as part of its ongoing "eco-imagination" campaign. Web surfers can print out a symbol that, when held up to their webcams, creates a 3-D hologram, floating before their very eyes, that demonstrates how green technologies such as

FIGURE 2–3. Augmented reality: GE uses 3-D digital holograms to demonstrate its "smart grid" green technologies.

wind turbines and solar energy systems can make life more cost- and energy-efficient (see Figure 2–3).

Augmented reality, or AR, is taking off. Papa John's recently affixed an augmented reality image on the back of 30 million pizza boxes, enabling users to hold the boxes up to their webcams and use their keyboards to drive an animated 1972 Camaro in 3-D to commemorate the car CEO John Schnatter sold in 1984 to raise money to open his first pizza parlor.

Frito-Lay printed a symbol on bags of its Doritos Late Night Tacos that, when held up to your webcam, "explodes" to reveal holographic images of either Blink 182 or Big Boi, as they perform hot new singles floating in midair right before your eyes.

For its part, BMW recently created an AR experience to promote its Z4 roadster. Users can drive a 3-D holographic version of the car across a blank canvas and even shoot out "ink" from the rear wheels to create their own customized artwork that they can then share on their Facebook pages.

Ray-Ban's website, meanwhile, features a virtual mirror that uses data points collected using your webcam to enable you to virtually "try on" sunglasses before you place a purchase. Move your head from side to side, and you can check out all the angles before you make up your mind.

And Topps trading cards has used the same technology with new baseball cards that you can hold up to your webcam to see a 3-D avatar of your favorite player, complete with sportscaster audio narratives. You can even hit commands on your keyboard to see your favorite sports stars swing the bat, throw the ball, or make a catch.

In these early efforts, the technology is certainly not glitch-free. But the point is clear: Nothing's impossible with enough ingenuity.

IF YOU'VE GOT IT, DON'T FLAUNT IT

If it already exists in another medium, why not keep it there? Paying off a thirty-second spot with its sixty-second counterpart is anticlimactic at best.

And don't pull a Bud Bowl. In one of Budweiser's annual Super Bowl campaigns, voters were able to sign up to be able to use their mobile phones to text in their vote for their favorite of the brewer's seven television spots aired during the game. So far, so good: Mobile makes television fully interactive—it's called "participation TV."

But the reward for participation in this case was merely a text link to an unaired TV spot. Thousands participated. But you have to wonder how many marveled that for all the trouble, all they got was the chance to watch yet another television commercial, but this time on a business card–size screen.

That's not to say video's bad. Sometimes, video content itself finds life online that could never exist anywhere else.

Informed by insights into Burger King's core customers—basically defined as mostly young, mostly male, who frequent BK five times a month, visit other fast food restaurants at least eleven times a month, and make up the same demographic that gravitates to video sharing sites—Burger King pulled a whopper on its customers.

Working with ad agency Crispin Porter + Bogusky, BK recently staged an elaborate hoax to help the burger giant's target audience understand what life would be like without the Whopper sandwich. And they did it to boost brand loyalty during the Whopper's fiftieth anniversary.

Customers were secretly videotaped as cashiers informed them that the Whopper has been taken off the menu, discontinued forever. The results—captured by award-winning documentary filmmaker Henry Alex Rubin—are hilarious. Irate customers react in dismay. Some customers are given sandwiches from other burger chains, eliciting responses that border on the obscene.

Yes, TV spots leveraged some of this content, but were, for obvious reasons, tame compared to the grittier online version, not to mention the often-profane YouTube spoofs they inspired.

In the campaign's first two months, a seven and a half–minute documentary video at whopperfreakout.com was played 4 million times on BurgerKing.com and, at this writing, has been viewed 376,550 times on YouTube. And according to *Communications Arts* magazine, "Whopper Freakout" was the most-remembered campaign in Burger King history.[5]

In fact, the campaign was so successful, BK followed up with *Whopper Virgins*, a TV and web effort that brought Whoppers to remote regions of the world to get reactions from the locals—in their native garb—as they taste a Whopper sandwich for the first time.

As the site for the initiative put it, "From a remote hill village in Thailand, a rural farming community in Romania and the icy tundra of Greenland," the mocumentary took "13 planes, two dog sleds and a helicopter" to produce, all in an effort to get a real opinion on Burger King "from people who don't even have a word for 'burger.'"

The logistics alone might win BK a Pentagon contract. Which is great for Burger King's irreverent client base, if not for international relations.

FIGURE 2–4. *"Whopper Sacrifice" rewarded Facebook users for dumping their friends— causing an uproar on the popular social network.* The BURGER KING® *trademarks and advertisements are used with permission from Burger King Corporation.*

Burger King was also among the first to recognize that digital means engaging consumers, not just entertaining them. BK's Subservient Chicken site—in which users can enter commands that are acted out in real time by a man in a chicken suit, ostensibly to pitch BK chicken sandwiches, set the early standard for viral experiences. Since its launch in 2004, the site has been accessed over 1 billion times.

With Crispin's help, Burger King is even reimagining—and famously tweaking—new platforms themselves. For instance, in a hilariously twisted take on online "friending," its "Whopper Sacrifice" effort rewarded Facebook users with a free Whopper sandwich for every ten Facebook "friends" they dumped (see Figure 2–4).

The campaign was pulled after dumped friends complained to Facebook—which could only have further endeared the brand to its audience.

Recent online banner ads use augmented reality to let users place the King's head atop their own in a pitch to sell cheeseburgers that was so successful, franchises complained. The company has even updated its website to enable you to customize which kinds of content to emphasize in a nod to the whole notion of "have it your way."

In celebration of Burger King's first Whopper Bar at CityWalk in Orlando, meanwhile, BK created an online Burger King Studio where its most diehard fans can design and purchase their own custom Burger King T-shirts.

And in a true feat, the fast fooder's branded Xbox video games starring the Subservient Chicken and the brand's creepy "King" character have literally redefined the brand experience while dramatically boosting burger sales.

These decidedly funky games feature "the crowned one" in a rambunctious bumper car rally; a goofy "pocket racer" motorcycle game; and a first-person mission-based adventure where you sneak up on people to surprise them with food. More recently, the King has been appearing in iPhone games, including one centered on Valentine's Day, in which players tap the screen to burst heart-shaped bubbles.

Collectively, these efforts sent a message: Ronald McDonald had better look out before somebody toasts his sesame seed buns.

In all, these games provided a nice way to connect with its joystick-loving audience at an emotional level. But more impressively, at $3.99 each, they literally took off—selling over 3 million copies, for $11 million in revenue.

YOU'RE NOT IN "ADVERTISING" ANYMORE

All of these examples illustrate a largely unspoken truth about the advertising industry in the century's second decade: None of this has much to do with what has traditionally been referred to as "advertising."

AKQA founder Tom Bedecarré recognized the changing world of marketing far earlier than most. As cofounder of San Francisco ad agency Citron Haligman Bedecarré, he realized more than a decade ago that the ad agency of the future must think of itself as much as a software company as a communications firm.

After reinventing the agency as AKQA, Bedecarré's initiatives have spanned everything from mobile apps that let you snap a picture with a camera phone and send it to Nike to instantly receive an image of a customized pair of running shoes featuring the two most prominent colors from your picture, to elaborate websites where consumers around the world can craft and submit new bottle designs to Coca-Cola, to fuel-efficiency apps for Fiat automobiles.

"It's such a changing business," Bedecarré tells me. "It's [about] constantly pushing the envelope and getting out to the newest technology or newest services that clients are looking for."

Ditto for New York City–based R/GA, which has infused technology into its DNA in order to help clients navigate the on-demand era.

Its work in recent years has included Nokia viNe, a mobile application that lets users tag physical locations with notes, music, videos, and other content that is presented in a streaming vine to others with certain Nokia phones.

"Software is a medium," says John Mayo-Smith, R/GA's chief technology officer. "Having people who understand software and a high-quality user experience is really important."[6]

All of this is to say that an ad agency without these capabilities is just as anachronistic as Don Draper and the rest of the folks at Sterling Cooper, the fictional firm of TV's *Mad Men*, which depicts the antiquated world of Madison Avenue advertising in the early 1960s.

For some time now, the conventional wisdom at most agencies has been to partner with experts in specific fields—social networking, gaming, mobile, or any other discipline—in order to "get the best people for the job."

But given the success of AKQA, R/GA, and so many other innovators, perhaps it can be argued that to be truly holistic in our approach, it's better to grow innovations from one's own stem cells, so to speak, than to try to graft on capabilities on an ad-hoc basis.

Some would no doubt argue that it makes the most economic sense to hire experts to execute as needed, rather than taking on more overhead in an increasingly competitive marketplace. But it should be pointed out that it's hard to have the original ideas themselves if your own team doesn't have a firm grasp of the technologies.

Without a cross-disciplinary team of in-house experts, who knows what opportunities you—and by extension, your clients—may miss.

"It comes down to the brains that you have working with you to make it a reality," John Butler, cofounder of Butler, Shine, Stern & Partners, tells me.

"The history of the ad agency is the Bernbach model—the writer and art director sitting in a room together coming up with an idea," he says, referring to legendary adman Bill Bernbach, cofounder of DDB and the man who first combined copywriters and art directors as two-person teams.

Now, all that's changed. "[Today, there are] fifteen people sitting in a room. Media is as much a part of the creative department as a writer or an art director. And we have account planners—we call them 'connection planners'—in the room throwing around ideas," he says. "That facilitates getting to work that is about the experience, about ways to compel consumers to interact with your brand in a way that they become like free media" by actively promoting the brand for you.

If his team worked on the old Bernbach model, Butler adds, they would never have created something like those cool MINI billboards that display messages to drivers by name that I described in the last chapter. The idea actually spun out of a discussion about 3-D glasses for print ads.

"Someone in the interactive group said, 'We can probably do that same thing with [radio frequency identification] technology.'" By using transmitters built into the billboards, and building RFID chips into MINI key fobs, "when a person drives by, it will recognize him and it will spit out a message just for him."

He adds with considerable understatement: "Through having those capabilities, in-house engineers, technical guys who know the technology and what's available, we were able to create something that was really pretty cool."

BRANDING'S WHERE IT'S APP

Today, one of the ways brands can best insinuate themselves into consumers' lives is through web and mobile applications that either deliver a diversion or a genuine utility through experiences that cannot be replicated in other media.

FedEx's Launch a Package Facebook app, for instance, enables users to send virtual goods—photos or links or other digital curios—to other Facebook users. The items arrive in a FedEx box that the recipient opens.

In its first two weeks, the app had 258,000 total installations on Facebook profile pages, and more than 15,000 active users who sent 1 million packages—helping it land the number one spot on Facebook's Most Activity rankings.[7]

Say what you will, but while the app may seem frivolous, it does provide brand reinforcement that's dead on to FedEx's positioning and value proposition—reinforcement that occurs every time a package is sent or received. In fact, according to *eMarketer*, brands are spending well over $40 million a year developing such apps.[8]

Nationwide Insurance has created an iPhone app that is essentially a mobile accident kit to help its customers in the event of an accident. Among other things, the app calls emergency services in the event of an accident, helps the user collect and exchange insurance information, stores the user's insurance and vehicle info for easy lookup, takes and stores accident photos, converts the user's iPhone into a handy flashlight, helps connect with a local Nationwide agent, and more (see Figure 2–5).

"Content and functionality are the new creativity—it's not about whether you have a whiz-bang rich media banner running," Andy Bateman, CEO of brand consultancy Interbrand New York, tells me. "Are you doing something that's actually helpful and useful to people?"

Not that it always works.

Without a doubt, many Facebook and web apps have short shelf lives, as enthusiasm hits hard, and then ebbs just as quickly, in a pattern that can be described as a precipitous bell curve.

The problem is that most apps are overly complicated and ill fitted to the flit-away nature of social networking sites—and because most are merely interruptive ads in an unwelcoming venue.

Even FedEx's fun little app quickly lost steam. Within six months of its launch, it was attracting only 1,500 users per month.[9]

Still, while apps made specifically for social networks present their challenges, even some of the most esoteric web utilities are generating excitement among users around the world. But you have to know how to do it right.

Japanese clothing brand Uniqlo has a utility called the "Uniqlock"—a web clock that has become a worldwide phe-

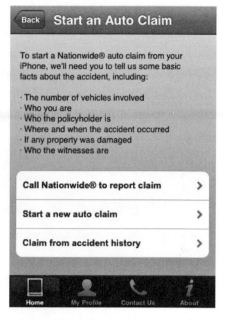

FIGURE 2-5. *The accidental innovator: Nationwide's iPhone app provides true utility when its customers need it most.*

nomenon on social networks, user desktops, and the iPhone.

The clock runs year-round, 24/7, and features video of dancers as they pirouette, plié, and otherwise move their bodies to communicate the time of day—hands or legs positioned to show high noon or 3:45 P.M., for example. It's all set to fun music, and the video is always timed to show off seasonal fashions. The web and widget versions of the clock have been viewed over 68 million times in 209 countries.

Additional activities are rolled out each season. The brand's recent Uniqlo Christmas Grid, for instance, enabled folks to modify the Uniqlo logo, twist it, divide it, combine it, and mix it around— all of which is then displayed with actions from other users around the world into a quaintly mesmerizing display. Within days of its launch, 116,345 people from 118 countries had added their touch to the grid over 65 million times.

FIGURE 2–6. The Target Gift Globe iPhone app puts gift ideas in the palm of your hand.

And just look at the popularity of iPhone apps like Target's.

In the runup to the holiday season, Target launched a free iPhone app that visually turns the familiar Target logo into a snow globe every time you shake the phone. When you do, you receive gift ideas and information on how to buy the gift at target.com or your nearest physical location. There is even a gift list you can check off once you've made the purchase.

"You could customize whether it's [a gift] for a teenage girl, or Dad or whoever, and then you shake it, and suggestions for that person for the price range you selected come up in the snow globe," says Bedecarré of AKQA, which created the app (see Figure 2–6).

Carnival Cruise Lines has had great fun with these kinds of apps as well. It recently rolled out "sidewalk aquariums"—interactive screens built into store windows—that enable passersby to use their mobile phones to design their own digital fish to populate the aquarium. They can even come back and feed their fish or just hang out with their new digital pets. The idea: Reinforce Carnival's position as a brand that brings fun to life.

We'll talk a lot more about apps of all kinds throughout this book. But in general, whether it's technically a widget, an app, or a utility, the idea can be applied to many kinds of amazing new experiences.

MAKE IT UNIQUELY YOURS

In all of the examples above, the experiences cannot be replicated in any other medium. And each is arguably ownable.

True, anyone can create interactive video content that's projected onto the sides of buildings, video cubes, and any number of other outdoor and online venues, but HBO's initiatives were intrinsically aligned to its brand positioning.

Several brands create experiences that let you send customized content to friends, yet CareerBuilder's are exquisitely tied to its value proposition.

Any brand can create a web clock. And yes, Uniqlo's clothes have nothing to do with telling time. But the brand's web experience presents its product lines in action, posing its models in a highly memorable fashion.

Likewise, anyone can create a game from their brand's characters. But Burger King's quirky take brings its characters to life in a way that's completely in step with its offbeat brand.

And offerings like Nationwide's "mobile emergency kit" are replicable by any number of brands in its category, but is perfectly matched with Nationwide's positioning as a go-to resource when you need it most, anywhere you may roam.

Indeed, every digital initiative should be viewed through a simple prism.

Don't do it in digital if it can be done better or more meaningfully somewhere—or by somebody—else.

Q&A

Alex Bogusky Tells All

Alex Bogusky, cochairman of Crispin Porter + Bogusky

IF THE ADVERTISING world has a rock star these days, it's definitely Alex Bogusky.

As cochairman of Crispin Porter + Bogusky, he has led the Miami (and now, Boulder, Colorado) advertising agency to national prominence with its breakthrough work for brands such as Burger King, Domino's, Coke Zero, and Microsoft.

The agency's recent work for Microsoft, for instance, has turned "I'm a PC" into a viable retort to Apple's longtime "I'm a Mac" TV campaign, pushing up PC sales while cutting into Apple's business by playing to bargain-hunting consumers.

But it is in the digital realm where the agency shines brightest. The agency's Burger King's Xbox games, Whopper Sacrifice Facebook app, *Whopper Virgins* viral videos, and that age-old favorite, Subservient Chicken, have helped BK become legendary for connecting with the fast food world's mostly young, mostly male clientele, while boosting sales most of the last five years.

More recently, Bogusky's work has included a system that enables consumers to place pizza orders to Domino's through TiVo, and a Coke Zero Facial Profiler application that makes use of advanced facial recognition technology to find people who look like you via Facebook.

For the effort, Bogusky has earned himself glowing profiles in *Business Week*, the *New York Times*, *Newsweek*, *TIME*, and many other publications—as well as a spot on bestsellers lists for his book, *Baked In: Creating Products and Businesses That Market Themselves*. He was recently named ADWEEK's "Creative Director of the Decade."

Bogusky, whose laid-back slacker-chic style has come to symbolize cutting-edge creativity (he once auctioned off the services of Crispin's interns on eBay), believes a new marketing era is here; one where successful brands piggyback on pop culture and (gasp) tap into the power of porn—and where the consumer is most definitely in control.

Rick Mathieson: You once famously described your mantra as "whatever it takes to make your clients famous." What makes digital experiences so powerful in fame-building, versus other channels?

Alex Bogusky: The power is just in the control that you've given the consumer.

It's not so much control over the creative, although that's part of it. But the idea that as you put content out there, if it's interesting and relevant, you get real-time comments, and you get even real-time alterations.

With Burger King, consumers are involved with [the King character] to all sorts of degrees. And in some instances, they're doing things that we'd never do.

You might see [a picture of] King's head on the Dalai Lama's body. There's the big sport of retouching that exists out there and people having fun with Photoshop.

Marketers for a long time have been fond of saying that the consumer owns the brands. But I don't think that they really believed it. Because they didn't have to believe it. Because the consumer didn't have the tools to [own it].

Maybe what they meant was the consumer talks about the brand or occasionally thinks about it, and what they think is what the brand is. But I think what's happening now is the consumer—whether you embrace it or not—is involved in the creation of your brand. So they're active participants—not just when you invite them to create content, but even if you just make something interesting—they just start to make content [around it].

I think there's power in being courageous enough to embrace that, and say, "Hey, a lot of wild stuff is going to happen; we're going to be brave enough to just roll with it." And entrust that it works out because that old saying "the consumer owns the brand" is true, and it's always been true, so this is no different.

I think a lot of our take on new media is that it's the same old thing. When we look at the work that we do, and themes that run through the work that we do, something like Subservient Chicken is a pretty basic old-school advertising message, which is "Chicken Your Way." It's skinned a new way, and it's served up in new media, and people find it startling, just because they're not used to it.

[Some marketers] also question, "Well, why would this work? How could this sell chicken sandwiches?" Yet somehow we came along to a point where they believe that you could watch a thirty-second commercial, and if you laughed, that might sell chicken sandwiches. It's funny because that was the conversation until all this other media came along.

In my mind it's just no different. You get the consumer to spend time with your brand—and, on average, they spend a lot more time with some of the more interactive stuff than they do with a thirty-second commercial or even a sixty-second commercial.

And I think that the old logic holds; that's a good thing.

RM: Clearly more marketers are catching on. But your work in particular has such a viral quality—it gets spread around fast. What's your secret?

AB: Should I say? We have a very specific definition for the word "relevance." And our definition of relevance is the conversation that pop culture is having with itself. We've bandied about the term, and we've used the term, and we've had people ask for "relevance'" and clients that want to be "more relevant."

And it was hard to lock down what that really meant. So we put a definition to it. There are themes that are going through pop culture. And they're unsettling themes, questions.

We find a little piece of that, and we try to hook our creative into that, so that when the work comes out, it's part of a larger conversation. And that it's going to stir a little bit of talk, because we're not sure about which way to go with this.

And with something like "Subservient Chicken," a lot of that technology came out of X-rated websites. That tension created, I think, a lot of what made that viral. There was nothing naughty about the site, but there was something about the fact that somehow people knew that a lot of this cutting-edge technology, like webcams and stuff, that that's where this stuff lives. So that provided some tension.

And then with things like the King, I think as a culture, we're used to using critters to sell fast food to kids, and we've not noticed that it's odd. And when you change the target, and you take the King and you start talking to adults with the same sort of methodology, it gives you insight into your own culture; it opens a little window and you're like, "Whoa, that's kind of freaky." It's stuff like that, basically, that we try to find and leverage.

RM: You've found a particularly willing client in Burger King. How do you make pitches for initiatives such as the *Whopper Freak Out* viral videos or the "Whopper Sacrifice" Facebook app? Those are daring moves for a family burger chain.

AB: We're pretty strategic and the work in general, the themes behind the work, can be traditionally strategic.

Once you have the idea, and you take it into some other technologies and other forms of media, it takes on a life of its own. The idea wants to live in different ways. Things that weren't possible in broadcast or print become possible online. And the conversation is usually not anything more than we probably have five ideas and we're saying, we've got this concept. This one leverages this aspect of the strategy, and this one does that.

It's usually a very business-oriented conversation, not a creative conversation.

RM: You've also made waves with the Burger King Xbox games.

AB: The thing I'm cautious of is product placement [in games], because I'm dubious of the idea that if I see someone drinking a Coke in a movie, that I'm going to be more likely to drink it. Or anymore than I would be more likely if I saw my friend drinking a Coke, actually probably even less so. Now, there are places where I think it's pretty effective, like with new product launches. In automotive launches, I think product placement is probably a pretty effective tool.

In the advergame area, I think the same thing. Sometimes it's really handled like product placement. I tend to like the notion that the brand has got a story, and that story can come out through a game.

[But these are] actually two separate things: One is, do you have a story that could even be a game, and then two, do you have the chops to make a good game? I think if all those things come together, it can be a pretty fun way for the consumer to interact [with the brand] and there're endless ways that you could turn that into anything, from branding to a form of couponing. Online, you could provide coupons for high scores and things like that, so you could drive people into BK, or whatever business you're doing advergames for. So it's pretty flexible. And I like it.

RM: In your view, what has been Crispin's most successful campaign in terms of digital, on-demand experiences?

AB: "Subservient Chicken" was definitely the one that was the most phenomenal. We do a lot of this kind of stuff, and most of it does really well. But that one just went into an insane realm.

It reminded me of when Budweiser did the "Whassup" [TV commercials, where a bunch of friends greet each other saying "Whassup?"]. I'm sure they try all the time to do "Whassup," but you can't necessarily do it every time.

We never officially launched "Chicken" when it first came out. We just sent it out to a few friends to say, "Hey check this out, see if it's working." And then ka-boom. And we were watching the numbers come in.

It reminded me of that old FedEx spot where at the dotcom they're sitting around waiting for the orders to come in, and a couple come in and they're like, "Oh geez, are we going to go out of business?" And then a couple more come in, and they start to feel good. A bunch more come in and they start high-fiving. And then a trillion come in and they start sweating.

It was very much like that. The site was being mirrored by other people to keep it from crashing. It was a really strange thing.

RM: What are some of the challenges marketers need to look out for in the age of so many transmedia possibilities?

AB: That's a good question. I think there are things that make it difficult, and one is where the money goes.

It's easier for me because I'm on the agency side and all creative is equally lovable. But when you take it over to the client, and they see where they're spending money, broadcast is still much more important in their eyes, simply because they're spending more money on it. Some of those [new] ideas start to feel unimportant because they're cheaper.

I think that's one of the biggest challenges. And I think the other challenge is, for us, our greatest successes are still when we control the media. And that doesn't happen with every client; we work through a lot of buying services. And we have great relationships with them.

But I think in the cases where we've been most successful, we are able to, on a very fast basis, adjust our media around ideas.

But when it comes down to where you're watching the money go, it's still all going to TV. And so that's where the attention goes, and by the time some of this other stuff gets approved, it's too late to do, because it's got a longer timeline.

So that's a real struggle—letting the work outside of traditional media get its due.

Don't Just Join the Conversation— Spark It

FOR ALL THE HYPERBOLE that surrounds Facebook, MySpace, Twitter, and other social networking outlets, many marketers may be shocked to learn that most consumers don't really want to have a personal relationship with your brand, much less hang out with people who do.

Yet the belief that consumers do hold such ambitions—or that they could somehow be coaxed to do so—has fueled wild enthusiasm for social networking sites as the ultimate in marketing platforms, a powerful way of facilitating communication and connections with and among a brand's most committed devotees and their friends.

The results so far have been mixed.

Yes, you can hang out on the Facebook page of Procter & Gamble's "2x Ultra Tide" detergent, and even share your "favorite places to enjoy stain-making moments!" with the twenty or so other folks who have done so over the last few years.

Or you could visit the Facebook page for PepsiCo's Quaker Oats and join 1,200 fans who are encouraged by the brand's unintentionally funny tagline to "Go humans, go."

You could also poke yourself in the eye with a stick.

"All brands want consumers to be their 'friends.' Oh, boy, do they!" Ted McConnell, general manager of interactive marketing and innovation at P&G, recently told the Advertising Club of Cincinnati. "[But] I don't want to be best friends with a brand."[1]

Despite such sentiments, by 2013, marketers are expected to spend $1.6 billion a year to tap into social networking sites.[2]

Brand initiatives can run the gamut from advertising banners placed on users' personal profile pages, to the branded apps users willingly place on their own pages, to pages created and hosted expressly by and for a brand, to clubs, and even to fully functioning storefronts in 3-D virtual worlds—and to everything in between.

To be sure, there have been successes. But the challenges may prove far more insightful.

THE NETWORK EFFECT

Today, there are well over 500 million members of social networking sites, including, it seems, at least 60 percent of wealthy consumers in the United States. According to a recent Wealth Survey from the Luxury Institute, American consumers with an average income of $287,000 and an average net worth of $2.1 million typically have memberships in 2.8 social networks, and average 110 connections.[3]

The allure of advertising within social networks has always been obvious and powerful, as social networking sites like Facebook and MySpace can offer exquisitely targeted advertising to their user bases. Need to target lawyers who are pet rock owners and drive Subarus, or brunette lesbians who vote Republican? No problem.

But advertisers have long been the bête noirs of social networks—essentially injecting themselves into other people's conversations. And after several attempts at making advertising work on Facebook, Bebo, MySpace, and others, many marketers are giving up.

"From a marketer's perspective, social networks look brilliant on paper," says Alistair Beattie, head of strategic planning at AKQA, London. "It's a switched-on crowd with a huge amount of time who hold brands close to them. The difficulty is that they regard this as their space. We have all become our own source of entertainment. . . . But there is a resistance to being advertised at."[4]

In fact, a study from research firm IDC found that just 3 percent of U.S. Internet users would be willing to let advertisers pitch products to their friends. The firm characterized advertising on social networks as "stillborn."[5]

As P&G's McConnell puts it: "I have a reaction to [Facebook] as a consumer advocate and an advertiser: What in heaven's name made you think you could monetize the real estate in which somebody is breaking up with their girlfriend?"[6]

Still, inspired by musicians who have long found often astounding success "friending" fans who seem to thrive on listening to their music and then discussing it with other fans, a number of marketers have sought to socialize their brands—not by interjecting themselves into other people's conversations, but by creating their own social network destinations.

Chrysler's Jeep brand has been actively and successfully using MySpace and Facebook for years. At Jeep's MySpace page, for instance, the brand's many friends can share their Jeep adventures with others, make friends, make plans, meet up, and get more information on the latest models.

For Jeep Compass, Jeep didn't even bother to put its own URL at the bottom of advertisements—it listed its MySpace page instead. Explains Chuck Sullivan, engagement manager at Jeep's digital agency, Organic, the idea is "to fish where the fish are."[7]

Which explains why a MySpace and Facebook page is now a must for most new major motion pictures, from *War of the Gods* to *Green Lantern*, where fans can express their excitement for their favorite films, download screen graphics, watch trailers, and build some serious buzz for the flicks well in advance of their premieres.

Starbucks, meanwhile, uses its Facebook and MySpace pages, along with its Twitter feed, in much the same way, and to promote upcoming drink specials. In one recent integrated campaign, the coffeehouse chain ran newspaper ads challenging consumers to seek out Starbucks posters in six major cities and be the first to post a photo of one using Twitter.

And MTV is heavily mixing its television content with social media. *What You're Watching with Alexa Chung* is a daily one-hour talk and music show in which viewers can interact with the host and her guests via Twitter, Facebook, and other digital venues, in a kind of Web 2.0 update to the text- and email-driven format of MTV's original audience participation show, *Total Request Live*. And no CNN or ESPN newscast seems complete anymore without viewer tweets appearing onscreen.

On the surface, these kinds of initiatives sound great—but often fall short.

AGAINST THE TIDE

The 2x Ultra Tide Facebook page I mentioned is just one example of an effort that in some ways has stained Procter & Gamble's reputation for marketing prowess. But it's not the only one.

P&G once launched a campaign to invite Facebook members in twenty college campus networks to become fans of Crest Whitestrips on the product's Facebook page. The effort attracted upward of 14,000 fans. How? By offering thousands of free movie screenings and sponsored Def Jam concerts.

As the *New York Times* puts it, "a brand of hemorrhoid cream could have attracted a similar number of nominal 'fans.'" Indeed, as the *Times* points out, within months, 4,000 fans had left the club.[8] Without expensive promotions, P&G discovered the tide was definitely against it.

But it's not as though P&G has somehow failed where others have thrived.

Out of the over 600,000 branded pages that Facebook Page Tracker monitors, a mere 57,000 have more than 1,000 "fans."

Of the biggest consumer product brands with millions of fans, even mighty Coca-Cola and Starbucks come in a distant second to a politician. Starbucks, for instance, has 3,703,584 to Coke's 3,526,967, while President Obama has nearly double that, at 6,486,228.

Somewhat surprisingly, at this writing, at least, Nutella comes in third among brands, with 3,157,966 fans. Which sounds astounding— millions of people signing on to become fans of a hazelnut spread. But to put it all into perspective, generic "pizza"—not a brand, just the topic—has more than any of these brands, with 4,460,139 fans.

While some brands seem to want to inject themselves into conversations, others are appropriating the conversations all together.

Mars Inc.'s popular Skittles candy brand recently turned its official website into an overlay of Skittles pages on popular social networking sites, essentially hijacking Facebook, Flickr, Twitter, and so on by simply floating a navigation widget over pages devoted to Skittles on these external sites.

The "Home" button brings you to Skittles' Facebook Page; "Chatter" brings you to the Skittles Twitter page; "Products" points you to the associated Wikipedia page(s); "Friends" points you to Skittles' Facebook friends. And "Videos" sends you to Skittles' YouTube page.

It's certainly a nice way to save money on site maintenance and updates. And it is kind of cool. But in this case, the brand brings very little to the table and abdicates all control over what might be said about the brand on the brand's own site. In fact, there's actually an age verification step and a warning about the possible content users may experience—on a site ostensibly designed to sell kids candy.

I guess "Tasting the Rainbow" isn't what it used to be. And things aren't that much better in social networks of the 3-D virtual-world variety.

A LIFE WORTH SAVING?

From the beginning, brands have been looking to score some real money in pretend worlds like There, Second Life, YoVille, and Utherverse. And for good reason. According to projections from Gartner, 80 percent of Internet users will participate in some form of online virtual reality world by 2012.[9]

What's more, in a typical twenty-four-hour period, $405,931 (that's real U.S. dollars) are exchanged in Second Life, an amount that is growing at 15 percent per month.

Indeed, at the height of hype around Second Life, there was a veritable land rush among brands such as Toyota, Sun, Starwood Hotels, Sony BMG, BMW, Philips, Warner Bros., Nike, and dozens of others, all hoping to create virtual venues where consumers could literally immerse themselves in the brand and its products.

Starwood's W Hotels opened Aloft—a virtual prototype of one of its real-world hotel chains—months in advance of its real-world debut.

American Apparel opened a massive virtual outlet where residents could purchase virtual versions of urban fashions for their avatars, and real-world versions for themselves, which could be shipped to their home addresses.

Sony BMG built a virtual building with rooms devoted to popular musicians like DMS and Justin Timberlake, where fans can mingle and listen to, and even purchase, tunes that they can then listen to as they make their way around the simulated world.

The *New York Times*, which actually has its own virtual-world news bureau, has run weekend getaway guides to Second Life in the "Escapes" section of its printed newspaper—pointing to many venues for fashion, food, and fun in-world.

Not to be outdone, Reuters, CNN, and other news organizations have their own news bureaus within SL to report on events therein.

But no sooner did the Second Life hype hit overdrive than brands started hitting the brakes. Turns out the virtual world's "Wild West" is just that—wild.

When Sun Microsystems held a virtual presentation with SL for attendees from around the world, it was overrun by avatars who stormed the stage and made much mayhem.

The Reuters news bureau was vandalized within two days of opening, sprayed with virtual graffiti.

And a group called the Second Life Liberation Army staged virtual attacks on Reebok and American Apparel stores in Second Life. According to the *New York Times*, the SLLA says it's fighting for voting rights for avatars—as well as stock in Linden Labs, which created and runs Second Life.[10]

But the biggest hurdle for brands in Second Life is far simpler, and far more disastrous: lack of traffic. While the world boasts membership in the millions, there are often so few residents in any one in-world venue at any one time that reach, much less frequency, is far less than advertisers have hoped.

Without warning, brands began pulling out of Second Life as fast as they had jumped in. Second Life storefronts for Best Buy's Geek Squad, Dell, and American Apparel have closed, as have others.

"There's not a compelling reason to stay," says Brian McGuinness, VP with Starwood Hotels, which closed down its Second Life operations.[11]

SOCIALLY ACCEPTABLE

Right about now you may be wondering if I'm completely discounting social networking as a branding platform. But nothing could be further from the truth.

If anything, the fearless brands that have dared to venture into these uncharted waters have taught themselves and the rest of us a thing or two about what works and what doesn't within many forms of social networks—at least right now.

Which brings us to Rule #3: Don't Just Join the Conversation—Spark It.

There are those who argue that brands should join ongoing conversations among communities of interest—think Tony Hawk's fashion label sponsoring a skateboarding club's Facebook group in addition to its real-world events, for instance.

That approach certainly works, and has been a hallmark of sponsorships for time immemorial. But to create truly meaningful online communities of interest around your brand requires that you go a step further—sparking conversations and interactions among your own consumer base.

In other words, if you're going to be part of the conversation, be the party that initiates it, through compelling experiences that take the following precepts into account.

HAVE A REASON FOR BEING

Just because social networking is hot, that doesn't mean its right for your brand. Don't just ask yourself what your social networking strategy should be. Ask *why* it should be, and why consumers should care.

Consumer care company Johnson & Johnson seems to have asked these questions, and come up with a good answer. Its social networking site, BabyCenter, hosts a hugely successful online community that reaches 78 percent of all online women who are pregnant or are mothers of children under twenty-four months old in the U.S.

"More moms go through BabyCenter in a month in the U.S. than there are babies born in the U.S. in a year," BabyCenter's Chairwoman Tina Sharkey tells me. Over the last few years, Sharkey has led BabyCenter as it has expanded its offerings to include expert advice, research, and articles based on a child's age. Most important of all, it has been actively fostering community among moms so women have a place where they can share pictures, find people like them, write blogs, share comments, pass on motherly advice, and more.

"The idea is to have the kind of engaged environment that you might find on the blogger platforms, like Facebook and MySpace, but very specifically targeted at the tribe of motherhood," she says.

Indeed, at any given time, Gwen might be writing a journal about how she's feeling in her third trimester. Shauna may be sharing photos from her son's first birthday party. Irina might be replying to another mom with a helpful diaper-rash–relieving tip. And Ashley is creating a group for moms who make their own baby food.

To the extent that J&J promotes its products, it's all handled as any ad buy from any advertiser would be—and the site even accepts advertising from other marketers.

"Just having that relationship with the global network and the global platform that reaches and engages with moms in these early stages of her life is a phenomenal asset for Johnson & Johnson to have in their portfolio," says Sharkey (see Figure 3–1).

On the other end of the spectrum, Sony's PlayStation Home is a virtual world designed solely and specifically for the rabid gamers who cotton to the PlayStation gaming console.

Think PS3 games where certain points or ranks unlock rewards inside the virtual world. Or tournaments and events around specific game titles.

As with Second Life, consumer brands seeking to reach the same audience as PS3—Red Bull, Diesel, and Paramount Pictures, among others—have already taken up residence within PlayStation Home, with their own game-related islands. Red Bull's island, for instance, features the game Air Racer.

Comcast is experimenting with a virtual world tied to its brand. Comcast Town is a virtual world linked to Facebook that enables users to kick back, socialize, and enjoy entertainment brought to them by virtual versions of Comcast's web, phone, and TV offerings, naturally.

Even brands oriented to very young kids are setting up their own stand-alone worlds. Cereal giant General Mills, for instance, runs

FIGURE 3–1. *Johnson & Johnson's BabyCenter is a hugely successful online community of mothers with children through age ten.*

Millsberry, an online virtual world heavily promoted on boxes of Lucky Charms.

Rendered in the style of cereal-box cartoons, kids take control of a virtual city, outfit their own avatars, design their own houses, and use a virtual currency called Millsbucks to buy toys, furniture, pay for haircuts for their avatars, as well as for activities and games. Yes, there's lots of promotion for products such as Trix, French Toast Crunch, and Reese's Peanut Butter Puffs. But also ample opportunity for kids to play math and spelling games, visit a virtual museum to learn about art, and engage in civic activities to better their communities.

This can work for business-to-business brands, too. Visa's Business Network, for instance, is a Facebook community that enables 50,000 small business owners to connect with each other and customers and exchange ideas, information, and opportunities with other small business owners (see Figure 3–2).

GIVE THEM A REASON TO KEEP COMING BACK

As I just described, Sony's PlayStation Home has a built-in traffic generator: gaming tournaments that attract avid gamers in hopes of winning prizes and bragging rights. Virtual MTV pulls traffic by enabling fans to attend special events with celebrities, play paintball, race cars, and chat with other fans from around the world.

Others soc-nets are trying to create their own reasons to keep people coming back.

At STAtravelers.com, customers can meet other people who love to travel, and who may be part of the vacation packages they purchase. They can read about other people's adventures through their own words, tips, pictures, and videos. And they can ask experts about travel-related issues.

FIGURE 3–2. The Visa Business Network brings a community of entrepreneurs together online.

There are even monthly travel prizes to Australia, Europe, Japan, and other destinations. And Twitter and RSS feeds will even send STA subscribers the cheapest flights so they can stop searching online for the best deals.

Reebok, meanwhile, has found success with its GoRunEasy website, a global community where over 20,000 runners find running partners, upload and share images, browse other runners' playlists, and share their favorite running courses.

And J&J's BabyCenter, of course, is designed from the ground up to offer tools, information, and social experiences tied to the age of one's child, from pregnancy to ten years old. Ovulation calculators, a baby name finder, and developmental information and articles for every step of a child's development—and all that advice and commiseration with fellow mothers—mean women have a reason to come back on a regular basis.

KEEP IT SIMPLE, SOCIAL—AND PREFERABLY EVENTS-BASED

Earlier in the chapter we talked about Jeep's presence on social networking sites. Jeep aficionados comprise a community that pre-existed outside of an online social network, and their digital experiences are designed to simply leverage the Internet to foster a way for the faithful to stay in touch and keep on top of the latest real-world Jeep Jamboree events.

In fact, the best model for social networking may very well be around specific, limited-time events—whether it's a Jeep Jamboree, an upcoming trip, or a product launch or movie premiere.

CBS's *CSI: New York*, for instance, has used Second Life as a platform for episodes in which characters from the show enter the virtual world to solve a crime. The show has used "machinima"—the technique by which avatars and sets within Second Life are filmed just as a movie is filmed in real life—to capture the action. The events have included online murder mysteries that the show's most avid fans can solve from within the virtual world (see Figure 3–3).

FIGURE 3–3. CBS's CSI: New York *has featured Second Life in some of its episodes, and has used the platform to enable viewers to immerse themselves in a virtual-world murder mystery.*

Along that same line, Anheuser-Busch InBev recently created a Facebook app that enabled 4,600 people participating in a Bud Party Cruise to see who else would be on the ship, upload photos of the event, and to keep in touch afterward.

Likewise, Land Rover used Twitter and popular Tweeters to promote the launch of its newest models during the runup to their debut at the New York Auto Show, reaching nearly 300,000 followers eager to get sneak peaks of the new cars.

Then there's the Tweetup. Pepsi, Panasonic, and the National Hockey League are just a few of the companies using Twitter to organize parties and events. When Ziploc wanted to promote its storage bags and containers, for instance, it worked with event company House Party to leverage Twitter to attract 14,000 people to over 1,000 "home organization" parties.[12]

Ultimately, who cares if this app or page isn't used much (or at all) six months from now? There will be any number of new social events for the brand to moderate as it reinforces its place in the lives of its constituents.

KEEP IT REAL

Debate is raging over whether it's okay to pay bloggers, Facebookers, or tweeters to post about your product or brand, a practice sometimes derided as "blogola." Mommy bloggers in particular seem to have been singled out for accepting free products, gifts, payment, or junket trips for posting reviews—practices that many view as especially pervasive among this group of bloggers. But mommies certainly don't have a monopoly on such things.

Holly Madison, the former Playboy Playmate and one of Hugh Hefner's three girlfriends on the reality TV show *The Girls Next Door*, was paid for endorsing Giorgio Armani products on her Twitter page, which boasts 175,000 followers. Likewise, that Twitter push for Land Rover mentioned above entailed paid posters as well.

In Madison's case, a company called IZEA, a "social media marketing" firm whose technology helps companies enlist celebrities and others to post about their products, played an active role in the promotion.

According to Ted Murphy, CEO of IZEA, these "sponsored conversations" can fetch anywhere from a few dollars per post to tens of thousands of dollars, depending on the reach of a particular Twitter feed, Facebook page, or blog. Launched in 2006, the company already boasts a network of 250,000 bloggers and clients such as Disney, Kmart, Paramount Pictures, Levi's, Sony Pictures, and others.

Murphy tells me the company has a strict code of conduct that, among other things, does not necessarily guarantee that a blogger or poster will say only positive things about your products. And everything must be disclosed, meaning it should be absolutely clear when a message is sponsored and paid for.

"A lot of people make this assumption that people are paid to post nice things. On our platform, we have what we call 'freedom of authenticity,'" he says. "We pay people whether they say good things, bad things, whatever it may be. We want them to share their honest and open opinions. We don't allow advertisers to put words in the blogger's mouth or say 'Hey, we want you to tell all your friends that this is the greatest product ever' or anything like that."

Still, it is hard to imagine a brand paying someone to say bad things about their products. But while my own personal view is that brands should avoid pay-for-say transactions with bloggers, it can be argued that this kind of arrangement is not fundamentally different than "program notes" in television news programs that promote upcoming shows, or "a few words from our sponsors" in entertainment programs.

The rule in anything you do should be to ensure complete transparency and provide full disclosure at the very minimum. Indeed, that's not just my view—that's the ruling of the Federal Trade Commission, which issued guidelines in fall 2009 that stipulate bloggers must disclose when they're compensated by an advertiser to discuss a product.

But be warned: Even then, there are arrangements that are completely ethical and transparent, but that still call their value into question by seeming less than authentic.

Drug maker Novo-Nordisk, for instance, recently teamed up with twenty-four-year-old auto-racing superstar Charlie Kimball to create a Twitter page called Race with Insulin.

Kimball, it turns out, has diabetes and uses Novo's drug Levemir to keep his insulin in check. With the Twitter feed, Kimball is able to talk about his life in racing, about his life as a diabetic building a successful career despite his condition, and about his life as a Levemir user. But interspersed with posts about, say, getting ready for bed before a big day at the Honda Indy in Toronto, for instance, are posts like this:

"Off to bed pre-Toronto. Just used my Levemir® FlexPen®. For Levemir® (insulin detemir [rDNA origin] prescribing info: [tinyurl])."

It's possible Kimball tapped out that post—complete with registration marks in their legally mandated positions, notes on the chemical composition of the product, and a conscientious link to an official brand website. But it sounds much more like corporate copywriting at its stilted worst. Which, in turn, casts the entire effort into question.

In my view, from a branding perspective it would be better for Novo to let Kimball write about his life without such artificial-sounding posts, or to create a social networking site that's openly meant to promote the drug among its community of interest, instead of trying to mix the two.

Bottom line: If you're going to engage in social media, keep it honest, open, and authentic.

MAKE SOCIAL APPS USEFUL

If you're going to create apps for Facebook and other social networking sites, make sure they're truly useful. In fact, we should probably call them "branded social utilities" instead.

Nike once created a Facebook application called The Baller's Network that enables pick-up basketball players to manage leagues, an effort that Nike has proclaimed will "revolutionize the way players around the world connect online and compete on the court." After six months, despite efforts to bring it global with support for three languages, the application had only 3,400 users per month.[13] Perhaps it was not useful enough in facilitating games.

In contrast, Pizza Hut recently launched a Facebook app, The Hut, that enables customers to place pizza orders without leaving their profile pages. There's even a sweetener—e-gift cards and the chance to win $50 gift certificates for ordering online.

The brand is clearly onto something. The Hut has already passed $1 billion in online sales,[14] and was the first major pizza maker to launch an iPhone app that lets you order food in a matter of moments, anytime, everywhere. In its first three months, the app locked in over $1 million in sales.

Facebook utilities like this will only help the company push more pies. Along the way, it'll collect valuable customer data it would never get with newspaper coupons or phone orders.

For its part, BabyCenter offers many useful apps and is extending them to mobile phones—including an app for monitoring one's ovulation cycle, called "Booty Call."

"We will send you fertility alerts of when you are ovulating, and tips and things to think about around your ovulation calendar," says BabyCenter's Sharkey. "And you can also sign up a spouse or partner so they'll get a text message that's based off of your ovulation cycle."

Which explains the app's provocative name (see Figure 3–4).

And which also brings us to our next tenet.

FIGURE 3–4. *BabyCenter extends its brand through useful apps like Booty Call for mobile phones.*

MAKE YOURSELF PORTABLE

Social networking today is more than about connecting with people when they're sitting at their desk in front of a computer. Increasingly, consumers want access to their networks, on demand, everywhere they go.

Coca-Cola's Sprite Yard, for instance, enables users to share photos, showcase a snapshot of their activities in the social calendar, chat online with friends, and enter codes printed on bottle caps to redeem for original content like ringtones and video clips.

"Being with them on their mobile phones is absolutely essential," Mark J. Greatrex, senior vice president for marketing communications and insights at Coca-Cola, proclaimed during the service's launch.

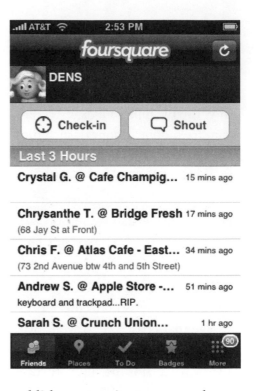

FIGURE 3–5. *Foursquare is a web and mobile social network that lets you meet up with friends, earn points, and unlock rewards for discovering new places, doing new things, and meeting new people—potentially with the help of lifestyle brands.*

Sprite, he said, is "trying to establish an omnipresent, on-the-go, everywhere relationship with teens."[15]

Even Facebook and Second Life are now available via mobile phones—enabling users to be alerted when friends are online, and to connect within the network while they're on the go.

Then there's Foursquare. The brainchild of serial entrepreneur Dennis Crowley, Foursquare turns nightlife into a game, with points and rewards for the kinds of activities members engage in during any given night on the town.

With Foursquare, players check in through an iPhone app or by text message or the web. This alerts their network of friends to their whereabouts—"Jan's at St. Michael's Alley; why don't you stop by for a drink," for instance.

Players get points for checking in at certain venues, early hours of the morning, or in the same real-world location as other players. Users can also annotate places with reviews and other information.

Lifestyle products such as premium alcoholic beverage brands could advertise—join the conversation—by rewarding points with free drinks. Or, they could spark the conversation by setting up evening or weekend itineraries for people who opt in to become the brands' "friends," or who belong to certain communities of interest. These brands can even offer up rewards like invitations to VIP events or after-hours venues (see Figure 3–5).

"There could be 'challenges' where if you go to four different places, then you unlock something that enables you to get into some secret party, or enables you to trade in for a gift bag or some other reward," says Crowley. "The possibilities are endless."

DON'T JUST TALK, LISTEN

Branded social networks are also an excellent way to solicit feedback from core constituencies—or, more powerfully, to spark conversations among members of your target audience.

Earlier, I was poking fun at some of Procter & Gamble's missteps. But the company has found tremendous success with social networks that empower its target customers, rather than make pitches to them.

BeingGirl.com is a P&G site designed for teen girls and sponsored by the company's feminine products brands. There's no overt selling on the site, which is designed to enable girls to discuss the issues they face at that age—music, cliques, dealing with parents, puberty, and so on.

What's more, girls can ask a professional psychologist questions that are then shared with the community, without revealing who the sender is. Answers are provided with subtle branding lines about how BeingGirl.com is brought to you by Always Pads & Panty Liners and Tampax Tampons. Members can also order free samples of the company's products if they want to.

According to P&G, this site is four times as effective per dollars spent as advertising. It's been so successful, in fact, that the company has now replicated the site in twenty-one different countries.[16]

Other companies have found that listening in on existing conversations can be powerful, too.

Computer company Dell, for instance, has a forty-member "communities and conversation team" that conducts outreach on Twitter and communicates with bloggers. And its DellIdeaStorm.com is a social website where consumers are invited to make suggestions for products and services. Of 9,000 suggestions, fifty have already been implemented.[17]

Likewise, Best Buy has enlisted hundreds of its employees to form its Twelpforce (or Twitter help force), which fields questions, offers suggestions, and even sends Twitter-specific promos to followers. In one recent initiative, print ads pointed consumers to the brand's Twitter profile rather than the corporate website.

Such sites also offer a way to identify serious issues that may be flying under the radar—or to mitigate criticisms and complaints before they become full-blown PR crises.

AT&T, Whole Foods, Southwest Airlines, Edmunds.com, JetBlue, and Comcast are just a few of the companies that actively monitor social networking sites to address complaints as quickly as possible.

"We're in a world where one person, by their actions, can make a company look bad," says Josh Bernoff, an analyst for Forrester Research and coauthor of *Groundswell*, a best-selling book about business and social technologies. "One person talks, and a bunch of other people echo and amplify what that one person is saying. Big companies now have to be worried about one individual with a microphone called a blog."

For evidence of that, Bernoff tells me, look no further than Comcast, which, despite efforts like Comcast Town, has been sparking the conversation in decidedly less productive ways.

There is, after all, the matter of the outraged customer who videotaped a Comcast technician who had fallen asleep on the customer's couch. Not very Comcastic.

The customer posted the video to YouTube where it was viewed 1.2 million times and garnered 750 comments. As a result, Comcast set up a Comcast Cares team to monitor third-party websites to respond to complaints as quickly as possible.

"The reason that was so damaging to Comcast, and the reason it got over a million views, was because it reinforced people's idea that Comcast's service wasn't that good, and so they passed it around and said, 'Yeah, see? This is a problem,'" Bernoff tells me. "It's a problem that Comcast has now tried to address, but it's an awfully big problem to deal with to change people's perspective on your service."

There are times, however, when the importance of online chatter can get overblown.

Johnson & Johnson's Motrin brand, for instance, caused an online ruckus when it ran television ads seeming to suggest that women who use babybjörns are wearing their babies as fashion accessories. Never mind that the ad was about alleviating pain for women who carry their babies. Social networks lit up with criticism, and the ads were eventually taken off the air, and Motrin apologized for the insult.

At the time, the incident was viewed as demonstrating the power of social networks to influence the way consumers view brands.

Yet for all the uproar, surveys from Lightspeed Research revealed that 90 percent of U.S. women had never even seen the ad, and once they saw it, 45 percent said they liked it. An additional 41 percent said they had no feelings about it one way or the other, and 15 percent said they didn't like it. Only 8 percent said it made them think negatively about the brand—compared to 32 percent who said it made them like Motrin more.[18] The point? Social networks can be echo chambers with little bearing on how everyday consumers view brands.

But make no mistake: In some circumstances, they can have a big impact.

Witness the "Twitterstorm" Domino's faced when a video surfaced of one franchisee's employees adding, shall we say, extra ingredients to its pizzas. Even Amazon fell prey when word got out that products categorized as "gay and lesbian" were pulled from its category listings. Both companies responded quickly—Domino's posted its own video apologizing for the incident and Amazon fixed a "glitch" that had caused the categorization "error."

Many brands are now trying to nip these kinds of issues in the bud to avoid full-blown PR crises. For instance, when writer Nicole Ouellette of Bar Harbor, Maine, ran into a brick wall with Best Buy customer service after trying to get a refund on a product she bought at a local store, she blogged about it at her Breaking Even blog.

According to Ouellette, a Best Buy "Internet relations" representative contacted her and quickly refunded the appropriate amount to her credit card.

In other words, smart move by Best Buy. But it leads to our final precept:

SOCIAL NETWORKING IS NOT A REPLACEMENT FOR CUSTOMER SERVICE

Sorry, but as sophisticated as it may sound to have brand representatives ready to monitor and respond to social networking chatter, it's far more useful to have highly trained, highly effective customer service in the first place.

If you want to get cutting edge, start there.

Virtually Amazing:
Sibley Verbeck on Building Brands In Second Life 2.0

Electric Sheep Company founder and CEO Sibley Verbeck and his digital doppelganger

HE MAY JUST be the coolest guy in Second Life.

Name the hippest virtual world initiatives from the likes of MTV, CBS, Sony, Nissan, Ben & Jerry's, and Yahoo!, and they may have less to do with Phillip Rosedale, the founder of Second Life's parent company, Linden Labs, and more to do with Sibley Verbeck, CEO of The Electric Sheep Company.

It was Electric Sheep, for instance, that helped bring Virtual MTV to life, while creating virtual-world experiences for Pepsi-Cola, Ridemakerz, and CBS's *CSI: New York.*

He's the real deal when it comes to virtual worlds. In 2003, he was selected as one of MIT *Technology Review's* top 100 technology innovators worldwide under the age of thirty-five.

In an exclusive interview, Verbeck discusses the appeal of virtual worlds for movie and television studios, why more brands seem to be abandoning Second Life for stand-alone virtual worlds of their own— and whether 3-D virtual worlds really make sense for brands hoping to tap into the power of social networking.

Rick Mathieson: You've created 3-D online virtual-world experiences for MTV, CBS, the NBA, and others. What do you feel is the appeal to content brands to extend the experience into worlds like Second Life?

Sibley Verbeck: In the case of television shows, it's really that the virtual world provides a whole different [experience] than the web or television or any other communication medium that we have available to us. It's very interactive, captures more of people's time when they use it, and it's a fantastic platform for advertising as well the online business models that a lot of these companies are pursuing.

RM: In the process, you've also integrated brands like Pepsi, Cingular, and Procter & Gamble's Secret deodorant into these experiences. What are the measurable benefits to advertisers?

SV: As with all advertising, it can be difficult to track all the way to the point of sale. However, with virtual worlds, you can do a lot more than you can do, for example, with television, which is obviously a popular advertising medium.

Not only can we track, we can also target better. We really do look at advertising less as just showing an ad, and more as engaging the user. For the example with Pepsi and MTV's virtual world, that has been a great campaign where users are actively choosing to buy virtual goods affiliated with that brand—whether it's a virtual Pepsi, or Pepsi-branded virtual clothing for your avatar. And then they're being rewarded in other ways as they do other activities in the virtual world with Pepsi merchandise, which you go around and wear or use or play with.

So [on the one hand, there is] Pepsi memorabilia sitting around in the virtual world that people may see, and you can track how many users see that—or at least get it rendered on the user's screen, whether or not they notice it.

The exciting thing is, unlike [TV] commercials, you can tell there are quite a number of users who are interacting with the brand because they actually pick the object up, or they do something with it. Or they use it and then they come back and use it again. Or they give it away to a friend. Those are actions that are far more valuable than interrupting programming to show an ad.

Of course, the science to it is the very beginning. You never have a full understanding what kinds of TV ads, for instance, really relate to what kinds of sales impact. But I think we will be able to get there as we're selling virtual goods, and eventually real goods, through the actual virtual-world platform.

RM: In fact, in terms of Pepsi, you have helped that brand run some significant initiatives within Second Life.

SV: Yes. One of the brand ideas that Pepsi had is the idea of being associated with adventurousness, the notion of trying new things.

So what we did was create a Pepsi skill ladder in the virtual world so that when you explored and tried new things anywhere around the virtual world—the first time you did some social activities, or played certain games, or went to a new place—you'd be rewarded on the skill ladder and you'd see your progress. As you go further through exploring the virtual world, you would get things like Pepsi t-shirts, hover boards, and so on.

RM: CBS has been among the most prolific in creating virtual world experiences tied to its television shows, including *CSI: New York*.

SV: That was a very exciting project. We really wanted to do something a little different, which was integrate with the show. Not just have something that was an adjunct to the show, really integrate with it. So obviously that show, *CSI: New York*, is about hour-long murder mysteries. And so we helped create an hour-long murder mystery where the investigators had to go into Second Life to help track down the killer.

Probably 40 percent of the episode was shot in Second Life, which is work that we did working with CBS and their production team. At the end, unlike most of those shows, the killer actually got away and viewers were invited to come into the virtual world and help solve the crime and continue the plot. And that continues to go on, and we're rolling out new mysteries every three weeks in the virtual world.

There are a lot of users—in the tens of thousands—playing those games, and the plot continues to go on.

RM: For a while, it seemed brands were jumping into, and then out of, Second Life at light speed. More recently, it seems brands like Coca-Cola, Sony PlayStation, and General Mills have created their own stand-alone worlds. Is this a trend?

SV: Yes, I think so. Everyone is searching for what brings a return in virtual space today. The technology's so new that Second Life is one of the few virtual worlds where you can go and do something, especially a smaller campaign, without needing to strike a major deal with the platform owner. So you see a lot of experimentation going on in Second Life.

But there are only so many users you see at any one time in Second Life, and it has its limitations as a platform. You only have an opportunity for so much return there. It can be great for learning, and if you do the right things you can get a great return. But some folks are saying, we want to really get out ahead and create our own platform that we can really bring our users and our audiences into, and that makes a lot of sense for many media properties.

That's because they want to make something really seem more like a video game, even though it may be a social virtual world. It's a closed universe, where they're publishing all the content, and controlling it. They're not relying as much on user-generated content.

RM: That's a big complaint about Second Life—that it provides too many venues, too few visitors to any one of those venues at any one time. How do you think this can be remedied?

SV: It's still very early. If you look at the whole virtual-world industry, the kids' virtual worlds have shown huge increases in their user base. So that's become a "mature" early-stage industry, if you will.

We're not there yet with other demographics. There are some in the teen space and there are some in wider demographics in other parts of the world. But certainly in North America and Europe, other than the kid space, you don't have virtual worlds that have a huge reach.

But I think that you will. We haven't had the "AOL Effect" yet of making them really easy [to access and negotiate] with a value proposition that a lot of people get and find really useful and that they want to return to.

RM: Once virtual worlds in general, and Second Life in particular, get through this period of disillusionment—when we reach Second Life 2.0—how do you think brands will start putting 3-D online virtual worlds to use in really amazing ways?

SV: Good question. It's always hard to predict those kinds of things. But I think there are a couple ways they could go. One is focusing less on branding and more on actual transactions. Actually, providing a shopping experience could be a killer app here. I think shopping in virtual worlds will be a bigger part of the economy ten years from now than shopping on the web is today.

RM: That's a pretty big statement. Retail brands like Brookstone are doing that now with a stand-alone virtual storefront. Are you talking about that kind of initiative?

SV: I don't know if that's going to provide the right experience or not. I think you really have to be in a wider virtual world. Because the biggest thing that the virtual world can provide, a shopping experience that the web can't, is social shopping—which is part of what a lot of people like to do.

You're still going to go for efficiencies and order a book from Amazon. But 3-D will bring some benefit to some types of products and customer service can be addressed there in a more user-friendly fashion.

RM: As technologies like Google Earth makes it possible to go into virtual worlds that are literally 3-D representations of the real world, where will that take these virtual-world experiences?

SV: We mentioned *CSI* earlier, and I think referring to the real world makes a lot of sense in that kind of scenario. But I do believe the virtual experience provides a different value than the real-world experience. You've just been hemmed in by the real world's physical limitations, and on a virtual-world platform, you shouldn't have those limitations.

I can imagine there will be some cases like mixed reality, where there is a real venue and events going on, and people are there—some virtually and some in the real space—and they can communicate with each other.

But I think those are very specific applications, and I don't see the true reality base for virtual worlds being used for nearly as many things. If you're going to build a bookstore on the virtual world, it doesn't make sense to make it look like a real bookstore.

RM: To that point, David Weinberger, the author of *Small Pieces Loosely Joined* and *Everything Miscellaneous*, once argued to me that links between people online are propelled by shared interests, not by a shared environment, and that text-based communities will be the primary way people make social connections on the web—not virtual worlds.

SV: Certainly, I think it's the case that half of that is true. Absolutely, you care a lot more about what someone else's interests are, and how compatible they are with you, and what their personality is like, than you do if their avatar happens to be standing next to yours at a given moment of time.

But fundamentally I think communication in a virtual world is a richer experience, and one that is closer to what our brains are used to. And there's opportunity for a more emotional connection between people when expressing themselves in a shared environment where you can have shared experiences.

I fail to understand that just because you want to have experiences with people to share your interests, why you wouldn't want to actually have shared experiences versus just sharing words across the globe in social networking sites.

We held a test event for Major League Baseball. People could go online as they do by the millions and watch baseball games and go into chat rooms. And they can text each other while they're watching a baseball game.

And we were [in a virtual version of the new Yankee Stadium, where a game was being] enacted live in real time with avatars as well as having the ESPN video feed on the in-virtual-stadium Jumbotron. Humorously, because the lag of the play-by-play of the ESPN feed, the avatars actually moved before the real players were seen to move in the video stream—so the appearance was the real people were "reenacting" the avatars. While the average length of user stay for [regular] online video [of the event] was nineteen minutes, the average user stay in the virtual world version of the same event was over two hours. People were sharing an experience and talking to each other while seeing each other and feeling that they were together in a place. That was really the only difference in the experience.

Yes, they had baseball in common, and then people found out they were fans of the same baseball team, i.e., they had even more specific shared interests. We were showing a Red Sox/Yankees game, but [some folks we were with] ended up sitting next to each other, finding each other, and talking about the Phillies.

You can do that kind of browsing for individuals, finding people, and then feeling like you've shared experiences with them in the virtual world. That affects what kind of virtual experiences will be successful. But not whether there is value to this graphical interface or shared experiences over just sharing text.

This is a communication medium that connects people around the globe in more of a way than we're connected now, with more personal relationships.

I think that's a powerful force.

Rule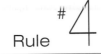

There's No Business Without Show Business

IT TURNS OUT Hollywood's best kept secret may be a video production house in Minneapolis.

Most television viewers would never realize it, but those "Story Until Now" recap specials that often air before the new season of heavily serialized television shows like *Lost*, *Grey's Anatomy*, and *Desperate Housewives* typically aren't produced by the writers and directors who make the shows, or even by the shows' networks.

Instead, Hollywood's promotions departments often turn to MET | Hodder, a Minneapolis-based production company that specializes in creating these programs—which are then packaged for broadcast and cable TV, DVD, computers, mobile phones, iTunes, Xbox game consoles, hotel and airline entertainment networks—and more.

"With some of your serialized programming, if you don't invest about three episodes in it, you don't get caught up very quickly; it's very exclusionary," founder Kent Hodder explains to me.

To that end, the specials are designed to make these shows accessible to new viewers while dialing in existing viewers who may not have seen an episode for several months between seasons. And the process can be daunting.

"We basically grab a thousand Post-it notes to look at every character, and the story beats they hit in every episode, and we map out all the story arcs within and across episodes, and story arcs across seasons," he explains. "Then we look at about three scripts into" the next season "and then reverse engineer exactly—and only—what you need to know" to get caught up to speed.

This can often mean compressing as many as forty-eight episodes into one.

"The reason I think we're good at this is because we can see the forest for the trees," Hodder says. "We didn't develop these characters, we're not in love with some of those really great storylines that they develop. We're truly, and somewhat dispassionately, looking at it as, 'Okay what does the viewer really need to know to really engage in next week's premiere?'"

In recent years, television producers have taken it all to far greater extremes, enlisting Hodder's help in creating online alternate realities for their TV shows.

For ABC Entertainment's *Lost*, for instance, Hodder developed a series of viral videos that were designed to bring verisimilitude to the cult favorite.

In the unlikely event you're unfamiliar with the show, *Lost* is about survivors of a plane crash who find themselves stranded on a mysterious island where time and space don't quite work the way they do everywhere else—leading the characters on an expansive, multifaceted adventure against forces who hope to control and capitalize on the island's unique properties.

Hodder produced faux public service announcements for the Hanso Foundation, the fictional organization behind the show's enigmatic plot, which ran during commercial breaks on ABC-TV. And he created a series of seventy video blogs featuring one Rachel Blake, a young woman documenting her investigation of the Hanso Foundation, as if it were a real-life organization.

The character quietly placed her videos on various websites, detailing her globe-spanning efforts to expose the organization's sinister activities. Fans would follow clues to locate the videos and post them on YouTube so others could follow the thread, and to point people to clues to the next video.

In a move that blurred the so-called fourth wall of drama, the woman even appeared at San Diego's annual Comic-Con sci-fi convention during a session featuring the show's producers in order to accost them for allowing Hanso to pay money to be featured on the show.

The producers retorted, "Lady, it's just a show"—to which she responded with questions about how they would explain any number of mysteries related to the foundation, including how it has managed to make itself seem fictional by being depicted in a fantasy TV show—much to the audience's glee. Footage was captured via camera phones by those in attendance, and eighteen different versions hit the Internet in less than forty-five minutes.

"We work with ABC in looking for opportunities to really explore these new mediums," says Hodder. "It's all about building awareness for a show first; second, getting [viewers] intrigued and building tune-in; and third, if possible, also rewarding existing fans and keeping their interest alive."

The effort was part of an ambitious initiative called "The Lost Experience" that we will discuss in more detail in a later chapter. For now, suffice to say that it is a conspicuous example of the most essential form of "branded entertainment" (also called "branded programming" or "branded content")—original online entertainment content that is designed from the ground up to put a brand's products center stage.

Madison and Vine Meet Cute, Fall in Love

As former MTV COO and author of *The Entertainment Economy* Michael J. Wolf once said to me as simply and plainly as he could, "There is no business without show business."

It is a dictum, of course, that has always been true for all forms of advertising, which live at the intersection of art and commerce. Advertisers have long sought to capitalize on, and hope to embed themselves within, popular culture—using celebrity pitch people, memorable jingles, and indelible images tied to what's hip, hot, and happening.

With the penetration of DVRs already nearing 50 percent for U.S. households, reaching consumers via scheduled TV advertising has grown harder and harder. As a result, product placement—whereby characters use real-world products—has become a bigger part of the TV viewing experience, as marketers work to thwart viewers who fast-forward through commercial breaks.

Obviously, those efforts are increasingly digital—and go far beyond just product placement—to an entertainment experience where the brand plays a starring role.

"'Branded content' is an extension of a brand, speaking a language that its consumers know and love, and actively seek out in a nonpassive way," explains Steven Amato, cofounder of Los Angeles–based advertising-and-content studio Omelet. "This generation is way too savvy to sit back and get a piece of information from a TV spot—they're going to TiVo [the show]; they're going to go right over it."

"The Lost Experience" was one example of entertainment that promoted a brand—in this instance, the TV show—as well as several third-party brands that paid for placement within the video adventures.

Earlier, I mentioned Suave's *In the Motherhood* and Dove's *Waking Up Hannah* online series, which are forms of branded programming. And there are many others.

Diet Coke's *Style Series*, for example, is an effort to position the low-calorie brand in the fashion lifestyle space. The series features live music events in venues like Times Square, which are combined with video segments on fashion tips that are simulcast on nearby electronic billboards, seventy-five different video Internet sites, and on mobile phones.

"The brand has always been a style-conscious part of the entertainment world," says Susan Stribling, director of communications for Coca-Cola North America. "Through talking to Diet Coke consumers over the past year or so, they look to the brand to be a sophisticated style-setter, so we started looking at different ways we could express that" through this digital series.[1]

For its part, fashion retailer American Eagle has its own long history of branded digital entertainment. Both its twelve-part series *It's a Mall World* and *Winter Tales*, for instance, were the creation of Milo Ventimiglia, the actor from NBC's *Heroes*, and his production company Divide Pictures.

The first series took place in a mall, and featured characters whose clothes were easily recognizable as American Eagle, while the second was a series of humorous shorts starring similarly coifed twenty-something characters relating their most memorable winter escapades—travel, parties, sports, snow fights—narrated by Ventimiglia, Pete Wentz, Kristin Bell, and others.

The series has run on AE's own online entertainment portal, 77e.com, which boasts a number of video channels, such as Spring Break, which features shows like *iJustine*, in which a hip young hostess interviews quirky college kids; and *New Music Weekly*, which showcases music videos from hot college bands.

"There's the art form that is emerging now, which is being able to understand a brand's audience so well that you can actually create entertainment that makes them want to come back to you," says Kevin Townsend, whose firm Science + Fiction has helped develop a number of entertainment initiatives for major brands—including *In the Motherhood* for Suave and Sprint, and *The Rookie*, a spinoff of *24* for Degree. "When compared to traditional ad campaigns, branded programming always compares favorably from a reach and relevancy standpoint."

It appears to have worked out well for American Eagle, at least. According to a study from Harrison Research, a survey of 1,277 thirteen- to eighteen-year-olds found AE is the third most popular shopping destination. Only Foot Locker and Aérospostale are more popular.[2]

Few efforts have been as ambitious as Scion Broadband (www.scion.com/broadband), which is an online entertainment portal sponsored by Toyota's Scion auto brand. You won't see Scions pitched much on this site, which features short films, Japanese anime, live music events, and short episodic TV-style shows. Instead, the site, which is managed very inexpensively, is designed simply to more closely align Scion with key influencers.

As Adrian Si, head of interactive marketing for Scion, tells me: "We've been very lucky that we've been able to associate ourselves with this emerging group of creative types—whether they're in fashion, film, arts, whatever the category may be. This is just another way for us to show how we are strong supporters of that group."

To connect with those audiences, Scion Broadband offers multiple entertainment channels, including Easy 10, featuring films from emerging directors; Music, with live shows, music videos, and documentaries; and Radio 17, with seventeen channels of hosted music and interviews. Another channel, The Skinny, includes interviews, art shows, and music events from performers such as Talib Kweli, Ghostface Killah, and DJ Jazzy Jeff (see Figure 4–1).

Some of the content has been quite ambitious. Scion helped produce such fare as Inform Venture's *Stomping Grounds*, a twenty-two-minute short film starring hip-hop legend Biz Markie as he takes a road trip back to his old hangouts in Long Island, introducing the people and places that have shaped his life and career along the way. Scion has also underwritten fictional fare like *The Fist of Oblivion*, an online serial featuring kung fu–fighting puppets directed by Roman Coppola, son of Francis Ford Coppola.

"Scion Broadband is a laboratory of experimentation for our brand," says Si. "To keep it fresh, we look for innovative and edgy

FIGURE 4–1. *Scion Broadband is an online entertainment portal designed to align the brand with cutting-edge creativity.*

content that will resonate with our audience and stay true to the culture of the brand."[3]

Though most content on the portal is advertising-free, some does work in some promotional angles.

In the case of *Stomping Grounds*, for instance, Biz Markie is driving a Scion xB on his trip down memory lane. But beyond funding for the film and a venue to show it, Scion takes a hands-off approach to content.

"There was never any pressure of any kind," Markie tells me of his experience working with Scion. "They couldn't be better to work with."

One-off viral videos, meanwhile, are short-form branded entertainment—a number of which have become global phenomena.

Dove's *Evolution* is probably the most famous. But there are many, many others—from Sony Bravia's series of viral videos (think color balls bouncing down the streets of San Francisco; paint-soaked buildings; and Play-Doh bunnies illustrating the rich color of Sony Bravia hi-def television sets) to efforts like Guitar Hero's *Bike Hero* (a bike-helmet–mounted camera captures the fun as a bike rider treks through a real-world musical course like the ones in Activision's Guitar Hero video games).

As Doug Scott, President of Ogilvy Entertainment, tells me, "Branded entertainment in its truest form really gives the brand a platform to elevate itself outside of the traditional sale of a product and into culture—giving it relevance with ownership of entertainment that is really multipurposed, and played out in a lot of different media to create an ongoing relationship with its customers."

Small wonder, then, that marketers spend over $22 billion a year on various forms of branded entertainment.[4] That includes efforts on television and in film, as well as online video, advergames, and more. But the digital realm definitely has its own dynamics.

In its best forms, it means creating content that either wouldn't or couldn't be used on television, either because of the expense, or because the content is so tied to a specific brand as to render it unviable as a television offering.

Back to the Future

Yet for all the talk of this "new wave" of digital entertainment, there is a familiar ring to it. As I mentioned earlier, Procter & Gamble created the first soap opera in 1933. And historically, Madison Avenue copywriters were writing scripts for TV shows in the 1960s.

We're really just going full circle. But that doesn't mean branded entertainment is an easy nut to crack.

How many times have we heard client or agency types say, "Let's create a viral video," as if just videotaping any old wacky idea and posting it to YouTube will automatically result in dramatic increases in brand awareness and market share.

Or how many times have we heard that a brand—no matter the category—needs to be a "lifestyle brand," as if adding cool graphics to its website and sponsoring music videos would, say, make a particular brand of paper clip "resonate with young people."

And then there's the eternal push to transform every brand's website into an "entertainment portal" that will result in massive increases in traffic.

Yeah well, good luck with that.

If you want a true shot at success, here are some basic guidelines for following Rule #4.

But before we begin, it's important to remember: You've got to have consumer insights that indicate that this is a powerful way to reach your brand's core customers and prospects. And the entertainment content has to be tied enough to your brand that you aren't just replicating what can be done on television or some other medium—or in any medium—by a competing brand.

Ask yourself: Why are we doing this? What is the objective? And what measurable result are we pursuing?

Once you've answered these questions, proceed with these precepts in mind.

YOUR BRAND IS A STORY; TELL IT

Don't just sell product, sell the problem it solves, the feeling it gives, the status it conveys, or the values it embodies. Entertainment value isn't enough—TV can do that.

Unilever's Degree deodorant's recent web series, *The Rookie*, a spin-off of Fox's *24*, takes the deodorant brand's attributes—"young, ambitious, and always looking for action"—and infuses them into the show's main character.

"We were able to anthropomorphize the Degree brand into *The Rookie* character in a way that allowed us to tell his story, which was to tell the Degree story," Science + Fiction's Kevin Townsend tells me.

Philips demonstrated the cinematic qualities of its Cinema Proportion TV through a stunningly spectacular interactive video experience, euphemistically titled *Carousel*, that takes the viewer through one continuous tracking shot of what appears to be massive assault on a city (and its overwhelmed police force) by clown-masked bank robbers. The action is frozen in time, but viewers are able to traverse the scene, making their way around flying bodies, bullets, and even through fiery explosions.

Definitely not PG, but the experience, from Tribal DDB Amsterdam, is enough to captivate grownups with the cash to cough up for a cinematic home television viewing experience. Indeed, so innovative is the short that *Carousel* was the first online video ever to win the Grand Prix for Film at the Cannes Lions Advertising Festival.

Honda's Dream the Impossible site, meanwhile, takes a more subdued approach, featuring short documentaries designed to celebrate "those who have the courage to turn failure into success, and to forge dreams into a better future" and to reflect Honda's own belief in the power of dreams. *Failure: The Secret to Success*, is about the fight to overcome organizational paralysis, *Kick Out the Ladder* is about inspirational metaphors, *Dreams & Nightmares* looks at harnessing "the transformative power of dreams" in order to bring innovation to life, and *Mobility 2088* asks noted thought leaders about how people will get around in the future.

"This is not a 'Go out and buy a Honda' campaign," Barbara Ponce, manager for corporate advertising at American Honda Motor, tells the *New York Times*, explaining why the carmaker launched the series during an economic downturn. Rather, she says, it is "communicating with our customers about what our brand stands for."[5]

"Consumers are going back to the basics, back to foundations, values," Ms. Ponce adds, "and this campaign is focused on our values as a company, the people who make up what Honda is about."

Best of all, Ponce says, each film cost an estimated $200,000 to $300,000—about 30 percent less than the cost of producing a regular thirty-second spot.

Estée Lauder's Clinique brand, meanwhile, has turned branded programming into a global operation, working with Sony Pictures

Television to produce online sitcoms built around young female protagonists.

Alternately called *Sofia's Diary* in markets like Portugal, Brazil, and Britain, and *Sufei's Diary* in China, the shows—all separately produced and featuring talent from each market—follow a fictitious eighteen-year-old girl trying to make her way at college. As any young woman primping for frequent nights out with friends, the character makes dutiful use of Clinique products, of course.

In China, the show is immensely popular, averaging about 453,000 views per episode. That has translated to 15 million online interactions since its debut, according to the company.[6]

Townsend says the way branded programming works best is to tell a story that connects with the audience and is true to the brand in a covert way, but to also have that programming embedded in a page or video player that features more overt brand messaging. This can also mean inserting "video billboards" at the start and end of episodes. This way, if viewers are so inclined, they'll click for more information while they're at the site.

In fact, for many of the programs Townsend's Science + Fiction has developed, viewers tend to do just that.

"We did a series for General Motors and MSN called *Fearless*, and one of the things we found was that there were certain episodes where people stayed on the site longer than the actual episode ran," he says. "That told us not only were they watching the whole thing, but they're watching it either again, or they're interacting with all the [messages] around it—which is ultimately what we want them to do."

It's a dynamic that no television ad buy can yet come close to replicating.

ACCENTUATE THE P-O-S-ITIVE

In the on-demand era, the best branded entertainment experiences are "POS" (personalizable, ownable, and sharable).

A site designed to promote Starz TV's *Head Case*, for instance, makes use of highly customizable video, enabling users to take a hilariously raunchy Rorschach Test during a therapy session with Dr. Goode, the show's trippy psychiatrist. Once the test is complete, the good doctor provides her diagnosis in a video segment. The results are riotous.

True North nuts took it further still. In the lead-up to the 2009 Academy Awards, for instance, True North nut snacks set out to "find the most inspiring personal story in America," and invited consumers to share their experiences for the chance to win $25,000 and see their stories become a TV commercial aired during the awards ceremony.

Stories could range from something that leaves a legacy, empowers others, or simply makes the world a more interesting place to live.

In the end, Chicago resident and former police officer Lisa Nigro, who runs the Inspiration Café, which serves the homeless with food, job training, and more, saw her story brought to life by director Helen Hunt, and broadcast worldwide to an audience of upward of a billion people. All while positioning True North as a snack with a moral compass.

In the case of Unilever's *In the Motherhood* and Clinique's *Sophia's Diary*, viewers get to own the content by influencing the direction of storylines and/or voting on plot resolutions via blog posts and text messages (see Figure 4–2).

Coca-Cola Europe recently explored a similar scenario on behalf of its Sprite brand, with its *Green-Eyed World* online series. The audience was able to follow and interact with twenty-three-year-old British singing sensation Katie Vogel—an appealing sprite herself—as she follows her dream of becoming a major star. By joining her journey online, the audience could influence her choices through commenting and voting directly on episodes of *Green Eyed World* videos using their own Facebook profiles.

For its part, U.S.-based tortilla chip brand Doritos even has its very own production house for branded programming. The studio, Snack

FIGURE 4–2. Suave's online series In the Motherhood *enabled fans to vote on upcoming story-lines—and even ran for a time on TV, in a version starring Cheryl Hines and Megan Mullally.*

Strong Productions, produces a wide array of entertainment content for the Doritos.com website.

Among other experiences, the studio's website Hotel 626—only available from 6 P.M. to 6 A.M. daily—employs users' webcams and phone numbers to make a creepy haunted hotel come to life in a provocative video-based game. As players navigate haunted hallways straight out of *The Shining*, the webcam secretly snaps pictures of their surprised faces at key moments—and then features the user as prey in a monster's Polaroid-style collection of victims. The ghouls who live at the hotel even call users on the phone to bring the chill factor into the real world. Personalization doesn't hit much closer to home than that.

Of course, none of this has anything to do with Last Call Jalapeño Popper Doritos chips—except that it's a perfect match for the product's target audience (fun-addicted preadolescent males). And it's embedded within a larger site that pitches the brand's snacks quite heavily.

VIRAL ISN'T A STRATEGY, IT'S AN OUTCOME

Far too many marketers set out to create "viral" games, videos, or other forms of branded content. Sorry, it doesn't always work that way. If you want to up your odds, spread the contagion through other channels. If the content's good, it'll catch fire.

"You can't make a viral video; you can end up with one," says Townsend. "That's one of our sniff tests on clients. When they say, 'Oh, we want a viral video' [we answer], 'Yeah, well, everyone wants a viral video—it doesn't mean you're going to get one.'"

According to Townsend, there are four key elements that maximize your chances:

● Star quality: Getting a celebrity attached to the project was helpful to the success of *In the Motherhood*, with Leah Remini, Chelsea Handler, and Jenny McCarthy.

● Preexisting tie-ins: *The Rookie* was built upon the action found on Fox's *24*.

● Cross-platform promotion: *The Rookie* was promoted in spots airing on Fox and ESPN.

● Community building: When you create something that's so inherently targeted at a core user group, and that they can directly influence, they become evangelists on behalf of the program.

True, Alex Bogusky's team at Crispin Porter + Bogusky simply sent links to the Subservient Chicken website and watched it become a phenomenon. But the more typical experience is like the one American Eagle experienced with its branded entertainment series.

Its first show, *It's a Mall World*, was shown during prime advertising segments of MTV's *Real World*. The exposure resulted in a 20 percent increase in AE web traffic on nights when the segments were shown, according to the *New York Times*. The audience pushed by the television exposure was ideal: 75 percent of those who watched *Mall World* episodes also made purchases at the AE website.

But while the brand's second series *Winter Tales* was just as entertaining, it didn't have an MTV tie-in and struggled to find an audience.

Anheuser-Busch has run into other challenges.

Its much-ballyhooed online entertainment portal, Bud.tv, carried several different channels of comedy, reality, sports, and talk, along with user-generated content and social networking components. And it launched amid much hoopla over original programming from top-tier production companies like LivePlanet (run by Ben Affleck and Matt Damon), TriggerStreet.com (Kevin Spacey), and Wild West Picture Show Productions (Vince Vaughn).

Without a doubt, it was the most ambitious example of branded entertainment to date. The site was designed specifically to burnish street cred with twenty-one- to thirty-four-year-olds by embedding the brand in an online destination built around quirky, slightly edgy diversions.

And it seemed like the perfect strategy. Over 700,000 people have downloaded Bud commercials from the company's websites, and 22 million have watched via third-party sites like YouTube.[7] With such popular online content, AB bet that it could "own" the entire experience for its most fervent fans.

Yet Bud.tv's goal of 2 million unique users per month never materialized. In fact, after a smashing launch propelled by a teaser on broadcast television during the Super Bowl, the site was a veritable hit for weeks on end. But before long, traffic dwindled to the point that the site sometimes didn't even register with some traffic reporting services. So AB pulled the plug.

Some blamed an age-verification requirement on the site, ostensibly meant to keep out minors. But it's more likely the online entertainment portal was undone by the costs and sheer effort it takes to produce original content and run your own television network.

"If the [TV] networks can't continuously produce that [volume of content], how can a beer company?" asks AB's VP of marketing, Keith Levy.[8]

Townsend views it differently. "Bud had a great idea, but they were three years too early," he says. "They built a mall when they needed a grocery store. They should have grown the audience, then grown the content from what the audience wanted."

Does the demise of Bud.tv mean the end of branded content for Anheuser-Busch (now AB InBev)? Of course not.

As they say, the show must go on—and the company plans to create content more specifically tied to its brands, and propagate it more broadly across as many different platforms as possible, which Levy says will include Hulu, Yahoo, Facebook, and many more.

Others are picking up the mantle. Condé Nast's Glamour has its own Glamour.tv video site featuring shows like *Mom's Working It*, *Tressed to Impress*, and *Beauty Wars*, all centered on style, fashion, and beauty—and all sponsored by Glamour's advertiser clients.

Adidas, meanwhile, has been trying a decidedly different approach, with its Adidas.tv, an online video player on the brand's basketball site.

In Adidas's case, the player itself is a widget that can be embedded in blog sites and personal profile pages. And content is comprised of short clips of star athletes showcasing their mad skills in recent games—a surefire approach with avid sports fans who want to share such clips with just about everyone they know.

Maybelline, meanwhile, sponsors Candace Bushnell's *The Broadroom* online series, starring Jennie Garth and Jennifer Esposito. Here, content plays out as any show would, but the sponsor offers makeup secrets from the set, user-generated video, contests, and more.

Time will tell if such efforts will move the needle for these brands—but as relatively low-risk, low-cost ventures, they can only help.

MAKE US LAUGH—AND BUY

While sites like Hulu serve up red meat in the form of even the grittiest television police procedural, the world of online branded programming today is still largely a happy place, filled with snarky humor, dumbass pranks, gee-whiz athletics, and laughter—lots of it.

"[Content] has to be interesting, funny, entertaining," says Omelet's Amato.

It should also move your business forward in some way.

Ultimately, many if not most brands will forgo creating branded programming, as well they should. In branded programming, solid metrics are hard to come by.

But in television, studies from Nielsen indicate branded entertainment can boost brand awareness upward of 20 percent.[9] So it stands to reason, some believe, that online branded programming efforts can do at least as much.

For computer maker HP, a host of initiatives—including a television-and-online effort called *Engine Room*, a kind of *Project Runway* for graphic artists coproduced by MTV, and *You on You*, a user-generated video contest letting consumers show others what they're all about—have helped boost awareness among the kind of hip, young consumers who traditionally buy computers from rival Apple.

Since it began engaging in such activities as part of a massive, multiplatform rebranding effort, HP went from being seen as a plain vanilla PC manufacturer to a bit of a cool maker—and has seen its market share jump to 25.3 percent, leapfrogging its competitors to become the number one PC manufacturer worldwide.[10]

"The secret to building brands in today's media environment is very much engaging the consumer with a story," says Ogilvy Entertainment's Scott, adding that brands must use the story to maintain "an ongoing dialogue with that individual through entertainment, through education, and through multiple forms of media."

For people like Kent Hodder and Kevin Townsend, that will mean many new branded programming initiatives for years to come.

"My primary ROI as an advertiser when it comes to branded programming is how does it sell my product faster in the next two quarters," says Townsend. "The ability to build a community, keep them there, and then feed them targeted marketing messages—that's a big win-win for everybody."

Q&A

Adrian Si: Rewriting the Rules of Branded Entertainment

NAME A SUCCESSFUL digital marketing initiative for Toyota's Scion auto brand, and Adrian Si is likely the man behind it.

Second Life? Been there, conquered that—by way of Scion City, where residents can test drive, customize, purchase, and drive virtual versions of their Scion xB. But Si certainly didn't stop there.

Working with social media firm Millions of Us,

Adrian Si, head of interactive marketing for Toyota's Scion brand

Scion created a site called WhatIsScionCity.com. It features six short films that use the technique known as "machinima"—cinema staged and filmed from within Second Life's virtual world environment, using avatars as the film's characters—with each film providing clues to the history of Scion City. In keeping with the brand's spirit of personalization, viewers can contribute their own research findings, with the idea that the masses will collectively unveil the origins of this "mysterious city."

And then there's the crown jewel of Scion's branded entertainment portfolio, Scion Broadband, which finances and showcases short films, music videos, animation, and other creative work designed to connect with the brand's target consumers in potent new ways.

Of course, for many brand marketers, a number of questions immediately come to mind.

Rick Mathieson: Why Scion Broadband? Why is a branded entertainment portal such a powerful marketing vehicle for a brand like yours?

Adrian Si: We've been very lucky that we've been able to associate ourselves with this emerging group of creative types—whether they're in fashion, film, arts, whatever the category may be. This is just another way for us to show how we are strong supporters of that group, and I think a lot of people say, "Hey, those Scion guys aren't in-your-face about marketing, they truly believe in this very creative, artistic community," and this is just one example.

We've found there is some power in having a video platform in which to share artists' passions and pursuits, as well as to spread the word to our users. It's been a really, really positive experience for us.

RM: Scion's model isn't merely advertisement. Your approach seems to be that this is targeted entertainment programming that just happens to be underwritten by a brand. What is the benefit of that kind of hands-off approach?

AS: We felt it would be better if we try to pick and choose, and provide content that we felt would be interesting to our target. That allows us a platform in which to support some of the new emerging artists, directors, filmmakers, and people that we've been working with throughout our history.

I think from [a marketing perspective] we've seen—especially for this younger target—that they're very savvy, and they can tell when something is authentic or not. And so for us, Scion Broadband is really about maintaining that authenticity with this target audience.

RM: Other brands have taken a cue from Scion—Adidas.tv, American Eagle, and the ill-fated Bud.tv, for instance. How do you at Scion Broadband, as one youth-oriented online entertainment network, differentiate yourselves from other emerging networks that will overlap your audience?

AS: First of all, we're completely different industries. From our perspective, we're not necessarily looking to differentiate ourselves. I think we have a core DNA that has always been about being authentic, not being in your face about marketing.

So as long as we hold to that DNA, it doesn't really matter to us what other brands are doing. For us, everything that we do is talking about, "Yes we're a car brand, but we're so much more than a car brand." I think as long as we stay true to [that DNA], that's all that we're really concerned about.

RM: But what happens when it seems like every brand out there gets its own broadband entertainment network?

AS: I equate that to thinking about the idea of a website. Ten years ago, companies started adopting websites. Now today, what company doesn't have its own website? Everybody has their own website. Now it's on to "What is the next big thing?" Basically it's just a natural evolution. Pretty much every large brand will not only have websites, but they'll have all this rich content. So be it. Who knows what the technology is that's around the corner that everybody will adopt five years down the road?

RM: For those looking from the outside in, how does Scion Broadband justify its existence over the long term? Is it a marketing expense, or will it build its own revenue stream?

AS: We definitely view it as a marketing expense. We're not looking at it from the perspective of ROI or building a revenue stream. There's a lot of buzz generated—a lot of positive buzz. It's great positive PR for us. At this point, those are the only things that we're thinking about. If we can associate ourselves with the fact that we're supportive of emerging artists and things like that, that's all positive PR. And if we get that, then we're happy.

RM: What sort of metrics in terms of traffic and demographics are you seeing from the site?

AS: Keep in mind that Scion in and of itself is a car company, so the vast majority of people coming to our site are really interested in the vehicle. [Scion Broadband] is just another outlet of things that we do. So we're running anywhere between 1,000 and 10,000 visits per month at the site.

By comparison, Scion.com itself gets probably about a half a million per month. From a percentage perspective, it's small.

But if you think about it, we do over 100 [live] events per month. Some of those events may only bring in fifty, sixty, seventy people. It's still good PR. And if it's among our influencer target, the good news is that they're sharing that information with their friends. So a lot of what we do is very viral and grassroots.

RM: In terms of content, do you have an editorial guru—someone assigned to keep an ear to the ground finding hot new filmmakers and musicians?

AS: We work with an agency that has very close ties with movie studios. So they have an ear to the ground in terms of what's hot out there.

We rely on them as experts to help us determine what some of the cool content should be. And then, of course, we review everything internally.

RM: What advice would you give to brands thinking about creating their own on-demand, branded entertainment portals?

AS: Bottom line: Think strategically. What is the purpose for doing video? Are they just doing video because they think "Everybody is doing it, and therefore we need to be doing it"? That's a bad reason to do it.

But if there's a specific strategy, and it supports the company and one of their objectives or goals, then I think that's the first step. Then the next step would be thinking strategically about what type of content makes sense to support those goals.

RM: Assuming we're talking about a lifestyle brand that wants to take this approach, how do you go to upper management and tell them, "Hey, we're going to have this expensive initiative that's not really meant to generate revenue, but will help us reach our audience in a meaningful way"? What are the things marketers need to get their management to think about?

AS: The first thing I would say is that it's actually not as expensive as you might think it would be, though obviously you make a very valid point.

I would not be able to go into my manager and say, "I'm going to spend a million dollars to create this site. And, oh by the way, we don't know what kind of traffic we're going to get. We don't know if anything will be converted or lead to any revenue stream." Obviously that's going to be a very tough sell.

I think what you need to be able to do is say, "Hey, here's an initiative that I think can bring us some really positive buzz. And oh by the way, it's not a huge expense."

To create a site that offers up content, really in the grand scheme of things, does not cost much at all. It's the cost of the content. And I think that there are a lot of creative ways that you can obtain content.

If you're going to go ahead and produce it all yourself, and you're going to go to large agencies [or studios] to do that, yes, that's going to be in the millions of dollars.

But I think the beautiful part for us is, when you're working with a lot of these emerging artists, the costs are a lot less expensive because they're really just looking for the exposure.

For us, that's an equation that works.

Rule #5

Want Control?
Give It Away

HEINZ KETCHUP never saw Chris Larrigan coming.

Caught in the hype around "user-generated video" and "consumer-created" TV commercials, Heinz decided it was high time it launched its own user-generated content contest. And so the "Top This" TV challenge was born, as a promotion that invited any American with a trusty Handicam and Hollywood dreams to create their own thirty-second commercial for Heinz 57.

At stake: up to $57,000 in cash and prizes.

Larrigan and his friends took the brand up on the challenge—to breathtaking effect.

At the time a fifteen-year-old high school student in Baltimore, Larrigan (not his real name) had long had an interest in filmmaking. He and his friends had even founded a comedy troupe that shot a number of videos ranging from a spoof of a Mont Blanc pen commercial, to rap songs about bacteria, to a comedy about evolution for science class.

For the Heinz contest, the troupe once again found inspiration in urban beats—crafting a rap music video that has the virtue of defying description.

Yes, there's the incessant beat. The head bobbing and the unnerving sight of white, upper middle class teens aping gangland hand signals. And inexplicable lyrics like "Yo Heinz is the ketchup with all unique flavors. . . . It's a sauce that repels alien invaders."

But steeped in elaborate green screen backdrops and produced with thousands of dollars' worth of hi-def equipment and software, it's a relatively well-produced affair, one that can only have polished the troupe's schoolyard cred—while simultaneously grating the already frayed nerves of the Heinz marketing executives charged with reviewing thousands of contest entries.

"What makes it funny is the fact that we're not very good at rapping," Larrigan deadpanned at the time. "So we decided a rap video, and doing it in the dumbest way possible, would be attractive in its own 'off' way."

That's certainly one way to put it. Years from now, when Larrigan's a famous auteur, he'll no doubt look back at the episode and laugh. He may even recognize the fact that he was caught up in marketing's first intrepid steps toward truly democratizing digital media. At least, that was the idea.

According to the Pew Internet and American Life Project, nearly 10 percent of online Americans have uploaded video to the Net, via YouTube or other video sharing sites. Over 15 percent of those between eighteen and twenty-nine have done so, and the younger you skew, the more likely the participation in user-generated content. Already, over 20 percent of online teenage boys have uploaded videos of their own creation.[1]

Over time, marketers began to realize online video was popular, and that consumer-created content either tended toward "Leave

Britney Alone"–style rants from celebrities' fans, "Don't Tase Me, Bro"–level shenanigans of people in ridiculous situations, or scathing spoofs of popular television commercials and brands.

It wasn't long before marketers decided that if you can't stop them, embrace them—by providing consumers with the tools to craft commercials for the chance to win prizes.

The idea: Entice hip young consumers to create their own videos with the hope that the made-by-a-regular-Joe dynamic will build interest outside the usual thirty-second spot, and that consumers will email the homemade ads to their friends and build big-time buzz for the brand. And today's consumers seem more than happy to oblige.

"It's a generational thing," says Steven Amato, cofounder of Los Angeles–based advertising-and-content studio Omelet. "It's powerful for brands, because it's powerful for consumers. Consumers of today don't want to be advertised to—so much so that they would rather make the ads themselves than sit back and have a passive experience with the brand."

The digerati like to call this kind of user-generated content (UGC) the cutting edge, but it's actually far from it.

"This label, 'user-generated content,' is new, but the concept dates back to the origins of advertising in general, it's as old as advertising itself," Norman Hayshar of Young & Rubicam recently told NPR, adding that testimonials and jingle contests date back to the 1940s.

Indeed, for all the hype, user-generated content has been featured on TV for nearly twenty years—in the form of ABC-TV's *America's Funniest Home Videos.*

In Hayshar's view, this new wave in UGC is being driven by two forces: the popularity of YouTube, and the TV show *American Idol.*

"Mix these things together, and what you've really got is a creative power-to-the-people movement that is reflected, as it always is, in the culture in advertising."[2]

But it hasn't been without its share of pitfalls.

Just ask Chevrolet.

WRITE-YOUR-OWN ADS GONE WRONG

It all started with a promotion on the NBC-TV show "The Apprentice," which pointed consumers to a website where they could select music and insert their own on-screen text into existing video clips to create their own thirty-second commercials for Chevy Tahoe.

Judging from the videos that quickly began circulating on YouTube, it was one SUV promotion that took a turn for the worse.

"If you want a gas-guzzling, road-hogging, global warming–causing ride, buy a Tahoe," proclaims one faux ad, after pointing out that the vehicle lacks basic Gen Wow features like an iPod plug-in.

Another declares: "This powerful V8 engine gets only 15 miles per gallon. In a world of limited resources, you don't need GPS to know where the road leads."

Yet another, entitled "2327," ties the SUV to the number of soldiers killed in Iraq at that point, as the spot's creator puts it, to ensure a steady stream of oil.

It stands to reason that a marketer engaging in this kind of promotion would recognize the dangers of putting a major brand in the hands of consumers.

But Chevy's not alone. One offer from Nike to produce customized shoes, for instance, reportedly ran awry when a consumer requested the words "Sweatshop" emblazoned on a pair of Nike running shoes. Factor in a product category as polarizing as SUVs, and you're just asking for the campaign to backfire, right?

Not in Chevrolet's eyes.

"We anticipated that there would be critical submissions," Chevrolet spokesperson Melisa Tezanos tells the *New York Times*. "You do turn over your brand to the public, and we knew that we were going to get some bad with the good. But it's part of playing in this space."[3]

In other words, in the idiom of brand marketers, "any publicity is good publicity," right?

Maybe. But given the dead-on messages of these spoof videos—and the currency they'd take on with all the tensions in the Middle East—and Tahoe's particular take on user-generated video may be more a cautionary tale than a laudatory one.

Since the Tahoe UGC launch, marketers have become more savvy about ways to enable consumers to become citizen marketers without turning the brand over to the public.

Here's how to do it right.

EMBRACE RISK, BUT ENSURE REWARD

In Chevy's case, just because you can do something doesn't mean you should. The fact that people may spoof your brand would probably go completely unnoticed to the general public. But the moment you become complicit in the act, well, the phrase "any publicity is good publicity" wears dangerously thin.

And even if you do have an appropriate brand for UGC, how do you give away control while simultaneously getting what you want?

Look to MasterCard. After years of seeing its popular "priceless" commercials ruthlessly parodied on the Web, the company launched an online sweepstakes at www.priceless.com that lets consumers insert their own on-screen text into a pair of existing TV commercials. The marketer than selected the best for broadcast on television, for millions to see.

Coca-Cola's "Essence of Coke" campaign enabled consumers to create and upload their own short videos about the essence of who they are for the chance to win prizes. And its Design the World a Coke website enables consumers to craft custom designs for the iconic contour bottle.

In what's now commonly referred of as "crowd sourcing," people from different parts of the world can connect and collaborate on digital bottle illustrations and also produce "mashups" that fuse two distinct designs into one final, finished look. First launched during the Beijing Olympics, the site has inspired over 150,000 designs and over 46,000 mashups (see Figure 5–1).

FIGURE 5–1. *Coca-Cola goes crowd sourcing: The Design the World a Coke website enables consumers to collaborate on designs for the brand's iconic bottle.*

MTV's Flux is a U.K.-based site where visitors submit their own videos—called "Killer Filler"—where they're voted on by the audience, for airing on cable during commercial breaks.

And both Dove and Doritos have created contests where consumers create their own thirty-second spots, which were voted on by consumers and by judges, for the chance to see them broadcast live during the Super Bowl and the Academy Awards, respectively.

"In today's increasingly reality-driven world, people are looking for new ways to interact with, help shape, and even personalize what is important to them," says Ann Mukherjee, group vice president at Frito-Lay.[4]

In the run-up to Super Bowl XLIII, for instance, Doritos offered a cool $1 million to anyone who could create a Super Bowl commercial for Doritos that trumps all other ads in *USA Today*'s annual Super Bowl Ad Meter, in which consumers vote for their favorite ads.

Joe and Dave Herbert, two brothers from Batesville, Indiana, did just that—triumphing over 1,900 other entries and astonishing the entire advertising world by beating out stalwarts like Anheuser-Busch in the Ad Meter rankings.

Their hilarious spot, called "Free Doritos," featured coworkers who throw a crystal ball into a vending machine in order to help themselves to free chips, and then run into trouble when one of them accidentally throws the ball into their boss's nether regions.

"We were hoping for this," Ann Mukherjee tells *USA Today*. "This is going to be the best million dollars we've spent at Frito-Lay."[5]

Indeed, according to the company, the effort generated $36 million in free publicity for the Doritos brand before and after the big game (see Figure 5–2). Small wonder that by 2010, Frito-Lay was offering

FIGURE 5–2. *The consumer-created "Free Doritos" Super Bowl spot topped* USA Today's *Ad Meter—and won its creators a cool $1 million.*

$5 million to anyone who could win the top three spots on the Ad Meter rankings during Super Bowl XLIII.

Wisely, in all of these examples, brand marketers required participants to submit their work for review.

In instances where content could be viewed and shared, tools for crafting ads were sometimes embedded in web pages where it was tough to capture and post outside the framework of their sites. Many were carefully vetted before sharing with the public. And all were monitored closely.

In other words, the companies gave users control, without giving them the ability, with apologies to Chevy Tahoe, to drive the brand into a ditch.

IT'S NOT CONSUMER-CREATED IF IT COMES FROM A PRO

In the case of the Doritos consumer-created promotion mentioned above, the winning entry, "Free Doritos," did come with a hitch. You see, the Herbert brothers are actually professional videographers with their own independent film studio, Transit Films, which offers advertising and animation services, as well as a game studio. Facts that most major news organizations failed to report.

As Dave Herbert tells me, the "Free Doritos" spot represented the second time he and his brother and friends had entered the contest—they were runners-up in a prior year—and that the idea was to help put their services on the map. They were obviously stunningly successful.

"When [Doritos] said they're putting up the $1 million price for the Ad Meter [winner], we did a lot of research on how the Ad Meter works, and tailored our commercial to exactly what we thought would achieve a high ranking," he says, reflecting on his observation that the everyday consumers who vote in *USA Today*'s Ad Meter tend to favor sophomoric humor. "Apparently that worked."

To be fair, this was indeed a grassroots effort—the brothers say they only spent about $2,000 to produce the spot, most of which was spent on food for the cast and crew, and $400 for the cost of a vending machine they bought on eBay.

About $100 went to five panes of vending machine glass the actors throw the crystal ball into—which meant their $1 million–winning spot had to be made in no more than five takes.

Of course, it stands to reason that people who are seriously into film-making—and who are actually good at it—would win such competitions.

But while brands themselves may make the contests open to all comers, the media should, perhaps, stop framing these promotions as if they mean a ticket to the big time for folks like Chris Larrigan and his friends.

In fact, popular past Doritos Super Bowl contest winners "Live the Flavor" (guy crashes car while eyeing attractive girl) and "Checkout Girl" (cashier and customer raucously bond over Doritos flavors) for instance, come from Dale Backus and Wes Phillips of Cary, North Carolina, and from Kristin Dehnert of Pacific Palisades, California, respectively. Backus and Phillips are professional videographers with their own commercial production company, and Dehnert is an award-winning filmmaker.

As a result, their entries look great. They're well shot, well cast, and well produced. Doritos' own ad agency couldn't have done better.

And that's a conceit that won't wash with consumers for long.

As I recently told National Public Radio, "It's ironic, because the people who actually end up winning these things are the people who could probably build careers in advertising, if they aren't already."

"For people who are looking to break into the business, it gives them a chance to showcase their work," says Herbert. "For us, it put us on the map."

Which is nice for the Herbert brothers, but when you factor in all those really awful yet truly consumer-created spots that are submitted along with gems like theirs, even brands might start reconsidering the open-to-all approach to UGC campaigns. There is also the question of what value these kinds of contests even bring to the brand.

In truth, brands can spend just as much money on advertising these contests as they would to simply promote the product. And once committed, they then have to assign resources to wade through a mountain of excruciatingly bad ads to get to one the marketer could have just produced in the first place.

In my view, if you're going to run these kinds of promotions, it's important to stay true to the idea of consumer-created content in an unambiguous way. You just need to be smart about how you do it.

Case in point: Medicis Pharmaceutical Corporation, which recently added a new wrinkle to the way it markets Restylane, a dermal injection that reduces the appearance of fine lines.

The effort: the "Hottest Mom in America" contest, in which participants could submit videos to the contest's website for the chance to win a $25,000 college scholarship for the munchkin, $25,000 cash, an interview with a prominent modeling agency, and yes, a year of free Restylane injections.

In such a scenario, there's very little incentive for "prosumers" to participate—the results are about the subject matter at hand—which, of course, is your mom. Who looked stunning in her video, by the way.

Likewise, Justin Timberlake's 901 Tequila recently invited consumers to post videos or photos about their "Big Idea" for marketing the brand—whether it be an ad campaign, a breakthrough promotion, a viral video, or whatever—for the chance to become 901's new Executive Vice President of Big Ideas. Apparently, this position entails a VIP trip for two to Las Vegas, tickets to a Timberlake concert, VIP access to after parties, an annual salary of zero, and the opportunity to get coffee for other 901 employees. Here, it's all about the idea Timberlake and his team are after, not the finished manifestation. So there's little incentive for professionals to get involved. Unless, of course, they're really into serving coffee for unappreciative colleagues.

Regardless of 901's desire for alcohol-inspired shenanigans or Restylane's full-throttle embrace of shallowness, these efforts exemplify UGC at its best: everyday people making videos for their favorite brands.

Ask yourself this: Are you really engaging your most fervent fans through these contests, or are you merely outsourcing the creation of professional ads?

"I don't know if they would ever change the name to 'prosumer'[-generated advertising], because the brands want to invite their consumers into it and participate and [to give everyone a voice]," surmises Herbert. But, he adds, "[The contests are] open to everybody, which does make it harder for the consumer—the average guy that picks up a camera doesn't really have as much of a shot to win."

If it's about the contest, keep it real.

DON'T THINK USER-GENERATED, THINK USER-PERSONALIZED

For all the attention UGC gets, there is much debate as to whether it's a lasting trend or a passing fad. To be honest, if yours is an offline brand, a far more interesting and entertaining approach is to use online channels to enable fans to personalize content built around properties they know and love, and to share it among family and friends.

Here again, look to MasterCard. As part of a "Priceless" television campaign featuring Peyton Manning, in which the football star offers up brutally honest "Pep Talks," the brand created a website where consumers could send personalized video greetings of Manning playfully chiding loved ones by name and personal foibles via email and mobile phone—all while promoting the brand.

A message to a golf buddy of mine might feature Manning intoning, "Hey Bill, I hear you suck at golf. To be honest with you, with a hook like yours, you really ought to just give up."

A later effort called "Suite Talk" did much the same thing, but dealt more directly with new offers from MasterCard.

NBC's hit TV Show *30 Rock* used a remarkably sophisticated solution that enabled fans to send highly personalized phone and email greetings starring Alec Baldwin addressing recipients by name and making fun of their occupation and physical characteristics, as the show's nutty boss Jack Donaghy.

In each of these scenarios, users typically type in the recipient's name and then choose from a selection of options about their hobbies, physical characteristics, career, or what have you. Sometimes you're able to enter a text message or even a photograph or video. Then the content is mashed on the fly and delivered to the recipient in a remarkably seamless way.

Indeed, in some of the most astonishing such executions seen to date, cable television network FX in the U.K. used truly amazing "personalizable video" technology to enable fans of the creepy serial-murderer-as-hero show *Dexter* to create customized faux television news snippets that name and even display user-uploaded pictures of friends as possible targets of the show's killer.

Such initiatives demonstrate many key benefits of on-demand media. They're easy-to-use. They're highly personalizable. And they're eminently sharable—immersing both sender and receiver in the brand experience in phenomenal (and potentially viral) ways.

No video camera or editing software required.

"Rather than have the message being created from the brand itself, it's always better for the brand to create a window that users can talk to each other through—so it's from your friend, as opposed to from the [brand]," says Dominick O'Brien, interaction designer for Glue London, a digital agency behind personalizable video efforts for clients such as the Royal Navy.

All of this said, if you're going to let consumers shape the brand itself for mass audiences, you could do worse than Jones Soda, which has essentially built its brand on consumer-influenced content.

The Seattle-based company long ago began enabling users to send in photographs to use as bottle labels. Today, it has over a million submissions and has used upward of 4,500 of the photos on its bottles—which consumers can collect and trade on the Jones Soda website. Even if your photo isn't selected, you can order a case of soda in your own custom bottles, featuring your image or design, for a small fee.

"We allowed the labels to be discovered, and that gave consumers a sense of ownership. It makes it more relevant to them and provides an emotional connection," Peter van Stolk, the forty-year-old founder of Jones Soda, tells *Business Week*. "With big soda brands, the 'Britney Spears model'—paying a lot of money to some hot artist to sponsor your beverage—is just so done. The wonderful thing about our competitors is, for all the money they have, they should be thinking more originally but they don't. If they ever do, I'm dead."[6]

I Want My ME-TV

Still, the lure of user-generated video contests seems to hold sway—for now at least.

For its part, Heinz found its "Top This" TV promotion was so popular that it received over 4,000 entries, with consumer votes giving the grand prize to Matt Cozza of Chicago, whose arguably professional-quality entry, titled "Now We Can Eat," won top honors—and $57,000 in cash.

"We know there are many loyal consumers out there who want to creatively express their passion for Heinz Ketchup," says David Ciesinski, vice president for the brand. "Clearly, people put a tremendous amount of time, passion, energy, and creativity into their videos, and it really showed."[7]

Indeed, the campaign is credited with contributing to double-digit increases in sales. Heinz was so pleased, in fact, it has since gone on to run subsequent "Top This" TV contests.

Which means Chris Larrigan may have many more shots at fame—and a $57,000 fortune—producing rap videos for everybody's favorite ketchup.

Q&A

"Obama Girl" Makes Good: Ben Relles's Racy Videos and the Democratization of Digital Media

WILL.I.AM HAS nothing on Ben Relles.

The lead singer for The Black Eyed Peas, Am entered briefly into presidential politics during the 2008 election cycle with his *Yes We Can* music video endorsing Barack Obama long before that seemed anything like a sure thing.

But Ben Relles, a then-unknown, thirty-two-year-old account executive at Internet advertising firm

Ben Relles, founder of BarelyPolitical.com

Agency.com, had his own idea for an online video—one that would tit-illate the electorate in unexpected ways—and become a pop culture icon in the process.

Indeed, unless you've been living on another planet—or have an unnaturally healthy aversion to political news—you no-doubt recall the viral video sensation *I've Got a Crush on Obama.*

The video stars actress Amber Lee Ettinger as "Obama Girl," who gyrates provocatively as she lip-syncs to lyrics (which include such brow-raising lines as "You tell the truth, unlike the right / You can love but you can fight/You can Barack me tonight/I've got a crush on Obama") from Leah Kauffman, and set to music from Rick Friedrich.

The video, posted on YouTube, was within hours the subject of reports from ABC News, MSNBC, and Fox News. At this writing, the political spoof has been viewed 12 million times via YouTube, and countless times on television news programs. And it gave Relles enough traction to found political humor video site Barely Political.com and create several sequels and spin-offs.

While we have yet to see "I Heart Mike Huckabee" or "I've Got A Crush on Kucinich," we've reveled in everything from *Romney Girl v. Giuliani Girl* ("I'm going to be wife four/he warms my heart just like Al Gore"); to *The Ann Coulter Song* ("Dad says she's starved for atten-tion/She's got the hottest Adam's Apple at the Republican Conven-tion"). In short order, the startup site was acquired by Next New Networks, which creates "micro-television networks" over the Internet for targeted communities, where Relles has also launched a spin-off channel called Barely Digital.

As it happens, "Obama Girl" was not Relles's first foray into user-generated content. He and friends Kauffman and Friedrich first made waves a year earlier with "My Box in a Box," a spoof of the "My [Junk] in a Box" skits on *Saturday Night Live.*

But "Obama Girl" took on a life of its own, and helped showcase a new reality taking shape in online media that Relles believes will have a transformative impact on our culture.

Rick Mathieson: How did "I've Got a Crush on Obama" come to be?

Ben Relles: We actually did a video called "My Box in a Box," which was also sung by Leah Kauffman, performed in the video by an actress, and that video was really successful. It ended up getting something like 6 million YouTube views. It was on MSNBC a couple times. So I called Leah and said maybe we can do some sort of follow-up to this thing. And then a couple weeks later, I called her up and said, "What do you think about a love song to Barack Obama" and she loved the idea.

RM: Did you hear anything from the Obama people about this? Were they happy, or were they worried about it?

BR: I [never] heard anything officially. We got emails from different sources saying "We love the video and I'm writing from the Obama camp," but they didn't come from Obama email addresses, so it's tough to tell whether it's actually from them.

It's actually a really complementary video and with the amount of political humor out there that's pretty scathing, when you look at the *Daily Show* and *Saturday Night Live* and all these programs, this was intended to be pretty lighthearted, and actually supposed to be pretty positive for Obama.

RM: You founded Barely Political.com when you were an account executive at Agency.com—not even on the creative side of the business. Did you always plan to become a purveyor of spoof videos?

BR: When I was six years old, I said, "When they invent the Internet, I am going to make YouTube videos." No, I basically did that more because I just kind of wanted to see what would happen if we put a little bit of money against it, knowing that there's this conversation already happening online about "Junk in a Box."

After that one, I had so much fun with it that it was like well, a), I'm having a blast. And b), I think this is where entertainment is headed.

But it's not just a TV show or a video, it's actually these characters that people can follow, whether they're in Second Life, or they're on TV, or they're on a Flickr page or wherever it is.

We have [a team] on board—in Amber Lee Ettinger who's the actress and Leah who's the singer and Rick [Friedrich] who's the producer—where I think we can keep creating content, and that the story can sort of develop.

RM: How much money did you spend on creating the original Obama Girl video?

BR: Not much. I'd say probably all in all about $2,000. I mean, $2,000 is still something, and I wouldn't have invested that if I wasn't confident in the idea, but when you look at the numbers, Barely Political is seeing somewhere between 10 and 15 million views per month. When you realize our videos are distributed on sites like YouTube and MySpace, Break.com, and Daily Motion, I guess $2,000 is pretty minimal.

RM: Not long after starting Barely Political, it was acquired by Next New Networks, giving you the ability to leave your old job to run the site fulltime, and in 2009, launch Barely Digital, which features video spoofs of the tech industry. Tell me about the evolution.

BR: We really want Barely Political to be a hub for edgy political comedy, a place where people go for political humor, whether we create original content ourselves or aggregate content that's already on the web, or ask for people who actually go to the website to submit some of their own stuff.

In a typical month we produce between fifteen and twenty videos, and those videos are getting between a few hundred thousand and sometimes a few million hits each.

While Barely Political is basically a satirical video site around the world of politics, Barely Digital is a site devoted to short videos about the world of technology. We cover everything from gaming to gadgets to Web 2.0 to really tech stuff—programming and coding in HTML and everything.

Our goal is to take the same kind of things that worked for Barely Political and apply that to technology, which I love and I think offers a lot of fodder for satire.

It's always been part of our plan to be able to cover other news stories that don't necessarily have to do just with Obama. And that was part of the reason we launched Barely Digital, because creatively it gives us new territory to play in.

RM: You started out making money by selling Obama Girl–related merchandise. But now as part of Next New, which sells advertising, you get a cut of ad revenues?

BR: Yes. For our first three months, I was handling everything on my own, and as a result, it was difficult to do all the things with the sites that we're able to do now. Because we joined Next New Networks, we had access to website developers and production facilities and an ad sales team and all the things that would have been difficult for me to do on my own.

After a few months of doing primarily Obama Girl videos, we were able to build out the channel and build a team that could create videos that were political satire beyond just Obama.

RM: *I've Got A Crush on Obama* is a perfect example of consumer-created content taking on a life of its own online. What does it mean to have an individual like you create videos that influence the national dialogue around a presidential campaign and now an administration?

BR: I think it's indicative of where things are headed. It's really interesting that in the last election, something happened that was somewhat similar, in that a group of people came together and they did a "Swift Boat" ad, and that was something that aired in a few markets and then became this huge critical thing.

But it wasn't something that one individual could have pulled off. Now, where we are today, we have a situation where somebody with a handheld camera, if they come up with an idea that's really original, can get it in front of millions of people literally days later.

And the amazing thing about this to me is: one) the power that an individual has, and two) the actual time it takes for an idea to spread has been compressed so drastically that we posted [Obama Girl] on YouTube on a Wednesday morning at 10 A.M. We had a call from ABC at 3 P.M., and then the next day Leah and Amber were running around the city doing national media. What is fascinating about the Internet, and why I love it so much, is that you have this opportunity to communicate with people, and for people to communicate with each other, that we just didn't have five years ago.

So yeah, it impacted the election. It impacted pretty much every walk of life. Probably the most interesting email I got was actually from a museum in New York that said, "We're putting together an exhibit on how media over the years have actually impacted politics, and we want to make your video part of this exhibit," which I just thought was a riot.

In terms of the presidency today, I think people are more interested in this presidency, because so much of President Obama's audience came from a younger generation that really grew up online, and came out of the grassroots level, which the campaign used so well. Obama is a pop culture icon right now. That gives us a lot of fodder to do videos that hopefully people will want to watch.

And looking forward, the political satire cycle revolving around elections gets earlier and earlier every year. And if Sarah Palin runs in 2012, she is just the perfect thing to happen to political comedy.

RM: Looking at the bigger picture, how do you think efforts like yours will impact the kind of content that we will all consume in years ahead?

BR: I think there will be a couple of shifts. One is, as the individual can create something and actually make money on it—whether it's

YouTube or anybody who's doing some kind of revenue-share plan—if an individual can create something and make back the money that they invested in it, I actually think you'll see the quality of content coming out of everybody across the country that has a camera and an idea really being elevated.

Because what we're seeing is, somebody says, well let's do this video about, whatever it is, Obama. Typically they're not going to invest more than a couple hundred bucks in it. When people start saying, "If we just get a little more talent behind this, we might be able to make back our money through the advertisers that these networks have relationships with," I think we'll see an even higher level of quality come out of all this consumer-generated stuff.

I think that's going to be one shift, and then the other element is I think we're going to see more and more entertainment take different shapes and forms, so people will be creating really interesting online games and people will be figuring out ways to create live-event entertainment on their own.

There's just a sense that the whole landscape shifts as the individual feels that, "Hey, with a good idea, I can come up with something that reaches a lot of people quickly."

RM: At the same time, is "user-generated video" really the right phrase for all this content? Most of the time, the really good content comes from professionals or semiprofessionals.

BR: The semantics of it are interesting because you hear new terms all the time. A term I'm hearing a lot recently at Next New Networks has been the "Pro Tail." Unlike the "Long Tail," which is all the user-generated stuff that finds its own small audiences online, the Pro Tail is the content out there that is done by people who are super talented and have content that's just itching to get out there.

I do think that [what] we're finding when we look for user-generated content is that there are certain people who just have a knack for creating things that work online, just like certain people have a knack for creating advertising.

To some degree, I think what's going on with user-generated content—especially from a political standpoint—is the democratization of the whole process, because anybody can get involved.

All this stuff is super cool, but it still tends to be a small number of people who figure out how to create something that's so different that people just have to share it with others.

RM: Do you ever feel like the Lorne Michaels of the twenty-first century?

BR: I would never go anywhere near that far. But it's funny because, I got my MBA in marketing strategy and then spent five years at marketing agencies. So a lot of the time, I feel like I'm faking my way through the role of video producer. But there is a lot of overlap.

Just like in advertising, you want to create things that people will talk about, and that inspire people, and that will differentiate yourself. You have to be different. It's all about the Big Idea, and there are a lot of parallels between that and trying to come up with online videos that will, hopefully, be odd enough or shocking enough or funny enough that people feel compelled to put it on their blog or send it to a friend.

It's Good to Play Games with Your Customers

MIKE BENSON didn't even know there was a name for what he was trying to pull off.

As executive vice president of marketing for ABC Entertainment, Benson had happily found himself with a phenomenon on his hands a few years ago, in the form of ABC-TV's cult-favorite television show *Lost*.

But he needed to figure out a way to keep fans of the show satisfied during what was shaping up to be a seemingly interminable break between seasons.

His plan: to launch an ambitious digital marketing campaign designed to be as frustrating as it was elaborate, involving a mind-bogglingly intricate effort to bring verisimilitude to the show's back story in the form of a vast online scavenger hunt.

He laughed when I reminded him during the height of the campaign that there was a name for such initiatives—

alternative reality games, or "ARGs" in the vernacular of online gaming communities.

"Someone called me and said, 'Oh, you're doing an alternative reality game—an ARG," he said, recounting the first time he'd heard the term. "And I said, 'What's that?' And they explained it to me. And I said, 'Well yes. I guess we're doing that.'"

In our look at Rule #4, we learned how MET | Hodder's *Rachel Blake* videos for The Lost Experience were hidden around the web, ostensibly chronicling the character's efforts to find out the truth about the show's mysterious Hanso Foundation, as if the organization were real.

But that was just part of the game.

A labyrinth of faux websites for other fictional organizations and individuals mentioned on the show was launched, many with so-called "Easter eggs" that would offer up clues to the next step in the mystery—some pointing to simple games, others containing coded messages complete with complicated encryption schemes.

Sprite television commercials flashed hidden passwords that could be entered at a special "Sub-Lymon-al" website (playing off the Sprite's lemon lime, or in the brand's lexicon, "Lymon," flavor) to access Lost Experience videos and websites.

Links on a Jeep Compass–branded site called LetYourCompass GuideYou.com sent visitors to YouTube videos about the game. Job listings at Monster.com included postings from the Hanso Foundation, which included anagrams with secret messages.

And TV commercials during ABC's *Boston Legal* led viewers to a site about paranormal psychology in which users could solve a puzzle that linked them to a secret "internal" Verizon forum where employees complain about undue influence from the Hanso Foundation on the inner workings of the corporation.

"Advertisers are starting to think more like a programmer," says Tracey Scheppach, senior vice president and video innovations director for media buying giant Starcom USA, explaining the appeal of the game to ABC's advertiser clients. "How do I create content that people will watch?"[1]

Overnight, Internet forums lit up with discussion of The Lost Experience, with users sharing clues, videos, and codes they'd discovered, in order to help others find their way through the maze of information. And the publicity the campaign generated exposed the game to millions around the world.

Indeed, the season opener for *Lost* saw record viewership, helping it become the second most popular television show worldwide, behind only CBS's *CSI*.

Small wonder that Benson has run a number of other *Lost* ARGs since then—including season four's Find 815, in which a character named Sam Thomas, an employee of Oceanic Airlines (the airline the show's crash survivors took on their ill-fated trip aboard Flight 815) beckons online communities to help him find his girlfriend, who was one of the passengers.

A special Find 815 website was joined by video clips on YouTube and *Lost* fan site DarkUFO, where users were invited to share clues on Thomas's Facebook and MySpace pages. Meanwhile, fake billboards for Oceanic popped up in nine cities, including Los Angeles, Sydney, Seoul, and others, all captured in photos shared on photo-sharing site Flickr. One of the billboards, in Ames, Iowa, was vandalized with the words "Find 815."

Then came The Dharma Initiative Recruiting Project, an ARG in which participants are invited to volunteer as recruits for one of the show's enigmatic organizations. A special DharmaWantsYou.com website informs volunteers that they would have weekly opportunities to complete a test that assesses their abilities in a particular skill— including "pressurized spatial judgment evaluation" and "numeric projection evaluation." And emails featuring videos with embedded codes for delivering secret messages to other recruits were sent to candidates (see Figure 6–1).

Some of Benson's branded games have been less elaborate. A Sawyer Nickname Generator, named for the show's sobriquet-slinging

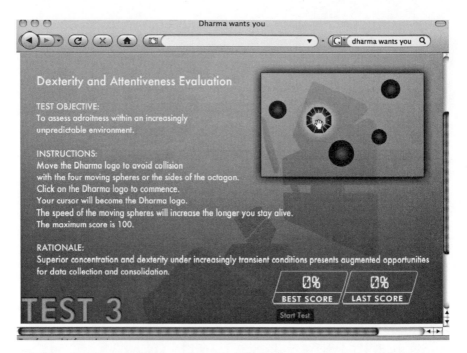

FIGURE 6–1. *DharmaWantsYou.com—an online recruitment site tied to the fictional Dharma Initiative—was just one element of The Lost Experience alternative reality game.*

southern con man, enables users to enter in names and characteristics to give themselves and their friends the same treatment Sawyer gives *Lost* characters he calls "Freckles," "Chopsticks," and "Bob's Big Boy."

Collectively, the efforts have helped *Lost* grow its viewer base in both first-run broadcast and now in syndication—polishing its reputation as one of television's most innovative shows and securing its place in the annals of broadcast history.

Along the way, they have also become the ultimate example of branded games designed to shape consumer perceptions and behavior.

Got Game?

Indeed, for consumers of a certain age, there's no better way to engage them than to play with them—in the form of branded games.

"With 72 percent of people playing one form of game or another, this is a medium that really can't be ignored by marketers," says Tim

Zuckert, CEO of Shift Control Media, which has created branded games for Coca-Cola, American Express, and Harrah's.

In his view, the most compelling reason for marketers to look at avenues like branded games is simple. "Consumers are increasingly empowered to turn away from traditional kinds of push-based marketing messages," he tells me. "Games offer a great opportunity for brands to bring consumers into their world, and to give people a reason to want to spend time with the brand voluntarily—and to recommend that other people do the same."

According to Zuckert, consumers tend to spend an average of twelve minutes with branded games—which is far longer than they'll spend with most other forms of marketing communications.

As we discussed earlier, Burger King's XBox games are among the most prominent examples of branded games, having sold three million copies and helping to boost the chain's burger sales by 10 percent. And games like AXE's Dirty Rolling helped establish the brand among its young male audience (see Figure 6–2).

But they're really just the tip of the iceberg.

Shift Control Media's series of branded games for Coca-Cola's recent "Happiness" campaign have gained widespread attention for taking characters from popular "Happiness Factory" television commercials and extending them into games in which players become factory "employees" who build love, fun, and happiness into the brand's products.

In one, players cap bottles as quickly as possible. In another, they play the role of a "kissie puppy" who "puts love" into each Coke. There's even a version of the game made for movie theaters, in which moviegoers move their arms to control the onscreen action.

Toyota Yaris, meanwhile, has its own Xbox game, designed to build awareness for the gas-sipping automobile among twenty-somethings. And Cadillac has had tremendous success with an Xbox game of its own.

Indeed, in groundbreaking efforts to appeal to younger audiences with its high-performing V-Series vehicles, Cadillac recently asked

FIGURE 6–2. *Burger King's nutty Xbox games reinforced the brand's quirky positioning and sold over 3 million copies.* The BURGER KING® *trademarks and advertisements are used with permission from Burger King Corporation.*

agency partner Arc to create a microsite where gamers can download a special V-Series Expansion Pack—software that lets them "drive" a virtual Cadillac within Project Gotham Racing 3 (known as "PGR 3" to its fans), a wildly popular title on the Xbox 360 gaming console.

Anyone who's ever played PGR 3 knows it rocks. For an automotive brand to extend its car into a fast-paced, adrenaline-pumping game is a perfect way to add street cred to the brand.

Within the first month, gamers worldwide downloaded the V-Series Expansion Pack more than 150,000 times, and logged 7,600 hours of racing the Cadillac V-series within PGR 3.[2]

A&E Television Network, meanwhile, recently launched a Facebook game based on its *Parking Wars* TV show, in which users park virtual cars on friends' profile pages, or "streets," while slapping tickets on cars parked on their own pages—and avoiding tickets themselves. Within weeks, the game had attracted more than 198,000 unique users, many of them repeat players, and generated more than 45 million page views.[3]

"We thought if we could find a clever way of increasing consumer interaction with the concept behind the shows, that we would increase curiosity in the show itself," says Lori Peterzell, A&E's vice-president for consumer marketing, goes on to say.[4]

Movie studios, in particular, find gaming a must-have component of many marketing campaigns. Marvel Entertainment, for instance, frequently creates games for franchises ranging from *Spider-Man* and *X-Men*, to *Iron Man* and *Thor*.

Family restaurant Dairy Queen, meanwhile, has been unconventional in its approach. In the branded game DQ Tycoon, players run their own Dairy Queen franchise. The stress-inducing game is part of a genre in which players are required to race against the clock to complete tasks—in this case, taking food orders, keeping inventories up to date, and dipping ice cream cones.

The $19.99 game is available at Target stores and aimed at the fastest growing category of gamers—women over thirty.[5]

These kinds of games are "popular with a group that skews very nicely with Dairy Queen," says Michael Keller, the chief brand officer for Dairy Queen International. "Women, a little bit more than men, are cravers of treats, and women, more than men, are the decision makers in the household as it relates to restaurants."[6]

Which means he's either got a hit game on his hands or he just ticked off a lot of stay-at-home moms. Or both.

PUTTING THE BRAND IN PLAY

The appeal of branded games is obvious: They represent a uniquely immersive, on-demand avenue for consumers to engage with the brand over and over again. And by making them sharable, they turn players into viral engines that spur competition among widespread social networks.

What's more, such games may help connect with audiences that are hard to reach through other avenues.

Recalling the Trix Rabbit, many believe videogames are strictly for kids. But according to comScore's Game Metrix, the average gamer is forty-one years old and has an annual income of $55,000+. And women make up 52 percent of the online gaming audience.[7]

To reach these consumers, many brands are creating branded games, or taking advantage of a related channel—namely, in-game advertising. In this milieu, commercial overtures appear within popular video games like The Sims or Grand Theft Auto—a practice that is expected to top $1 billion in ad spend by 2012, according to the Yankee Group.[8]

Indeed, according to a separate Gartner study, over 20 percent of tier-one retailers will have some form of marketing presence within online games or virtual worlds in that timeframe.[9]

In the eyes of many gamers, such advertising makes games set in the present day seem more realistic. Imagine characters sipping Pepsi, or wearing Nike shoes that enable them to run faster when purchased. Indeed, new transaction capabilities may enable players to actually buy real-world versions of in-game products and have them delivered to their home address.

Typically, in-game advertising can be targeted to specific player segments, and can even be bought for specific campaigns. Sony and ad network IGA Worldwide, for example, allow ads distributed over the Internet to be inserted into PlayStation 3 videogames just as one might buy a flight of television commercials. Imagine, for instance, a billboard ad for the movie *Shrek Forever After, Newt,* or *Pirates of the Caribbean 4* appearing on roadside billboards within a car racing game in the weeks leading up to their world premieres. A week later, the ads might be dynamically replaced with promotions for running shoes or even other video games—purchased just as a flight of commercials are bought in the television industry.

Even presidential politics is taking to the nascent channel. During the 2008 election cycle, the Obama campaign famously placed an ad buy within the Xbox racing game Burnout Paradise in an effort to influence the youth vote.

Perhaps more against type, rival John McCain's camp got into the action too, with a so-called "advergame" called Pork Invaders, in which players zap pork barrel spenders in a spoof of that 1980s classic, Space Invaders.

To be sure, in-game advertising is a powerful outlet for many brands, but that's not to say there aren't issues. Any advertisement within a game is as intrusive, if not more so, than a television or radio commercial. And one has to wonder if attention will be paid to any advertisement when players are facing a frag-or-be-fragged scenario.

Indeed, games built around a brand and its value proposition or positioning provide a far more direct connection between brand and consumer than in-game advertising ever will.

That is, if you follow some important guidelines for playing games with your customers.

A GAME MAKES SENSE FOR ANY BRAND—EXCEPT WHEN IT DOESN'T

Branded games may or not represent an opportunity for some brands in some categories—as we've seen, automotive brands in particular can turn racing games into virtual test drives, for instance.

But be smart about it. While Pampers could no doubt create a humorous game around diaper changing, it's a genre that other brands—Depends Undergarments, for instance—should probably avoid.

Likewise, while a first-person shoot-'em-up game might seem natural for a gun manufacturer, it might make for a, shall we say, "touchy" political situation.

That said, if done well, even sensitive topics like medical care can be extended into games as an engaging way to get consumers to get more involved with their own health care and, perhaps, turn to the associated brand for help.

In the U.K., for instance, Prudential Health, created a game, The Health-O-Meter, which enables players to get a rough idea of their fitness level in a lighthearted way.

Players are asked questions such as "How much alcohol do you drink in a week," with multiple-choice answers ranging from "I don't touch the stuff," to "I sometimes have a cheeky one at the weekend," to "I can't remember the last time I was sober."

At the end of a series of questions, the Health-O-Meter offers up a fitness score and information on how PruHealth can help the player live a healthier lifestyle.

DON'T JUST PROVIDE A DIVERSION, DRIVE HOME YOUR VALUE PROPOSITION

Microsoft has found huge success with the Microsoft Office Trivia Challenge, a Concentration-style game designed to showcase the new capabilities of Office.

At this writing, over 65,000 users—mostly middle-aged office workers—have downloaded the game. What's more, 47 percent of these people say they have played it at least four times. Some 22 percent say they have played it more than ten times. And 50 percent say they learned something about Office's new functionality.

Meanwhile, online travel company Orbitz has its own online gaming destination, called OrbitzGames.com, which at this writing features games like Flick Football, Bing-Bing Pinball, and a Squeal & Burn car driving game. All are designed to help players discover great deals on travel while associating Orbitz with fun vacation packages.

According to the company, the site not only builds awareness for the brand, but also drives significant traffic to Orbitz's main website, and even generates transactions.

For its part, Discovery Channel has artfully used games to promote its upcoming television programs.

In the run-up to its annual *Shark Week* programming block, the network recently launched Sharkrunners, an online game that puts players in the role of marine biologists on a trek to find out everything they can about these deadly creatures of the deep.

The game, created with the help of game company area/code, is perfectly suited to the Discovery brand. Players control research ships while the position and movement of onscreen great white sharks correspond with real-world telemetry provided by GPS units attached to actual sharks in the wild.

Players log in, select a crew and an "approach technique," and then collect data from the sharks. Since it's all in real time, players receive email and mobile text alerts throughout the day when their boat is within range of a shark. It's fun and educational at the same time.

More recently, Discovery has even created its own expansive ARG, called Frenzied Waters. In this game, players fan out across Twitter, Flickr, Facebook, and other sites—not to mention real-world cities from San Francisco to Miami Beach—to seek out answers to eleven clues to a mystery involving an event that happened in Ashbury Park, New Jersey, in 1916 (needless to say, it involved sharks). Some participants were even mailed physical items such as newspaper clippings about their own deaths by shark attack, bloodied swim trunks, and beach closure signs.

Suffice to say, it would be hard for anyone playing either of these games to resist at least some portion of *Shark Week* programming—much less fail to know it was coming.

DON'T FORGET A CALL TO ACTION

Before designing your game, define what it is you want your audience to do, feel, or think about your brand once they've played.

At the very least, your game should prompt a positive association. But ideally, it should lead people onto the next step in the buying process.

Doritos, for instance, recently launched an alternate reality game in the U.K. in which players take part in a highly immersive interactive video experience to try to guess a mystery flavor called "ID3" while thwarting a gang of international identity thieves.

Players make their way through dozens of decisions to navigate three separate video experiences created by ad agency AMV BBDO and Upset Films. Players unlock the video episodes by entering the codes on specially marked packages of Doritos, and are then engaged with in a cinema vérité–style video experience presented from the participant's point of view. The game even integrates user-uploaded images and other content to personalize the sensation of being recruited, against one's will, to take part in a sting operation that plays out over each successive episode. Each code entitles the player to a certain number of lives—though, with a mind-numbing array of possible paths, that means needing to acquire as many codes (by purchasing more and more Doritos) as possible. At stake: bragging rights and up to £20,000 in prizes.

Meanwhile, a client of ours, Internet security solutions provider SonicWALL, recently came to us to develop a game designed to illustrate how futile it is to thwart incoming threats to enterprise networks without the company's particular brand of security solutions.

As part of an integrated print and online campaign, the game, The SonicWALL Network Security Challenge, features conveyor belts carrying symbols of incoming data packets—envelopes symbolizing email, and toolboxes symbolizing applications, for example. A scanner on each conveyer belt reveals the content of the packages, and players have to stop viruses and other attacks by hitting a "destroy" button while letting acceptable packages through.

At each level, more and more conveyer belts carry faster and faster traffic—ultimately forcing the player to realize they will fail without SonicWALL solutions. And game play was paid off by linking players to information about how the brand's solutions can help remedy the challenges of this business critical enterprise operation.

"Brands should look to games as a form of integrated marketing that can dovetail with some of the other activities that they're doing in both traditional and digital marketing," Zuckert explains. "These days, marketing departments, like every other functional area within the organization, are looking long and hard at every investment that they make. Games only make sense when they're part of an overall, integrated approach, as opposed to being a stand-alone or one-off."

As the SonicWALL and Microsoft games mentioned above indicate, it turns out the workplace may be an ideal gaming environment for brands, especially the business-to-business variety.

In a study from PopCap Games, researchers estimate that as many as 80 million white-collar workers play casual online games. Of those surveyed, nearly a quarter (24 percent) say they play games "at work"—with fully 35 percent of CEOs, CFOs, and other senior executives acknowledging that they play while at their desks. Indeed, 61 percent of these senior executives say they play once a day, if not more frequently, compared to 51 percent of other white-collar gamers.

"It's not surprising that today's business professionals are casual videogame users," says Carly Drum, a recognized expert on workplace issues and managing director of Drum Associates. "The face of today's executive workforce is definitely changing: We're seeing employees who are much more technologically savvy and familiar with all forms of new media, from social networking to blogging and beyond.

"So, it's natural that some business executives would also look to casual videogames that they can play on their PC, mobile phone, or BlackBerry during a work break, as a way to quickly relax and recharge their batteries, so to speak."[10]

All of which points to some great opportunities in turning fun and games into serious business—if you give gamers a reason to take immediate action.

Indeed, though primarily designed to build brand awareness, Rick Wootten, SonicWALL's director of e-business and e-marketing, tells me his company's games—including Network Security Challenge and a particularly popular game called The Phishing IQ Test, a visual quiz to test one's ability to recognize a phishing attack—have collectively been downloaded over 1.2 million times and have became serious lead generators for the company by opening up dialogue with prospective customers.

GAMES ARE BEST PLAYED WITH OTHERS

In most of the examples above, sharing the game is a key ingredient of the experience. In Microsoft's case, nearly 25 percent forwarded its Office game to a friend or colleague, for instance.

According to Time Shift Media's Zuckert, it's not uncommon to see pass-along rates of 40 percent or more.

"If I pass something on to you, the only cost that's involved for the brand was the cost of me finding the game in the first place," he says. "So, in essence, that 40 percent pass-along is not only free media to the brand, but it's also delivering a higher value to them because the pass-along is coming with an implicit endorsement from the person who's doing the passing."

Increasingly, these games are no longer just about online connections.

Coca-Cola's Fanta orange soda recently used augmented reality technology to create a virtual tennis game that can be played by people using their mobile phones.

Players can go to a microsite to print out a special graphic symbol that, when held it up to their camera phone, creates a 3-D hologram of a virtual tennis court—overlaying the physical world around the player. They can then hit a virtual tennis ball using the phone as a virtual racket, à la Wii. They can even compete against others by connecting with another phone via Bluetooth. It's cheesy and a lot of work. And it's just the kind of funky experience kids love (see Figure 6–3).

"Fanta's brand positioning is about focusing on moments of enjoyment throughout your day, and the mobile phone is with you from when you wake up until you go to bed," says Jeff Arbour, SVP of North America operations for The Hyperfactory, which created the game for Coca-Cola. "We thought [this was] a light, easy game that represented the brand's identity and personality."

Or, as Prinz Pinakatt, group interactive marketing manager for Coca-Cola Europe, tells me: "It's a perfect representation of what Fanta stands for, which is playful imagination."

FIGURE 6–3. *The Wii is so last week. With Fanta's augmented reality game, players print out a special form that, when viewed through a camera phone lens, creates a 3-D holographic mobile tennis game that connects players via Bluetooth.*

None of this is lost on ABC's Benson, of course. As he learned firsthand, when branded games are designed correctly, players become viral agents—as has been the case with his games associated with *Lost*.

While his effort was aimed squarely at the show's "super fans," the game was artfully designed to engage casual viewers, too.

"By utilizing the Internet, the exposure that we've had, not only here in the United States, but across the globe, has been phenomenal—in the millions—beyond anything that we thought we were going to get," he says.

Starting on the next page, we'll find out exactly how he did it, and what it has meant to his brand.

Q&A

Mike Benson and the ABCs of Advergames

Mike Benson, executive vice president of marketing at ABC Entertainment

THANKS TO Mike Benson, *Lost* can be found in some pretty strange places.

Benson, the executive vice president of marketing, advertising, and promotion for ABC Entertainment, oversees all marketing communications for the network's blockbuster primetime and late-night television lineups, where he has helped launch shows such as *Lost*, *Grey's Anatomy*, *Desperate Housewives*, *Ugly Betty*, *Flash Forward*, and many others.

A longtime entertainment marketer, Benson helped reposition VH1 for a more adult audience in the 1990s by helping to launch such shows as *Behind the Music, Pop Up Video,* and *The Rock & Roll Picture Show.*

Since coming to ABC, he has twice been named *ADWEEK's* Entertainment Marketer of the Year, in part because of the game-changing digital innovations he has brought to bear for *Lost.*

Rick Mathieson: What does an initiative like The Lost Experience and your subsequent alternative reality games—or ARGs—portend for the future of advertising and promoting shows as well as consumer products?

Mike Benson: I look at our marketing as a 3-D chess game these days. From a television show standpoint—and it's probably no different than if you're an automotive or any other type of advertiser—the days of doing an on-air promo and a *TV Guide* ad are long gone.

It's about really having to understand your product, your audience, and how you are going to connect with them.

I think [an ARG developed with this understanding] does a couple of different things. It really takes advantage of what we're seeing with consumers these days. People used to gather in different [physical] places, and now they can gather online in virtual communities. When you have something like The Lost Experience, it's allowing people who are engaged by a certain type of content, and it engages them further—and hopefully makes them even bigger fans. The interesting thing for advertisers is that it really gives them other platforms to play on as well.

RM: How did the first Lost Experience get started?

MB: The Lost Experience grew out of something that we started after the first season of *Lost.*

It was interesting because when we launched *Lost,* we really looked at the program as creating this great mystery. We really wanted the audience to believe that, "Hey, you know what? Maybe there was a plane crash. And there are a whole bunch of stranded survivors on an island that nobody knows about."

When we started marketing the show, whether we put messages in bottles and placed them all over beaches, or we had websites and other things, what we found was that there was an audience out there that was hungry to become much more engaged in the program than just simply watching it.

As we saw the core audience develop over the first season, we figured it would be interesting; what if we did some things online that gave the audience more of *Lost* but from a different perspective?

So we actually started to bury web addresses, in the final episodes of *Lost* after Season One, that took people to Oceanic-Airlines.com and other [sites] that would help people discover more about *Lost*. And that was really the beginning, when we saw how popular this could be, and the kind of hits that we were getting on this website. Within the first day or two we had a million hits on a website, which is pretty phenomenal. There's an audience out here that wants to participate in this.

We took that idea and grew it. We sat down with the show producers and we really wanted to make something that was in line with the show; that was truly organic, that wasn't just a game. It was really looking at marketing as content.

RM: How did you line up advertisers to help pay for it? Was it a value-add to buying TV spots during *Lost*?

MB: It wasn't part of a plan to go out and sell advertisers; we wouldn't say to them, "Well, in order to be in The Lost Experience you have to buy so many spots," because what we were doing was really experimental.

What we looked for in advertisers were people that were willing to experiment with us and take some chances, not only with how or where they would be exposed, but how they'd be integrated into this in a way that would be organic to The Lost Experience, organic to the show, and something that consumers would buy and appreciate.

We weren't really out to make money on this. We wanted to figure out if this would work.

RM: What sort of metrics did you see?

MB: The exposure has been phenomenal. And I think the other really interesting dynamic of this—and it really goes back to the television show—is that *Lost* is a global brand. And by utilizing the Internet, the exposure that we've had, not only here in the United States, but across the globe, has been phenomenal—in the millions and millions—beyond anything that we thought we were going to get. Within the first week, the Hanso Foundation website had tens of millions of hits.

So you look at that kind of traffic. And it's not only coming from the United States, but it's coming from all over the globe.

RM: Since the first Lost Experience, you've done numerous initiatives like the Find 815 promotion and The Dharma Project Recruitment Project. What are you learning that is refining these initiatives as you go along?

MB: That's a great question. One of the things that I learned with [the first] Lost Experience is that I think it went on too long. When you stretch something out between the end of a season and the beginning of a new season, where there are five months in between, it gets really difficult to sustain.

I actually believe a period of silence is really good. Build your story to a big crescendo at the end, leave them wanting more, and give them a little break before you come back again. I would call them more "ramps" than "bridges."

What you need to do is ramp people either out, or up and into things.

RM: How does a medium like television navigate a world of "now" media?

MB: When you have shows like *Lost, Desperate Housewives,* and *American Idol,* these programs prove that broadcast television is still as important as it was back when there were [only] three networks, and that you still need programs that bring people together in a community.

Broadcast television does that. There's no other medium, including the Internet, that can do that, because you still need some way to tell everybody that you can watch something happen and be part of a community for one hour. Thirty-five million people can come in and watch one show.

Then, the fun thing about technology—whether it's mobile or broadband Internet—is they can talk about it right afterward. It's sharing your thoughts and your experiences with people you know, and people who have like interests. I think that's what makes the Internet so interesting and technology today so exciting. And it makes it happen so much faster than it used to.

"What did you see?" "What did you like?" "I can't believe that happened." It's like, "Can you believe so-and-so cheated on so-and-so?" on *Desperate.* Or, "So-and-so was shot in that episode." Or, with *Lost,* "What happened here? What did it mean? What do you think—are they in purgatory?"

The exciting part for us is figuring out we've got a great premise for a show. How do we articulate that in all kinds of different ways? And whether it may be doing something on a beach, or putting a poster up somewhere, or creating a scavenger hunt on the Internet, it's really about creating whatever experiences we can for a potential audience.

RM: What advice would you give to marketers who may be looking at the success you've had and want to try something like this?

MB: I really believe that it takes some willingness to experiment and understanding that some things will work and other things won't.

A lot of advertisers are finding really new, unique, creative ways to get their products out in front of a potential audience. Branded games are one example of this. And whether you are an automotive or a soft drink or a packaged goods [brand], you start to find other opportunities where you can creatively and organically [showcase] your product, probably even more effectively than something that you could do on television, just because you've got a little more latitude.

I also believe that you have to let go every once in a while. I won't use names, but I think the thing that was most interesting for me personally when I sat down with some of our partners in The Lost Experience, is the ones that I thought were going to be the least innovative were the most innovative. And the ones that I thought would be the most were the least.

Some of the older companies that have been around for a while, that you really wonder, "Are they going to get it?" They seem to really grasp what is going on in our culture today. And some of the newer companies were just very inflexible. They did not want to bend at all.

At the same time, you've also got to be aware of what the consumer will and will not accept. They know when they're being sold—especially with the *Lost* audience. They're so hardcore. When they see something, they're just, "Okay. I'm just being sold something here."

And I think that there's an audience out there that can appreciate real creativity, and that will accept and buy an advertiser's product if it's done right.

But if you don't do it right, they're going to write you off—fast.

Products Are the New Services

YOU MIGHT NOT recognize it by taste alone, but Coors Light isn't just a beer anymore.

It's a portfolio of Facebook apps that enable you to access maps that direct your "brew crew" to nearby bars—or MySpace pages where you can locate happy hours in your geographic area and upload pictures of your posse for the chance to win prizes.

For that matter, Chantix isn't just a smoking-cessation drug anymore, either. It's a service that connects you with a personalized website and easy-to-use tools to track your progress, as well as access to support groups and on-call coaches who can help you squelch your addiction.

Your daughter's Webkinz isn't just a stuffed animal. It's an online virtual world where she can take care of her virtual pet, earn KinzCash, and play games. It's been so successful that even Barbie now has her own virtual world, called BarbieGirls.com, where girls can customize their dolls' looks, shop at an online mall, and hang out together at a place called "The B Cafe."

Even your Special K cereal is far more than a lowly bowl of corn-flakes these days. It's an online weight management service and social network called "The Special K Challenge," where you can share your frustrations and triumphs with others, and customize a meal plan that is, not coincidentally, built around Special K products ranging from Cinnamon Pecan Special K Cereal, to Peaches & Berry Special K bars, to Pink Lemonade Special K2O protein water mix.

The service will also give you telephone wake-up calls to motivate you to eat healthy. You can even get expert advice from celebrity blog-ger and model Gabrielle Reece.

Indeed, as many of the examples in this book demonstrate, in the digital age, differentiation may come less from the quality with which your products are manufactured, and more from the on-demand dig-ital services they deliver to your customers.

Product Plus

The poster child for products as services has long been Nike+ run-ning shoes, which don't just cushion your soles. They interact with your iPod Nano to monitor your workouts and offer instant stats and feedback.

On the running trail, the system measures your time, distance, pace, and calories burned. It'll even play your favorite power song when you're in need of instant motivation. At the gym, it'll do the same thing on the bike, elliptical trainer, or treadmill. Whatever the venue, all that data is uploaded to nikeplus.com so that after you sync your iPod with your PC, you can track your progress over time.

The product was first launched in 2006 and continues to evolve. By 2010, the Nike+ site had added more personalization and social net-working functions. Runners in networks are ranked based on how much and how far they run. The site will make shoe recommendations based on interactive questionnaires. Users are able to share running info on Facebook and Twitter. And the service will even suggest potential running partners.

Indeed, runners have found Nike+ so compelling, it has helped Nike's share of the running shoe category skyrocket from 48 percent to 61 percent in just three years, according to *Adweek*.[1]

But all of this may be just the tip of the iceberg. According to a patent application recently filed by partner Apple, the application may soon deliver a whole new level of service interaction.

According to the filing, new Nike+ running systems (or, conceivably, those from other shoe manufacturers) would compare the runner's progress against a reference performance typical of a person having similar physical characteristics. It would monitor the wear on shoe performance, to make recommendations on running technique (not to mention alerting the runner when it's time to buy new shoes). And it would feature GPS location awareness, to report elevation gain, speed, heading, calories burned, and more.

Last but not least, the system would even enable marketers to send offers from stores and other establishments that the runner passes during a workout. Which could be a problem, at least for me, if that means receiving offers as I run past bakeries and fast food outlets.

Yet what's perhaps most interesting about the Nike+ system in its current incarnation is that it didn't come from Nike or Apple. It came from an ad agency—R/GA in New York.

The thirty-three-year-old agency has a storied history of blurring the lines between product and product marketing—making them, in practical terms, synonymous.

Thanks to R/GA, your Nokia N-Series mobile phone isn't just a multimedia smart phone. It's a channel for Nokia viNe, a mobile application that combines GPS, camera, and media player to enable users to leave photos, videos, and songs and tag them to physical locations for others to find with their own phones, or to share with friends in real time.

Bob Greenberg, the founder of R/GA, believes in what he calls "a new world of ubiquitous content on demand." As Barry Wacksman, R/GA's executive vice president and chief growth officer puts it, "We are now in the era in which brands must create new transformational technologies [and] think about how to create new ways to serve [their] customers."

"Rather than use a website as a piece of brand communication, pegged to the look and tone of the TV spots and print ads like a set of matching luggage, why not add some useful functionality," he adds. "Technology is something that is invented. If it's any good, you use it. If it's insanely great, it changes your life."[2]

SPECIAL DELIVERY

This kind of digital invention is taking many forms, thanks to many brands and their agencies. We've already mentioned how Domino's enables Facebook users to order that Cali Chicken Bacon Ranch pizza without ever leaving their personal profile pages. Now, even TiVo's in on the action.

If you're anything like me, you long ago came to cherish your DVR for setting you free from television schedules and commercials (talk about changing your life). Yet while you can now program your DVR—and even view your recorded content from your computer or cell phone, anywhere, on-demand—you may, like me, come to find yourself wondering, "Can't this miracle machine also just close the deal and deliver a piping hot pepperoni pizza, too?"

The answer is now "yes"—hallelujah and amen. Through an interactive TV solution, TiVo subscribers can use their DVRs to order Domino's pizza for pickup or delivery and (here's the genius) track the timing of deliveries (see Figure 7–1).

"Interactive TV, in general, is the future," says Rob Weisberg, VP-precision and print marketing at Domino's Pizza. "To give the average consumer the opportunity to order pizza while never getting up from watching Sunday football . . . is pretty amazing."[3]

FIGURE 7–1. Couch potatoes of the world rejoice! You can order Domino's pizza via TiVo, and even check on its delivery time, with a few clicks of the TV remote.

And by "amazing," he of course means "a freaking dream come true."

At their most essential, these kinds of services recall Rule #2—moving beyond repurposing content to rethinking everything about the way you market your products in the on-demand era. In this rule, we take the next step—rethinking the product itself.

It's that kind of (re)thinking that led CBS to create a "social viewing" service that answers the question, why just watch TV when you can chat about it, too?

The service, available at cbs.com, enables groups of viewers to collectively interact with streaming TV content in "social viewing rooms" that mash up video conferencing, live chat, and live streaming to create a "communal" experience when watching CBS shows like *Two and a Half Men* and *The Amazing Race.*

Friends can log on, watch shows, and participate in polls and quizzes, and even throw virtual objects like tomatoes and kisses at the screen.

"In the past when you watched videos online, it was a very isolating experience," Anthony Soohoo, senior vice president and general manager of CBS Interactive, told the *Hollywood Reporter.* "This takes people 3,000 miles away and makes them feel like they're sitting on the couch next to each other. The social viewing room is a next-generation social media platform that lets users engage with each other and the content they are watching in a fun new way."[4]

While uptake has been slow so far, the service is a step toward associating the brand more firmly with Twitter-based communications so common to television shows' fan bases, and of single-event–based online social viewing experiences like those from MLB.com for specific games.

Indeed, in my view, CBS's social viewing rooms would be much more compelling if they integrated fan Twitter feeds into the experience, so as to better capture the ongoing—and never-ending—online discussion around popular shows.

Obviously, music and entertainment brands in particular have found adding on-demand services to their products—music or video content—can help build fan databases that can then be leveraged to increase ratings or ticket and album sales.

Fans of songstress Taylor Swift, for instance, were able to go to TheTaylorNation.com, where the first 10,000 fans to order a limited box-set edition of her music could upload their own photos for a mosaic image to be featured on the album artwork and CD.

Along the way, the artist has collected contact information for thousands of fans to whom she can pitch future offerings.

As these and many other brands demonstrate, products are the new services. And to fully take advantage of Rule #7, you've got to also apply Rule #2—don't just repurpose, reimagine—to do it right.

Here are some considerations to take into account.

THE PRODUCT IS JUST THE BEGINNING

Brands need to realize that products are the jumping-off point for building relationships with customers. Digital channels enable you to turn products into on-demand services that help consumers make the most of your product, reach their goals, entertain themselves, or connect with other like-minded consumers.

Polar, for instance, offers a popular line of sports watches that let you track your heart rate and calories burned during workouts. The watches are great—I've used one for years. But the watch is just the beginning. At PolarPersonalTrainer.com, users can upload and analyze their fitness routines, get help when choosing a type of exercise, access training programs tailored to their individual level and goals, challenge themselves and friends, and find new training partners through the Polar community.

This isn't all just about health, of course.

Technology giant HP has been especially active in extending its products into services. The company has been an early innovator in so-called "cloud computing" technologies that enable its computers to be the interface for services ranging from customized magazine printing that enables everyday consumers to have their own personal magazines published, to video conferencing for consumers and businesses, to templates for customized arts products such as paper dolls, baby cards, and tour books designed by singer Gwen Stefani.

"We're always trying to find new ways of doing things that accentuate the idea rather than just doing technology for technology's sake," says Derek Robson, managing partner of San Francisco–based advertising powerhouse, Goodby, Silverstein & Partners, reflecting his agency's role in helping to develop many of these services. "And I do think most of the best work has a kind of an application and a kind of utility to it."

Sometimes this is all just played for laughs. Unilever's AXE deodorant brand (known as Lynx in the U.K.), for instance, mixes fun apps with a little offensiveness in what it calls "Digital Ice Breakers."

At the Lynx Effect website, you can download the Facebook Chocolate App, which lets you dispatch a tiny chocolate man that invites girls to "lick, nibble, or bite" him from your profile page, tied to Lynx Dark Temptation deodorant.

There's the Cheerleader Countdown widget, with which you can count down the next event you're planning—whether it's "Beer O'Clock," a big night out, or a holiday. At one point, there was even an app that turns your mobile phone into a "Fit Girl Finder," designed to let you "show to the girl of your dreams that it has scientifically picked her out as the fittest [in the U.K., that's akin to 'hottest'] girl in the room."

IF IT DOESN'T ADD VALUE, IT'S NOT VALUABLE

To be clear, a content-rich website alone is not a service. In the Web 2.0 era, consumers chafe at brochureware, no matter how interactive it is.

To make your digital service useful, it either has to offer an entertaining diversion, or it has to enable your customers to actually accomplish something inherent to the purchase decision—with bonus points if that actually facilitates that purchase or adds value to it afterwards.

STA Travel has been a real innovator in that regard. We mentioned earlier how the youth-oriented travel company has harnessed the power of social networking. The company has also been aggressive in turning its products—travel packages—into services.

The Dallas-based company has launched a number of online travel tools that help make the vacation planning experience as easy as possible. There's a special travel offer widget that sends the latest offers direct to the user's desktop or web page; a travel to-do list to make sure the user is ready after he or she has booked a package; a weather comparison widget to compare the weather where the user is now with where they're headed; and a trip countdown widget that counts down those days, hours, and minutes before the big getaway.

Each of these widgets can then be personalized and customized according to the tastes of the user. If you're flying to the Caribbean for vacation, you can customize the widgets with a beach theme.

"If you look at most mature categories, the way you can continue to generate decent margins, and the way you can continue to deliver increased value and increased relevancy to customers is to take your products and turn them into services," Andy Bateman, CEO of global brand consultancy Interbrand, tells me.

Even turkeys can create value-added services. Just look at Butterball.

The company's "Turkey Talk-Line," an 800-number call-in line first launched in 1981, helps over 100,000 consumers navigate the often panic-inducing ritual known as Thanksgiving dinner.

In the last few years, the brand has rounded out its offerings to help consumers perfect everything from their Turkey with 7-Grain Bread and Squash Stuffing to their Chocolate-Pumpkin Cake with Broiled Coconut Pecan Frosting.

In addition to the 800 number and the Butterball website, consumers can now read up on tips for everything from basting to deep-frying their birds via blogs and a mobile website; participate in live chats with Butterball experts; and get answers to questions via "Turkey Text" messages by mobile phone.

"When the Turkey Talk-Line started in 1981, the phone was the best way to give people the important turkey-cooking information that they were looking for," says Bill Klump, senior VP-marketing for Butterball. But he tells me the digital age not only enabled new kinds of services—it necessitated them.

"Now, as new cooks emerge we as a brand needed to evolve and provide expert holiday advice the way consumers want it—online and on-the-go," he says. "The offerings we launched in 2008 were an extension of the Butterball Turkey Talk-Line that allowed us to provide helpful holiday information to Thanksgiving cooks the way they consume it—anytime, anywhere" (see Figure 7–2).

In this way, the product becomes a service that, with luck, will result in far fewer spoiled Thanksgiving feasts.

FIGURE 7–2. Talkin' turkey: Blogs, a mobile site, and live chat mean Butterball's not just a bird, it's a holiday service.

On the other end of the spectrum, it's hard to say how Sprint's This Is Now widget dashboard adds true value, but it does demonstrate the power of the product it advertises.

Created by Goodby's Robson, "This is Now" is a dashboard with a wide array of widgets featuring such ephemera as the number of coffee cups being produced per minute worldwide, the number of 911 calls being made, your share of the national debt, the number of Post-it notes being produced, the top words being used online (at this moment, "next" and "back," ironically). And so on.

It's all backed by an audio track of a soothing, mildly robotic female voice dropping such bon mots as, "It's currently now in all time zones" and "Buckle up and enjoy the millisecond," along with obscure factoids such as "Just now, your body made 50 million new cells," and "In the last second, your hair grew five millionths of an inch."

Users can also use the Buzz Meter to compare search words for what's hot online at the moment, watch top videos at YouTube, and place purchases from hot new bands (see Figure 7–3).

It's all a lot of fun, and designed to promote Sprint's mobile data card for laptop computers, which enables you to stay on top of anything and everything, wherever you are—right now, on demand.

THE BEST SERVICES DON'T JUST PROMOTE PRODUCTS—THEY POWER THEM

Your offering—whether digital service, web app, or mobile-based—is not just a marketing platform (the fact that it exists is the promotion), it can, and often should, be central to your entire offering.

Apple could have simply manufactured its popular iPod MP3 players. Instead, it created iTunes—a music, and later, multimedia service completely removed from Apple's core business, computer device manufacturing. iTunes enables the iPod to become a personal content service (and with the iPhone, a personal communications tool), not just a content playback mechanism.

According to some estimates, iTunes and the App Store account for over $3.5 billion in revenue for Apple[5]—and drive consumer purchase decisions on who knows how much of the $40 billion Apple makes on its computers, iPods, and iPhones.[6]

Amazon's Kindle, meanwhile, is essentially an iPod for books. The product (the device) delivers a service (book downloads) for, as is the case with the iPod/iTunes ecosystem, a tidy fee—a factor that no doubt played a role in the development of Apple's own tablet device, the iPad.

There are other modalities, of course. In an interesting partnership with Facebook, online jewelry retailer Blue Nile created an app that enables you to sign up for an account, make a wish list, and then place a branded widget on your Facebook profile where all the people in

FIGURE 7–3. *Now hear this: Sprint's widget is meant to demonstrate how its mobile broadband service keeps you in the know about what's happening now.*

your social network can see it. Your more generous friends can then click on items to place a purchase for you, if they are so inclined, and have the items sent to your physical address.

Whatever your application, your digital service should be a valuable asset for your customers and, ideally, enhance or even power the experience of owning your physical products.

Forget that and you're back to square one.

Agent Provocateur:
Goodby's Derek Robson on Reinventing the Ad Agency

Derek Robson, managing partner of Goodby, Silverstein & Partners

Photo: Claude Shade

CALL IT "How Goodby Got Its Groove Back."

To be sure, Goodby, Silverstein & Partners, the legendary San Francisco–based ad agency behind such classic campaigns as "Got Milk" and the Foster Farm Chickens, had found itself in a funk—and felt increasingly irrelevant in an emerging, transmedia world of social networking, user-generated content, mobile, Internet video, and more.

So a few years ago, the agency set an ambitious goal to completely revamp itself for the digital age. "Our goal is to be unrecognizable twelve months from now," creative director Jamie Barrett said at the time.

The idea: transform an agency known primarily for eye-popping television spots into one badass, multiplatform marketing machine.

It was well worth the effort.

In less than a year, Goodby saw revenues leap 20 percent to $102 million. At the start of its transformation effort, 80 percent of the twenty-five-year-old agency's revenues came from traditional advertising campaigns, while less than 20 percent came from digital initiatives. Today, after three years of reinvention, those numbers are nearly flip-flopped, with 60 percent of revenues now coming from digital initiatives, and 40 percent from traditional.

Now, a team once vexed by what it called "Crispin Envy"—for all the attention Crispin Porter + Bogusky receives for its groundbreaking work in digital media—has found its own footing, and then some.

While many have driven the transformation, no one has received more credit as a catalyst for change than Derek Robson, forty-two, whom Goodby recruited from adverting agency powerhouse Bartle Bogle Hegarty in London.

As the agency's new managing partner, Robson immediately began implementing strategic changes that have helped the agency retool, reconfigure, and recalibrate itself for an extraordinary new era—and helped agency cofounder Rich Silverstein overcome his very worst fear.

Rick Mathieson: Why was transformation so necessary for Goodby, which has always been one of the indisputable leaders of the advertising world?

Derek Robson: We had become acutely aware that the world was changing incredibly quickly around us, that the media landscape was changing dramatically, and the things that had been very good about the company's DNA since its birth—the ability to tell stories—was still incredibly relevant, but it needed to be applied in new ways as we moved forward.

Alongside that, you had the rise of a different kind of [ad] agency. Crispin had arrived on the scene to become a very significant player. You didn't have to be a rocket scientist to realize if we weren't going to move forward, we were going to get left behind.

RM: I think there's a parallel for a lot of brand marketers who are asking, "How do we move beyond great TV spots?" How has this reality impacted the way Goodby works to help its clients connect with consumers?

DR: The truth is, now there are large audiences whose first and most relevant experience will come not in a traditional media. Younger audiences [are] spending more time playing computer games, more time on the web. And brands are being defined not just in traditional media, but outside of that media.

You look at things like the Apple brand and iPod. That's a brand that is defined much more by an online experience than it is by an offline experience.

There's nothing particularly revolutionary about this, other than trying to understand where people are, what they are doing, where they are consuming stuff, particularly in terms of media, and then following those people and understanding how they use that media in a more in-depth and interesting way.

RM: Agency co-founder Jeff Goodby has described you as a great catalyst for the dramatic change within the agency. What is it about you and your background and your skill set that Goodby was able to leverage so well?

DR: I was managing director of BBH in London. My background is as a planner, so I'm a strategist by background. I think in many ways because that's what I was, my approach to these things is much more about analysis, about looking at the problem from lots of different angles, weighing it out, proving things out in fact, in numbers, rather than lots of opinion. I think opinion is great, and has its place. But when you're trying to get a company to do new things, you have to prove to people with facts.

I'm not a particularly threatening character. I'm not somebody who goes around thumping the desk. I do think the way that you change companies is by actions more than talking.

And I think I was given the opportunity, probably as the first outsider to be in that partner group maybe ever, to look at the agency in a way that you can't if you've been here for ten, fifteen years and all you know is the way that it is.

I think many people could have done what I've done. It just happened to be me that was the person who was doing it at this moment in time.

RM: So your outsider status—your fresh eye—and your planning background led you to do things like conducting internal and external analysis of the agency.

DR: I spoke to people inside the company about the state of the company. I spoke to people outside the company about the state of the company. And then I did something that probably had not ever been done before, because it hadn't needed to be done before, which is to literally look at all the work that we had produced for all our clients. Not necessarily from the standpoint of what does the work look like and is it creative, but more about how much time does it take us to actually get to a piece of communication that we can sell to a client, and how many bits of television are we making, how many bits of Internet work are we creating.

And I looked at it to a certain extent more like a factory, to work out whether we have the right machinery in place to make the factory work properly.

As we went through, it changed almost at a level that would be staggering in our industry. We went from 17.5 percent of our work within new media to 50 percent in the first year. Now, our digital production department is as big as our broadcast production department. And our output is now 60/40 in favor of nontraditional interactive work.

That's a massive change. Not just in what we produce, but also, you've got to try and mirror that change with the resources you have. And you've either got to shed some resources and get some new resources in, or you've got to reskill people on the move. And that is a more complicated task, but that's one of the things that we've managed to do very successfully.

RM: One of the more interesting moves you have made was to merge media and account planning into one department.

DR: It's not rocket science to put the two disciplines together, because they share so much data and so much insight from the same sources. I felt that they should be more like an art director and a copywriter—they should work together to develop strategy, because the art of crafting strategy is no longer just about message management, or what you're going to say to consumers, but also where you're going to say it.

The earlier that that dialogue took place, the more likely we were to get more interesting strategy, and the more likely we were to produce more interesting work.

That was the theory anyway. I do think it's absolutely the right approach.

RM: What client work has best represented Goodby's transformation in your mind?

DR: Culturally one of the most difficult things that happens is to get creative people to understand [that] the world is no longer just defined by television.

The thing that happened, and has been happening for some time here, is that our work was much more diverse than even we knew it was. And I think as we began to change, the way we tackled problems and the way that we looked at problems was completely and utterly holistic in a way that I'd probably not ever really experienced before. Because television is the place where a campaign idea is normally articulated most clearly, and then from that work it falls out into other media.

Some of the best work we're doing is quite simple stuff, like the Warrio ad we did on YouTube. The [video] game's all about shaking through an obstacle course. And the YouTube video for the game starts shaking, and then the entire YouTube page, including everything outside the video window, shakes and falls, and it's a very simple and beautifully executed idea that involved what would be considered old/new media, rather than things like the augmented reality we did for GE, which is at the cutting edge of new media.

At Goodby, we're always trying to find new ways of doing things that accentuate the idea rather than just doing technology for technology's sake. And I do think most of the best work around has an application and a utility to it.

You look at things like Nike+ from R/GA, and Crispin's work with Domino's, where you can order a pizza through TiVo—these are communication ideas that are utilitarian and also business-sensitive. They generate revenue in their own right, and they're obviously very smart communication.

You have to apply the [right] technology to the right project, and that's what we've tended to do.

In Hotel 626 for Doritos, for instance, we're trying out technology that hasn't necessarily been executed on the Web before, using your phone and your webcam [in a haunted house experience]. Put on some headphones and it'll scare the bejesus out of you.

RM: So many agencies—especially larger ones—are recognizing they've got to master digital, not just react to it and try to play catch up to the cool thing some other agency did six months ago. Where do they start?

DR: God, that's a big question. The thing you've got to start with is by asking "What are we good at? What's part of our DNA that defines what the agency actually is?"

The thing that is very easy to do—and to a certain extent we did it, too—is that you look at the people around you that are doing well, and you ask why aren't we like them? I don't mind saying this, we had "Crispin Envy." Which is to say we were obsessed by how well Crispin Porter + Bogusky was doing. And I genuinely believe that actually that was part of our issue—we weren't looking at ourselves. We were looking at somebody else.

The answer to the question of how do we make the agency better is not by looking at Crispin. It was by looking at ourselves and what we've historically done well, and then applying that kind of DNA to a new way of looking at the company.

And it just so happened that we have always been a great storytelling agency and the art of telling stories and building brands is as enduring now as it was when the agency was founded by Rich, Jeff, and Andy [Berlin].

The big thing is look at yourself. What are you good at? What makes up your brand? Then you've got to get everybody to understand and to believe that you've got to live in the future. You can't live in the past.

What I think is brilliant about Rich and Jeff in particular is that at no point did they talk about the past. They were only interested in what was going to be in the future.

Rich summed it up on the first day. I said to him, "What's your biggest fear? What is the thing that we most need to solve?" And he said "I fear that we will not be relevant." And I think that kind of clarity of understanding about what needs to get done, a definition of what the problem is makes it easy to work out what the solution should be.

We're far from done. Structurally we are a long way from where we need to be for the future. There's no perfect agency model.

There's no perfect agency structure. You do these things as the world around you changes.

RM: As that world changes, how do you think marketers should prepare themselves?

DR: At the end of the day, technology is interesting and important, but the thing that defines great marketers and great brands and great clients is having great ideas.

Hyundai came to us with a great idea around how people are afraid about the economy and when they can buy a car or not. Hyundai came up with a plan that essentially allows the consumer to give the car back if they lose their job.

That's a great marketing idea. I think more often than not, clients go "I need to be on Facebook," or "I need an iPhone app," or what have you. And that is fueled, one, by what they read, but also by what is current, rather than thinking, "What have I got inside my brand that's really interesting to communicate, and that comes from a place that's grounded in something important?"

A lot of advertising agencies try and solve problems that actually need to be solved by [the client's] marketing department, not by communication. Better marketing will lead to better advertising and communication, and people just need to be interested in what the new world looks like and spend some time in it, surfing around it and spending time.

I think the most critical thing for agencies and clients is, as these new things come to the fore, you've got to constantly want to have a go at doing things, even if they aren't necessarily that successful. The constant striving for experimentation.

I think the one thing you can say with a degree of certainty is that the consumer will be much more in control, and that will continue to the point where they're pretty much defining their experience in all the media they're in.

Reaching them requires an idea that is executed through the right channels, not just applying new channels and technologies. And sometimes, that [idea] resides inside your [client's] company, and not inside your agency.

Mobile Is
Where It's At

IF YOU NEED to be convinced of mobile's ascendency as a marketing platform, just look what it's doing for the product categories most associated with geeky, tech-savvy edginess.

Women's underwear, for instance.

When U.K.-based lingerie retailer Bravissimo ran a recent television, radio, and direct mail campaign, consumers were invited to seek product information by dialing an 800 number, by visiting a website, or by requesting a brochure by texting a certain keyword, such as "Curvy," and sending it to a mobile short code.

Turns out texting was by far the most popular avenue for responding to the promotion, accounting for 45 percent of all responses.

What's more, the texting, or SMS (for "short message service"), component helped the brand track campaign effectiveness across a wide range of media—including print, television, outdoor, and more.

As Jo Lee, marketing director at Bravissimo, puts it: "Assigning a unique keyword to each advertising placement across all media channels enables us to see exactly where leads come from to help determine how successful each has been in generating response. This is valuable information when planning future campaigns."[1]

Women's wear wasn't the product category that immediately came to mind when you thought mobile marketing? That's the point.

While mobile seems forever poised to be "the next big thing," it long ago became a fundamental tool for brands seeking to boost the effectiveness of campaigns for product categories ranging from computers to canned soup, and from cereal to yes, brassieres.

In fact, mobile has emerged as the channel that most embodies the idea of the on-demand brand.

Just not in the way most marketers realize.

You Make the Call

Today, there are over 3 billion Internet-enabled mobile phones worldwide—far more than the 1.2 billion personal computers with active Internet accounts.[2] Indeed, the mobile phone is the first truly interactive device that everyone has, everywhere they go.

Recall the Burger King Syndrome that I discussed in the Introduction: "Have it your way, or no way at all"? Well, mobile means never having to say you're out of touch. Consumers can access their content, their communications, their transactions, and their applications their way—anytime, everywhere.

Many of the examples in this book have already demonstrated the power of this medium as a part of integrated marketing campaigns, and as the platform for many blockbuster applications. Without a doubt, "mobile marketing"—marketing via the mobile platform—supercharges virtually any effort to connect with consumers where they live.

But it remains wildly misunderstood.

One notion that has been popular from the very earliest days of mobile marketing is gaining new currency as the iPhone and other so-called "smart" phones with geo-location capabilities attract more and more attention. It's the idea that we'll all soon be walking down the street and get pinged with an offer for, say, fifty cents off our next latte at the Starbucks nearest to our physical location.

Heavy yawn.

Sure, it sounds cool when it's Starbucks sending you a mobile coupon. But the moment you're walking down the street and thirty-five different retailers ping you with offers, it's going to get very old, very fast. We will never put up with that kind of intrusion.

Opting in to receive such coupons doesn't make much sense, either. Why do you need to be physically near a store to receive a coupon?

Other scenarios include ones in which you use your phone to run a Google search for the nearest pizza parlor, and are presented with an interactive map of nearby options, complete with directions and special offers.

Very nice, but perhaps not as compelling as it seems at first blush. According to Chet Huber, head of OnStar Corporation, which has been offering a location-based search function in cars long before the capability migrated to the mobile phone, most local searches aren't for general categories (pizza, gas) but by specific brands (Round Table, Chevron), offering fewer real opportunities to other marketers than you may think.

And then there's the display ad scenario, which essentially transfers banner ad models and video spots from the old-school Internet and television to the mobile world. Advertisers have the pleasure of being able to buy ad space on networks of mobile websites or ad-supported applications. And you get the pleasure of squinting at tiny ads while you're already straining to view content on your phone.

I don't know about you, but as a marketer, I don't view such a notion as very compelling. And as a consumer, it's even less so.

TINY ADS, BIG RESULTS

Make no mistake, however: I am decidedly contrarian on many of these matters. There are many marketers who disagree with me—especially in the mobile advertising space. And they point to the success of many ad campaigns delivered to smart phones as proof of the model's efficacy.

One iPhone-based banner ad campaign for Land Rover, for instance, enabled consumers to quickly connect with an exclusive Google Maps page pointing them to the nearest Rover dealer.

The campaign involved 400,000 impressions (or instances when the banner was rendered onscreen) that resulted in roughly 11,500 click-throughs. Of those who clicked through, 88 percent watched a video of the car, 1,100 users (around 9 percent) punched in their zip codes to locate a dealer, and 3 percent used a click-to-call function to call a dealer directly. "That's excellent results—that's significant," says Mariana Solano, advertising-communications manager for Land Rover North America.[3]

Another banner ad campaign, for Kotex of all brands, invited consumers in Australia to click through to download a humorous video based on an extremely popular television campaign for the brand. The effort scored a 28 percent response rate.

As Nick Baylis, CEO of the New Zealand office of M&C Saatchi puts it: "It's inevitable that mobiles will become a major video channel. It's just too good an opportunity for advertisers not to investigate."[4]

And then there's Porsche. In a four-month "test drive," mobile marketing outperformed other efforts to convince car buyers that Porsche is an affordable luxury.

Mobile was only added to the campaign at the tail end of an eighteen-month-long integrated campaign meant to quash the notion that the German-made sports car was out of reach—a nod to research that showed people thought Porsche automobiles cost more than they actually do.

A mobile advertisement on Yahoo's and Weather.com's mobile web pages conveyed messages such as "You can own one, click to see how" or "Can you afford a Porsche? Just say 'I can.'"

Clicking through led to an "I Can" mobile website where respondents could choose to see models and their prices.

As it turned out, mobile delivered 22 percent of the total web traffic generated by the entire digital campaign, with a click-through rate that was up to six times higher than online display advertising.

What's more, mobile generated three times the volume to Porsche's call center than online advertising did, and twice as many dealer look-ups. In fact, the mobile site logged 40 percent higher visit rates to sections about prices on models than did online ads.

"We had never done any extensive mobile campaign before, so going into this, we didn't know exactly what to expect," says David Pryor, Porsche Cars North America's VP of marketing.[5]

According to Pryor, the mobile component got about 10 percent of the overall budget, and the cost per click was up to four times less than online. Online display advertising got 70 percent of the budget, and traditional search got 20 percent.

Needless to say, mobile will get more of Porsche's budgets moving forward. Indeed, with worldwide mobile ad spending projected to reach $13 billion by 2013, it's going to play a bigger role in a lot of campaigns.[6]

Still, it might be useful to do a quick reality check.

Yes, response rates for mobile are high right now—especially when compared to the average response rate for traditional Internet banner ads, which has hovered around one half of one percent for over a decade. But mobile response rates will go down as more people venture into the mobile medium. Already, 70 percent of mobile subscribers say they don't recall or respond to mobile advertising, according to Nielsen Mobile research.

And even if the acolytes of mobile advertising are all correct about its potential, I can only say "so what?". Mobile is so much more powerful than that.

Taking ad models from one medium and applying them to another isn't very compelling—even when location awareness is thrown in.

"I think the biggest mistake with mobile is to try and take the Internet and deliver it on a mobile device," echoes Andy Bateman, CEO of global brand consultancy Interbrand.

In my book on mobile marketing, *Branding Unbound*, I put forth a concept I call "mBranding"—the use of the mobile medium to create differentiation, generate sales, and build customer loyalty as never before possible. It's not (just) about delivering a commercial message through mobile phones as part of an integrated marketing communications campaign. It can also mean creating unique, branded experiences that engage consumers in amazing new ways—or that serve them anytime, everywhere.

The following precepts demonstrate how many brands are using mBranding to keep Rule #8—often to astonishing effect.

DON'T INTERRUPT, ACTIVATE

Yes, an increasing number of brands are advertising via mobile ad networks—promising to bring a new level of ad clutter (and irritation) to the most personal of consumer devices.

But others are finding that instead of thinking of mobile as a new advertising distribution platform, it's far more powerful as a response, or "activation mechanism," to commercial messages we experience in other media—print, broadcast, direct mail, outdoor billboards, and more.

Now, there's no reason for consumers to ever again have to try to remember a URL the next time they happen to find themselves sitting in front of a computer, much less try to recall a phone number or physical address after experiencing a commercial message.

With mobile, everything in the physical world becomes interactive. Which means consumers can use their mobile phones to respond to— that is, to activate—a promotion right at the point of impression.

This usually means entering a short code, those four- or five-digit numbers featured in advertising, as in the case of Bravissimo and its "Curvy" brochure discussed in the beginning of this chapter.

And many brands—including Quiznos, Subway, Pizza Hut, McDonalds, and others—enable consumers to sign on to receive "mobile coupons" and to place food orders through texting-based services like GoMobo and Cellfire.

Propelled by a tough economy, Juniper Research predicts over 200 million people will use mobile coupons by 2013, signing on to services that send them coupons that can be redeemed by showing their cell phone screen at the point of sale.

But mobile interactivity is taking on many forms.

In Europe, marketing for Ford's youth-oriented economy car Ka recently included a 3-D augmented reality experience activated by pointing your mobile phone at a direct mail package.

As part of the car's "Find It" campaign, special direct mail packages were distributed to bars, clubs, music events, and colleges. The packages featured special symbols like the ones used in the tennis app mentioned in our discussion of Rule #6. When the consumer views the symbol with a camera phone, a 3-D hologram of the Ford Ka appears on the screen, as if floating right in front of the consumer.

When you move the phone at particular angles, a URL—GoFindIt.net—is revealed, taking you to a mobile website featuring films, music, and photos geared to the target audience, and designed to infuse Ka with cool.

"It's my personal conviction that [very soon] every medium-to-large marketing campaign in pretty much every industry will have some sort of augmented reality piece to it, because it's fairly easy to do," says Prinz Pinakatt of Coca-Cola Europe, which has created augmented reality experiences for Fanta and other beverages.

"If you think about it, we sell 1.5 billion drinks a day. If we just take the Coca-Cola logo and turn it into a Quick Response or QR logo, that means we generate one billion additional contacts with our consumers. All we have to do is tell consumers, 'Show your logo into the camera phone and you're going to see something fantastic.'"

These and other kinds of QR codes—so-called "smart codes" or something like them—may very well be the future of mobile marketing.

When a QR code, a kind of 2-D barcode, is featured in print, broadcast, outdoor, or direct mail advertising, all the consumer needs to do is aim a camera phone at the code. Click, and the symbol activates content or services. It might launch a website with product information. It might instantly download a video or music clip to the phone. It might instantly dial up a call center agent. It might download a coupon. Or it might place an immediate transaction for, say, movie tickets or travel.

Papa John's pizza has been hugely successful in the mobile space, earning over $1 million in sales through its mobile website in its first three months of operation. In fact, more than 20 percent of all Papa John's sales now come online or through texting, widgets, or smart phone mobile devices. Small wonder the company is experimenting with QR codes in direct mail fliers so consumers can scan them to receive coupons or place orders.

Coca-Cola Mexico, meanwhile, labeled 40 million Sprite bottles with QR codes that automatically call up the Sprite website on the phone browser, which presents users with a trivia question. Get the answer right, and you instantly find out if you've won one of millions of prizes—including food from Domino's Pizza, DVDs from Blockbuster, and more.

Even Hollywood's getting in on the action. The movie poster for Tim Burton's animated science fiction movie *9* featured nothing but a giant QR code, which you could scan with your camera phone to link to exclusive video footage and commentary from the director.

And the book jacket for MTV reality TV star Lauren Conrad's novel, *L.A. Candy*, featured a QR code that, when scanned, linked users to video of Conrad talking about the inspirations behind the book.

TEXT SELLS

As sexy as such capabilities sound, the vast majority of Americans are not yet using smart phones that enable such high-concept experiences, let alone downloading apps that let them access multimedia content via smart codes or other new-fangled technologies.

But over 100 million Americans—including nearly 58 percent of all mobile subscribers between the ages of twenty-five and thirty-four, and the *vast* majority of everyone under that age—actively use text messaging. And they aren't afraid to use it in response to offline advertising.

In the U.K., a recent survey from mobile operator O2 found that one in three mobile users have already sent a text message to a five-digit short code, primarily in response to TV and radio advertisements. And 50 percent of mobile subscribers between the ages of eighteen and sixty express interest in responding to offline campaigns via text message.

Of the consumers who are interested in using SMS in this fashion, almost three quarters (74 percent) say they would use their phones to request a brochure, 70 percent to check product availability, two thirds to help locate the nearest store, and over half to book tickets or request further information from an advertiser.

Indeed, certain brands have discovered that simple text messaging is activating their print, broadcast, and outdoor advertising as never before possible. And it's catching on everywhere.

Exhibit A: Calvin Klein.

The famed fashion brand recently created a lot of buzz with a teaser campaign for its new fragrance In2U. Giant digital billboards in Yonge-Dundas Square in Toronto invited passersby to text their answer to the question: "What are you in 2?"

Responses were then displayed in twenty-second ads for all to see. The campaign ran for two weeks before revealing it was for the Klein fragrance. And thousands of people participated.

"It's good that brands are recognizing the power of user-generated content, and the cell phone is a great way to bring that communication to new outdoor environments, such as the busy streets of downtown Toronto," says Nussar Ahmad, director of mobile partner Addictive Mobility.[7]

What's more, in-store signage prompted consumers to visit a special CK In2U mobile website for the chance to download wallpapers (screen graphics), request free samples, view a list of retailers carrying the fragrance, and the chance to win an iPod.

Nearly 50 percent of consumers who sent a text to the site signed up for the promotion and requested a sample.

"This is the first time a premium fragrance brand such as Calvin Klein has used mobile to offer samples to consumers," says Christophe Spencer of OMD UK, the agency behind the promotion. "We can obtain data from customers who are interested in our client's products, and from the data we collect we can remarket special promotions back to our customers."[8]

Indeed, even the ultimate driving machine has discovered the ultimate activation mechanism.

As part of its recent "Hug the Road, Hug the Sky" campaign, BMW placed short codes on outdoor signage in fourteen major airports throughout the United States. A consumer who texts a keyword to the code instantly receives a link to a mobile application promoting BMW's new convertible.

The app includes a BMW video—or a gallery of still images, depending on phone capabilities—and a button to schedule a test drive at a local dealer.

Working with Boston-based Cielo Group, BMW has been able to track the campaign's effectiveness at each location through the use of keywords.

The company is mum on response metrics. But it says the results have been enough to continue the use of such signs ever since (see Figure 8–1).

Television, print, and outdoor aren't the only media mobile can activate. Just look at radio. When a local Daisy Maids housecleaning service in Salt Lake City used mobile as a response mechanism in radio commercials, it not only got a large number of people to respond, but the leads were so qualified that 80 percent of the those who responded via mobile signed up for maid service.

FIGURE 8–1. The "ultimate activation machine": BMW uses mobile as an activation mechanism for outdoor advertising as part of its "Hug the Road, Hug the Sky" campaign.

Here's how it worked: A country radio station in Salt Lake City offered an exclusive sponsorship opportunity tied with a promotion to give away four tickets to see country star Brad Paisley in concert.

Daisy Maids purchased the sponsorship, and using technology from mobile solutions partner HipCricket, all text entries received a confirmation text message with a request from Daisy Maids to text the word "CLEAN" for information on their housecleaning service.

According to HipCricket, the station received over 24,000 text message entries, and, more importantly, the advertiser received responses from over 700 people who went on to text in the word "CLEAN" for more information. Of these, 560 people opted to use their services.

Entertainment brands in particular have discovered the joy of text. Kid Rock, Rascal Flatts, and LilWayne are just a few of the music artists that use texting to create "mobs," or mobile fan clubs, that the artists can use to communicate with fans on an ongoing basis.

As with many live concerts and sporting events, fans use SMS to interact with the band onstage and send song requests, shout-outs, and other messages, all via electronic displays. But others take it a step further, by using solutions like those from Palo Alto, California-based Mozes Inc., to enable audience members to instantly sign up to fan clubs where they can link to text, voice, and web content centered on the band—both during the concert, and on an ongoing basis as new content and offers are developed—all within a trusted, spam-free, ad-free network.

"[A band like] Rascal Flatts gets a couple of things out of it. [First,] they have the ability to connect with fans during the show, and make that event more engaging," says Mozes founder and CEO Dorrian Porter, a client and friend of mine. "Second, they use that as a great vehicle on which they build their database marketing efforts to be able to keep in touch with fans after the show is over."

Indeed, in the lead up to the band's album, *Unstoppable*, Rascal Flatts alerted its mob when a new track was posted to iTunes, and enabled them to call into their Mozes voice lines to hear clips before anyone else. Not only did the album sell 351,000 copies in its first week, but the secret single broke the iTunes record for Country song downloads in one week (see Figure 8–2).

New Kids on the Block, meanwhile, has found new life thanks to Mozes. During a recent tour, the band collected an average of nearly 1,000 new mobile members each night in what Porter calls the "point of inspiration"—an invitation from the band to join its mob. Over a three-month period, the band accumulated over 30,000 fan club members, and now communicates with them on an ongoing basis, informing them of show dates, ticket sales, and in-venue offers.

As Porter tells me, text messaging doesn't just mean delivering short messages. With Mozes, messages might point fan club members

FIGURE 8–2. *Rascal Flatts fuels fandemonium by using text messaging to build and tend to its "mob," or mobile fan club.*

to digital "lockers" where they can experience multimedia content online that they may or may not be able to access on the phone.

In fact, the solution is so powerful that at this writing, music artists and other entertainment properties have used Mozes to connect with 2.7 million individual consumers. That's roughly 1 percent of America's cell phone subscribers.

"A simple text message can lead to an ongoing experience that's much bigger than a text message, and I think that that's only going to get bigger and better as time goes on," says Porter, adding that while a new Mozes iPhone app adds new capabilities to the equation, "the simplicity of being able to access a text message can lead to some pretty engaging campaigns."

APPS AMPLIFY

FedEx, ESPN, 1-800-Flowers, Godiva, and Barnes & Noble are just a few of the major brands that have created downloadable mobile applications for use with iPhones and other smart phones.

As with many of the mobile apps we've described so far, these utilities enable consumers to interact with the brand directly, and to place transactions through a far simpler interface than doing the same thing by visiting a website via mobile phone.

Building on its mobile website and QR efforts, Polo Ralph Lauren developed an iPhone app that invites users to view seasonal collections via video highlights of runway shows, behind-the-scenes videos about the inspiration for each collection, and exclusive photography. The app also includes domestic and international store locators that instantly connect the user to any Ralph Lauren store in the world. More recently, the brand created an app that enables consumers to design custom rugby shirts—complete with a selection of patches, numbers, and letters—and purchase them via mobile phone. They can even upload photos of themselves modeling their creation, which they can share via the app's "Make Your Own Rugby" gallery, email, or Facebook.

The FedEx Mobile for iPhone enables users to quickly track the status of a package, create shipping labels, get quotes, find the nearest drop-off center, and request a pick-up, right from the handset.

Benjamin Moore's Color Capture iPhone app lets you snap a photo of anything—that bucolic meadow, that radiant sunset, or maybe just that neighbor's house you love—and the app will show you the closest matching colors in the Benjamin Moore catalog (well over 3,300 in total). Shake the phone, and the app will provide coordinating colors, as well as directions to the nearest Benjamin Moore retailers.

ESPN MVP, meanwhile, is an app that enables sports fans to instantly access up-to-the-minute scores, news, commentary, and video and radio clips on Verizon smartphones.

Not to be outdone, MLB.com At Bat is an app that enables users to view live games on their iPhone or iPod Touch devices and access game day audio, stats, real-time box scores, in-game video highlights, and more.

For 1-800-Flowers' part, it's using BlackBerry and iPhone apps to enable consumers to browse and even place purchases in under thirty seconds. Ditto for Godiva.

But Starbucks is among the brands that are taking it a step further. In one mobile app, Starbucks customers are able to manage their loyalty card accounts through mobile phone. They can add money to their account via a credit card, and check their balances on the go. Which is all fine and good. But more important, the brand is testing a system that makes the mobile app itself the loyalty program. Cashiers simply scan the mobile phone screen to deduct a purchase from the user's prepaid account, with no need for a physical card at all.

According to Gartner Research, the number of consumers using mobile phones to shop will increase at an average of more than 25 percent per year through 2012. Gartner expects Asia and Europe will take the lead, though the United States could put the trend into hyperdrive. But this is not just about direct shopping.

Kraft's iFood Assistant, for instance, delivers recipe ideas and how-to videos—featuring brands such as Kraft Grated Parmesan Cheese, Kraft Classic French dressing, and so on, of course—and helps manage shopping lists.

"When we look at consumers, we think that they're busy and they're looking for food-planning tools that can make their lives easier," says Ed Kaczmarek, director-innovation, new services at Kraft. "We developed iFood Assistant as a downloadable app so they can use it anytime and anywhere."[9]

Indeed, at this writing, the app, at ninety-nine cents, is among the top 100 most popular paid iPhone apps and is number two in the lifestyle category—proving that if you deliver real value, consumers are not only willing to put up with overt marketing messages, but they're even willing to pay for it.

Other brands merely want to extend popular Internet experiences to mobile apps.

As we touched on earlier, Nike PhotoiD lets you use your camera phone to snap a picture of virtually anything and send it to a short code to receive a reply that features a rendering of a customized shoe that uses your picture's two most dominant colors as its highlights (see Figure 8–3).

Then there's Audi, which has its own mobile game app that uses the iPhone's accelerometer to enable players to steer a digital version of the Audi A4 through a series of progressively challenging courses—a virtual test drive, if you will.

On the other end of the spectrum, Kia Motors of America recently lived up to its brand slogan, "The Power to Surprise," by launching a branded radio station on a mobile social music app—imeem—in conjunction with the launch of the 2010 Kia Soul. Featuring playlists that include hits from Gym Class Heroes, Minus the Bear, and The Get Up Kids, the station is designed to bring some cool to this up-and-coming auto brand.

The power of such apps cannot be underestimated.

At their most basic, apps are akin to having a Pepsi- or Macy's-branded web browser on your computer, one that directly and exclusively links you to the brand's products or experiences.

Not that it's all business. One app for Coca-Cola's Fanta soft drink, called the Fanta Stealth Sound System, lets teens talk to their friends in secret. The application uses high-pitched frequencies that can only be heard by young people—frequencies so high that they are inaudible to people over age twenty-five.

Fanta's prerecorded sounds included wolf-whistles, warnings, and "pssts," along with messages like "cool," "uncool," and "let's get out of here" to enable the youngsters to enjoy a little mischief at everyone else's expense.

It's important to not push it too far, however. Pepsi's Amp energy drink created an app called Amp Up Before You Score, which gives guys pickup lines and cheat sheets for approaching twenty-four different types of women, ranging from Goth Girl to Women's Studies Major to Cougar.

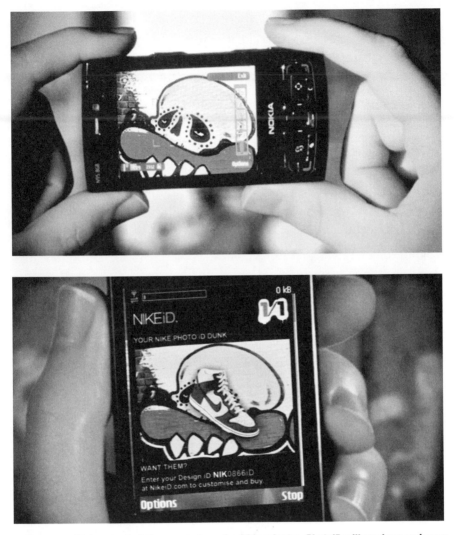

FIGURE 8–3. *Picture perfect: Snap a photo and, within minutes, PhotoiD will send you an image of a customized pair of Nike shoes using the two most prominent colors in the photo.*

"Is she an Artist? Quote some Picasso. Indie Rocker? Here are her favorite songs. Sorority Girl? Good thing you know the Greek alphabet. Know what makes her tick before you open your mouth, so she'll like what she hears when you do."

Selecting Cougar, for instance, prompts the app to present nearby hotels for a rendezvous. There are even hints for hitting on married women—and a "brag list" for sharing conquests via email, Facebook, and Twitter.[10] Reaction was so heated to the app that Pepsi ultimately decided the game wasn't a score for the brand, and pulled it from the iTunes App Store.

Such unusual missteps notwithstanding, looking out five years, one can envision a world in which mobile apps serve as the primary interface that consumers use to interact with many brands.

"You want to move beyond advertising because advertising is just shilling, it's just selling a product," Carl Fremont, global head of media for digital marketing powerhouse Digitas, tells me. "You really want to move beyond that and actually get into a valuable experience."

Indeed, marketers may have little choice. By 2020, mobile apps alone "will be as big or bigger than the Internet," peaking at 10 million apps before leveling off, according to Ilja Laurs, head of mobile app store GetJar, which already processes 14 million downloads monthly.[11]

Small wonder Procter & Gamble decided to ditch mobile banner ads for Vicks and launch an app that consumers can use during cold and flu season to monitor weather conditions and get tips and offers to battle that runny nose.

As Doug Levy, CEO of imc2, an independent digital agency, puts it: "Placing ads on mobile sites is just a media placement compared to finding the applications consumers want [in order] to interact with the brand."[12]

PLACE IS THE SPACE

The integration of outdoor and mobile gives "a brand a huge opportunity to initiate a relationship with the consumer via the mobile device and [provide] ongoing value to continue that relationship over time," says Jeff Arbour, vice president of Hyperfactory, which has spearheaded numerous mobile marketing initiatives for clients such as Coca-Cola, Toyota, and Vodafone.

For premium vodka brand 42Below, Hyperfactory used pop-up projectors to project images of an actor on buildings and signs near popular nightspots in various cities around the world. Passersby were invited to send commands to the images via short code that would essentially tell the actor what to do, in real time. Send "jump," and he jumps. Send "act like a monkey," and he acts like a monkey. You can use your imagination about where things went from there.

"Mobile and billboards complement each other perfectly," says Arbour. "As more digital billboards are present in urban environments, we'll see a lot of connection between phone and board to initiate some sort of action. There's a huge opportunity for brands to take advantage of that."

While mobile delivery is very popular, another up-and-coming form of place-based communication is called "proximity marketing," which typically involves transmission devices built into signs, billboards, or kiosks that invite passersby to activate the Bluetooth function on their mobile devices to receive promotional content when they are within thirty feet of the promotional signage. You already see them at many malls, for instance, inviting shoppers to access the latest offers from stores.

One proximity campaign to promote the *Transformers* movie series in theater lobbies resulted in over 54,000 consumer-initiated interactions. Each consumer spent between two and ten minutes engaged with the digital media, which involved watching the movie preview and partaking in a series of free mobile downloads—including animated screensavers and ringtones.

Forty-seven percent of people who were invited to connect to the content did so. And an offer for an in-theater promo for a candy bar voucher achieved a redemption rate of 38 percent.

Meanwhile, the Royal Albert Hall in London has discovered that even the tech-savviest mobile consumers want to party like its 1699. The stately classical concert hall recently invited concertgoers with Bluetooth enabled on their phones to receive a short video that includes a link to access a free download from each night's performance via home computer.

In my view, there's a right way and wrong way to conduct proximity marketing.

Promotional advertising that visually or audibly invites users to accept content is fine. But pinging phones with unsolicited messages is unacceptable—and is no different than the geo-location–aware mobile ad pitches I poked fun at earlier.

In the mobile world, your brand needs to earn the interaction, whether you're pitching a motion picture, an automobile, a video game—or even women's underwear.

BMW and Beyond: "Activating" Traditional Media through the Power of Mobile

Dean Macri, founder and CEO of The Cielo Group

WITH MOBILE, the sky's no limit at all.

Over the last few years, mobile marketing firm Cielo Group—whose name aptly comes from the Spanish and Italian word for "the heavens"—has been making a name for itself by developing mobile campaigns and applications that give brands a direct channel to consumers through compelling informational and entertainment experiences.

An innovator that has run mobile initiatives for the likes of Budweiser and BMW, the Boston-based firm understands that mobile display advertising in and of itself is uninteresting, no matter how location-based and behaviorally targeted it gets.

Instead, as Cielo Group founder and CEO Dean Macri puts it, mobile is at its most powerful as an "activation mechanism" for the advertising we experience in traditional media—print, broadcast, outdoor, direct mail, and more.

Rick Mathieson: Why aren't we seeing every major brand using mobile as a response, or "activation," mechanism in traditional media yet?

Dean Macri: I think what's happening still is that the traditional media buy—the commercials and the time purchased for TV—is still really not integrated with the budgets, and in some cases, not even with the ad agencies that handle the interactive and the mobile campaign. Mobile is still a victim of these walls that exist between agencies that focus on traditional advertising like TV, and the emerging digital advertising agencies who talk to the interactive people at a brand, and talk to the people who own the digital budget.

RM: There has been a lot of focus on mobile advertising—ad banners and video spots appearing alongside content accessed through mobile devices—which is ultimately not very interesting. Why do you think so many marketers are intent on turning mobile into the wireless version of the Internet or television?

DM: Because that's what they know. It's a simple concept. It's almost a cultural mindset of [looking at] how we use the Internet and applying it to how we might want to use cell phones.

And the truth is, I really don't think people browse when they're using the mobile phone. But they will use that mobile phone as a direct response mechanism the way they use other forms of digital media. Mobile marketing is not about browsing websites. Mobile is about injecting traditional ad media with a direct response, driving consumers to a microsite or deep link with a call to action that's activated through a mobile phone.

RM: And sometimes those links lead to branded mobile applications, like the kind you've developed for BMW, which was activated through a call to action on outdoor billboards.

DM: That's right. Saying mobile is not about browsing, that doesn't mean that the experience can't be highly interactive, very graphical, and have a user interface and content and an experience that is as entertaining as you might expect on the web. You don't have to settle for a text-based, menu-driven, this-is-your-grandfather's-mobile-website kind of thing.

When you key in a short code and click off a print ad into a mobile call to action, you should be linked into something that's highly interactive, in a web application like what we did for BMW, which streams video and allows every consumer—not just those that have GPS or location-based phones—to key in his zip code and get a click-to-call response [that dials up] a dealer, where they can book a test drive.

[As the popularity of iPhone apps shows], the ability to download a little application that persists on a mobile phone can drive value or utility or content that the consumer wants to use every day. And if the consumer is using it every day, that means the advertiser gets to interact with that presence or that applet and therefore, the consumer, through their phone every day.

Suddenly, what begins with looking at a traditional print ad in a magazine can mean clicking from that ad as a direct response through your mobile phone to a downloadable app. And that app injects new value into the print ad, uses the print ad to drive a call to action, and ultimately creates a branded presence that lives directly on the consumer's phone.

In BMW's case, they ran a series of campaigns beginning first with the BMW 3 Series vehicle and going into the 535 and the 550. These are campaigns that went back-to-back over the course of a year, and the campaign was principally an airport billboard, with brightly lit signs that appeared in these gate areas in fourteen airports around the country. On those billboards was a keyword and a short code. The keyword would be an identifier for the billboard or the airport itself. Using keywords, we were able to track how many people looked at which sign in which airport.

And consumers basically sitting in the gate area could text in the keyword to the short code using any kind of phone they wanted. It didn't have to be a smart phone or anything like that. They could text in, for example, bmw.lax. We would then say this is a consumer that was looking at the LAX airport, so we're beginning to track. We would then reply back with a link that would bring the consumer to a landing page that would stream video.

That landing page, of course, would have to detect what kind of handset they had. If they had a handset that could support video, then they would get a menu choice for video. If it weren't a video phone, they would get a little menu choice as an alternative that would allow them to browse a photo gallery.

And of course, they were getting menu choices on this highly graphical [wireless web]site to view information about the car, and also to click in and talk to a dealer.

RM: What kind of response have you seen?

DM: The response rates were very good. You've got to understand that there are thousands and thousands of people sitting in a gate area on a given day looking at these billboards in fourteen airports. And roughly half the people who responded via mobile phone actually made a call to a dealer. So, I think that the response was so high because we're using the mobile phone to capture people at their peak emotion, when they're looking at a billboard sitting in a gate area, thinking, "Gee, when is it my time to own a BMW?" And for BMW, it gave them the ability to track and measure their traditional investment, which they were going to make anyway. Mobile became a way to boost the ROI of what is typically a static out-of-home investment.

Now, while this app was campaign specific, the future step is adding a menu choice that allows consumers to download a BMW app to the phone that continues the relationship with content that is entertaining and valuable to the consumer.

RM: What kind of content?

DM: BMW, like other major consumer brands, acquires content, and produces content, as a way to build community. You'll often see some of this content on their website. If you were to go to Procter & Gamble and CoverGirl, you would see content from *America's Top Model*, for example.

Brands like Red Bull spend a tremendous amount of money producing content around the events they sponsor, the athletes they sponsor, and so on. And they are always searching to capitalize on that content through the convergence of digital media and the long tail that comes from that.

In mobile, consumers have to pay for most content, particularly premium content, whether that's a skateboarding video or a NASCAR video. The consumer brands who are already advertising in those events through sponsorships have access to that content, and can use it and make it available to consumers for free in exchange for the ability to build a relationship with them on the phone.

So the content still is king. The question is, how do you get it to a consumer so that they want it, so it's valuable to them, and so they don't have to pay for it and yet the owners of the wireless networks still get their money.

RM: You've led initiatives like this for Nokia Sports, for instance.

DM: Yes. Nokia Sports is how we got our start. Prior to Cielo, the company and its operation was loosely known as Live Sky, where we were streaming motor sports content over Wi-Fi networks to pocket [devices] in the stands at race car events. We began working with Major League Baseball to stream baseball content to fans in the stands, and Major League Baseball Events Media asked us, "What can we do to get onto mobile phones?" And in those days, and when I say those days, not more than four years ago, it was not common at all to stream video to mobile phones.

It was a struggle, but we brought Major League Baseball to Nokia, and Nokia was releasing handsets that had streaming video, and they wanted to have access to premium content that would sell the handsets.

And we pitched the idea of a sports application that would be pre-installed and made available for download that would make use of video highlights, real-time scores, live audio, everything you would find on MLB.com would be on Nokia Sports on the phone.

It started just as MLB on Nokia, and then we began to add other sports leagues with the NBA, and it really took on a brand of its own, called Nokia Sports.

RM: In this case, the app was branded to a handset manufacturer, but it could really be applied to any consumer brand.

DM: That's right, you've got it. There's no reason why today we can't have Taco Bell Sports. Taco Bell is a very large sponsor of MLB. They have access to certain content. They could acquire additional content as a result to their sponsorships and it can be available to you on your [iPhone or other] phone. It could be Taco Bell/MLB on your phone.

RM: What is the most important thing that marketers need to consider when they think about using mobile as an activation mechanism, or as they start to think about creating a branded mobile app?

DM: They already need to begin thinking beyond just text messaging, that text messaging should be the link between their traditional media and this app, whatever it might be. But they need to realize that [ongoing text dialogue alone] doesn't build relationships with [consumers,] and that having a more interactive presence on the consumer's phone will accomplish that. Once they begin understanding that, then it becomes a very easy leap. It begins with wanting to move beyond text messaging, and then showing them what they can do with an application that leverages content they already have.

RM: Depending on whom you talk to, mobile marketing is either set to explode, or is still in for years of continued experimentation before we see it on a mass scale.

DM: I think you're going to see classes of explosions. I think you're going to find those companies that have done their tests and learned from them are going to be doing super creative things very early. But in terms of the sheer number of people who are doing those kinds of creative things, it's not going to be huge.

The brands that are doing text messaging, text to win sweepstakes and contest entries, and things like that, you're going to see a lot more of that.

The early leaders are going to be doing the really creative things, and then the rest of the world is just going to begin getting into text messaging.

It's still evolutionary, I don't think there's any one big bang. Back to the point we discussed at the beginning—I do feel that for anything significant to happen in terms of mobile becoming the kind of medium that the ad world expects it to be, you still need to see more coordination between the traditional media buyers and those who control the digital budget. Because it is in the traditional world that mobile has its greatest power, its greatest value, and its greatest ROI by activating otherwise static traditional advertising.

I think traditional media has a huge power of mass market reach, and [when] discovery from mobile applications starts to become prevalent there—on [print and broadcast advertising and] product packaging, for example—that's the point when you're going to see huge, huge value.

Always Keep Surprises In-Store

THE BRAND experience doesn't stop at the storefront door—or at least it shouldn't.

Yet for all the advertising and marketing that brands engage in to entice shoppers to open their wallets, more often than not, actually buying the product is lackluster at best—often disconnected from the brand experiences that got shoppers into the store in the first place.

In the digital age, brand marketers—both physical world retailers and their product marketer partners—are beginning to understand that personal connectivity is now pervasive. Just as consumers want to be able to buy from you on demand, wherever they may be, they also want access to their digital lives when they actually do make it into your physical store.

And they want experiences that bridge the gap from the virtual to the physical, from clicks to bricks, that can make all the difference in whether—and how much—they spend there.

Already, advertising networks that display brand messages on seemingly every available wall, kiosk, and monitor account for 10 percent of the revenues U.S. malls generate for themselves. In the Middle East and Latin America, malls can derive over 30 percent of their income from ads from product marketers, according to Cincinnati-based research firm Marketing Developments.[1]

In other words, the interruption advertising so loathed and ignored elsewhere is now invading the actual shopping experience to an unprecedented degree.

But there's a better way.

In-Store, Out of Site

Today, a growing number of store brands and their product-marketing partners are recognizing, acknowledging, and acting on trends ignited by the on-demand revolution.

Look no further than Nike. Remember the Nike PhotoiD digital experience we discussed in the last chapter—the one in which you can take a photograph with your mobile phone, send it to a short code, and receive an image of a customized sneaker that uses the two most prominent colors from your photograph?

Nike has long run an expanded online version of this experience at NikeiD.com, where consumers can select the materials, choose the colors, and customize the fit of Nike shoes and sportswear—and then place a purchase.

In a twist, Nike has taken this idea and put it into reverse—enabling in-store customers to design and customize shoes and products at Niketown stores in New York and London.

Interactive kiosks and displays immerse shoppers in the brand, providing a high-resolution visual of their custom shoe design, and then deliver the shoes to the shopper's home or to the store. What's key here is that the in-store experience offers exclusive design and material options not available in the online version.

At Polo Ralph Lauren's Madison Avenue store in Manhattan, passersby attracted to new fashions shown in window displays can tap on the window, which is outfitted with a thin touch foil material mounted on the glass that turns it into a touchscreen interface.

Window shoppers can then live up to their name—calling up a projected image of different clothes, displayed on the actual window. If they really like what they see, they can use a conveniently located credit card swiper mounted on the outside of the window.

"I really wanted to find a way to make that amazing technology a retail reality," says company senior vice president David Lauren.[2]

Even individual product brands are getting into the act.

Procter & Gamble's CoverGirl brand, for instance, created a mobile application, ColorMatch, that recommends shades of makeup based on complexion, clothing, and accessories colors. The idea is to provide a tool when women are at the makeup counter, where they wouldn't have access to a computer.

Look for several brands to begin leveraging the mobile-to-store channel to influence purchase decisions. In recent tests, Visa created mobile apps that enable shoppers at nineteen Safeway and eight Mollie Stones stores to text short codes to Visa for advice on wine and food pairings (see Figure 9–1).

In another initiative, diners at local restaurants can text Visa to receive voice messages from the establishment's chef about that evening's menu.

One could easily imagine such offerings as branded services from Zagat's and other guide brands.

Spectator Mobile, on the other hand, is a mobile-optimized version of winespectator.com, tailored specifically for wine-buying information on the go, especially when at a restaurant or in a store.

With Spectator Mobile, members of WineSpectator.com can search for scores and tasting notes in *Wine Spectator*'s database of more than 200,000 wine ratings, view vintage charts of all the major wine

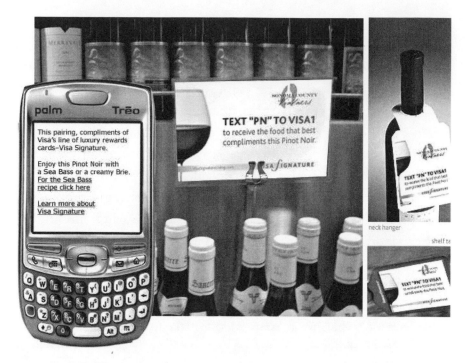

FIGURE 9–1. *Mobile apps like this one that enables shoppers to send text messages for advice on food and wine pairings demonstrate how brands can leverage consumer technologies to enhance the in-store experience.*

growing regions to determine the best years to buy, and reference their customized shopping lists and current cellar inventories via a Personal Wine List feature.

"For everyone who has wanted specific wine-buying information on the go, our mobile site is designed for you," says Marvin R. Shanken, editor and publisher of *Wine Spectator*. "It brings our website's most popular wine-buying information and repackages it in a simple, easy-to-read mobile interface."[3]

For their sakes, retailers had better catch up. Amazon's audacious iPhone app Price Checker enables shoppers to compare store prices with Amazon's, and even place an order if a better price is to be had online.

But retailers do have a few tricks up their sleeves.

THE RISE OF SOCIAL RETAILING®

Social retailing was first popularized by Tom Nicholson, the legendary retail visionary whose firm, IconNicholson, has revolutionized the in-store experience for brands like Prada.

As shoppers make their way around Prada's Epicenter stores in New York and Los Angeles, for instance, digital readers embedded in furniture scan the Radio Frequency Identification (RFID)–based smart tags on clothing items. The readers access codes from the tags that correspond with content in a database, and then automatically display the content—video of models wearing the fashions, as well as designer sketches and information about cut, color, fabric, and availability—on the nearest video display.

In dressing rooms, shoppers can access much of the same content via an interactive touchscreen display. When in default mode, the display plays video—dubbed "aura"—showing content associated with the selected clothing collection, including the images and inspirations that led to the design.

And while the shopper tries on the clothes, the dressing room's mirror takes time-delay video and replays the action in slow motion so the shopper can take in the full effect.

Social retailing takes it all a giant step further, by mashing up this kind of innovation with social networking, enabling shoppers to connect in real time with friends outside the store and to share their shopping experiences.

"Social retailing is a concept that evolved out of our work building personas based on youth shopping needs, behaviors, and current technology trends," says Rachael McBrearty, vice president of creative strategy for IconNicholson. "[It offers] a vision for how they can reach the audience at the center of the social computing craze seen in websites like YouTube and MySpace, to connect in-store shopping with the online world in a way that is new, entertaining—and completely relevant."[4]

In a pilot at Bloomingdale's in New York City, changing room mirrors were outfitted so you can try on a shirt and instantly send a video to your MySpace page or friends' cell phones or computers to get their vote on whether it's "fly" or "forgetaboutit."

The system even enables shoppers to view others' past purchases (with appropriate permissions, of course), and view options that aren't available in the store but that can be purchased online and then delivered.

"We always look to keep Bloomingdale's at the leading edge of retail innovation," says Frank Doroff, senior executive vice president at Bloomingdale's. "Today's young tech-savvy shopper expects to be connected 24/7 with her friends when she shops. [These forms of] 'social retailing' enhances that ability to connect and I expect will draw new, younger shoppers to our stores."[5]

"Essentially, social retailing really is nothing more than taking a lot of those features and activities that are happening online today and finding a way to move those into the physical environment," Nicholson tells me.

Indeed, companies like Zugara are enabling stores and brands to capitalize on new AR technologies to enable shoppers to "try on" clothes superimposed over their own images captured on their webcams, and to solicit feedback from friends.

Still, one might ask: Do these kinds of experiences increase sales, or create a new, very distracting layer to the in-store shopping experience? Will reaching outside the store result in more sales inside?

It's hard to say at this point. Some believe people who find such experiences engaging will stay in the store longer, which inevitably leads to more items purchased.

There's even a name for this type of experience: It's called a "weenie."

That was Walt Disney's term for a visual magnet or focal point that draws people in and becomes the capstone that defines an experience. Think Sleeping Beauty Castle, the centerpiece and wayfinder so central (literally) to how we experience Disneyland.

Today's weenies are increasingly digital—and solutions like these can enrich the in-store experience to amazing effect.

To that end, here are some tenets for bringing Rule #9 to life.

BRICK AND MORTAR IS THE NEW CLICK AND ORDER

Think of it as Facebook meets the mall. Today's shopper is growing accustomed to living seamlessly and simultaneously online and offline. They want the instant gratification to purchase what they want at your store, at home, or on the go. But make no mistake: While in the store, they want to connect with the posse before they open the purse strings.

The Bloomingdale's pilot is just one example. Fashion retailer Nanette Lepore uses these technologies in what it calls the Lepore Looking Glass.

This in-store mirror interacts with on-clothing RFID tags at the company's SoHo store.

Hold, say, a Lepore "True Confessions" silk top in iris or a "Naughty Flirt" tweed jumper in onyx up to the mirror, and a transparent video monitor housed within the mirror's glass reveals itself to play animated scenarios featuring the brand's whimsical Lepore Girl mascot, who up-sells accessories and complementary items.

With the help of IconNicholson, Lepore is going further still. One recent pilot could even project images of other clothes onto the mirror so it overlays the shopper's reflection.

The shopper could then quickly "try on" fashions and stream video to far-flung friends for feedback via the web and mobile (see Figure 9–2).

It gets better. Groups of teen shoppers can even use the mirrors to access each others' video feeds in other dressing rooms to give each other feedback in real time.

ANTICIPATION IS THE BETTER PART OF VALOR

New in-store technologies enable retailers to actually anticipate what consumers might want, based on their past purchase behavior and on what shoppers physically pick up while in stores.

The same systems built into store walls and fitting rooms to detect what items shoppers are carrying around can also access databases that can display complementary recommendations on monitor screens. Should the shopper provide personal information, such systems can tie

FIGURE 9–2. Facebook meets the mall: Social Retailing® mashes up social networking with real-world shopping to enable customers to connect with friends outside the store and even try on virtual versions of fashions those friends might recommend.

the suggested product mix to past purchases, personalizing recommendations to boost sales potential.

One can imagine such messages as "Like that top? It would go great with those Lucky jeans you bought last month."

These same kinds of technologies are increasingly used in supermarkets. Stop and Shop, a chain in the Northeast, has started deploying "smart carts" in selected stores. It calls this cart a "Shopping Buddy," and it features a wireless touchscreen device.

Swipe in a loyalty card and the system will automatically access your buying history and provide any special offers from your preferred or competing brands. You can access the grocery list you entered from your home computer. And as you walk the aisle, additional coupons and promotions pop onto the screen.

Throw items into the cart, and the Shopping Buddy scans them so you can pay for your items at checkout without having to stand in line.

While these kinds of offerings are picking up steam in the United States, they're already making major inroads abroad. According to Gartner Research, nearly 50 percent of European retailers expect to offer these kinds of services to customers by 2015, while nearly 40 percent expect that customers will use their own mobile devices in-store to access similar information. And nearly 25 percent of stores will introduce self-scanning technologies in that timeframe.[6]

THE STORE IS A SERVICE

It's easy to imagine Shopping Buddy technologies making their way into Banana Republic or Barnes and Noble.

But instead of tricked-out shopping carts, a far easier route might be a mobile application that could fulfill many of the same functions.

The Gap, for instance, has an iPhone app called "StyleMixer," which enables users to get in touch with their inner fashionistas by mixing and matching images of apparel to build outfits, which they can then share with friends on Facebook for feedback, as well as using it to find the nearest Gap location carrying the garments. As they walk past the store, they can turn on the app to receive a special offer.

Now imagine version 2.0 or 3.0 of this app—a "Gapp," if you will—that takes this all a big step further. You activate it as you enter the actual store, and instantly, you receive the latest offers based on your stated interests and past purchase history. "Welcome back to The Gap; if you liked those straight-fit plain-front herringbone pants you bought last time, you're going to love our new collection of blazers" appears onscreen, along with a map showing you the location of the items in the store. If you've preselected the option, this same information is sent to a device in the sales clerk's hands, so he or she can better serve you based on your preferences.

See an item you like, and you simply use the app to scan the barcode so you can access shopper reviews or send the item out to your friends for feedback. Try the item on and snap an image of yourself in the dressing room's mirror to show friends how the item looks on you. Then, should you decide you want to buy the item (despite what your lame friends said about how it looked), you simply walk out the door—without ever digging for cash, writing a check, swiping a card, or standing in line. The charges are automatically applied to the credit card information you entered into the app's interface, and the security devices attached to the items are instantly disabled.

High-end cosmetics retailer Sephora has already taken a step in this direction, launching a mobile service that allows shoppers to easily browse product reviews from other consumers.

Reviews are now a key part of the shopping experience—and play a major role in building confidence in purchase decisions for everything from L'Oreal lipstick to Lamborghinis.

According to Nielsen, eight out of ten shoppers now routinely read online product reviews before placing purchase orders. And 40 percent cite online customer reviews as one of the primary reasons they have bought from a retailer, online or off.

Perhaps most important of all, consumers are two and a half times more strongly influenced by customer reviews than by a salesperson's advice.[7]

The beauty of Sephora's solution is that the service is primarily accessible when the consumer is in the store or mall, as he or she accesses the reviews by looking up a keyword or SKU (the string of alpha and numeric characters used for inventory management) on product packaging.

The capability began as a feature on the Sephora website, where it became an instant hit. According to Julie Bornstein, senior vice president for Sephora Direct, the migration to mobile was a no-brainer.

"We knew it would be a popular feature, but the order of magnitude blew us away," she tells me. "It made us realize how much our clients love to talk about product. Instantly it became a very useful feature for client shopping, to help them make their purchase decision. We also were thinking about how we could extend this service to clients in our store."

Indeed, in some ways, the translation to mobile made the service far more useful than its traditional web counterpart. When they're in-store, customers simply pull out their mobile phones and go to the Sephora mobile site, where they select by product category, or simply enter the product name or the twelve-digit UPC code they see on packaging. Instantly, they can read product reviews from other customers—and there are many—to get a feel for whether the product is right for them.

You'd be surprised how many people can get supremely passionate about, say, Philosophy brand's Cinnamon Buns body wash. And yet a quick look at the mobile site reveals 132 different reviews, featuring comments ranging from "Kinda smelled like cardboard," to "Smelled so good my husband wanted to drink the bottle."

According to Bornstein, social shopping applications—whether through store infrastructure or mobile phones—are not the threat to physical stores some retailers may fear.

"I think it's acknowledging and capitalizing on the dynamic [that's happening anyway]," she says. "I don't think it will ever replace having these highly trained people in our stores to really provide advice."

For that matter, there's no reason individual product brands couldn't develop similar apps that work with participating retailers—upping the chances devoted customers continue to purchase from their favorite brands, no matter where they shop.

Ask yourself: How does the linkage with your brand come to life within a retail setting? Start there, and define the apps that make sense for your brand.

THE STORE IS A PLATFORM

As I mentioned earlier, malls and stores are making serious money by allowing product brands to advertise in their venues. And they should. Most recognize that the brands they carry have a vested interest in helping them sell. Digital signage is certainly a valuable medium for actually selling ad space to product partners.

Indeed, venues such as Safeway, Wal-Mart, Kroger, and Costco now deliver mass audiences that television could never dream of. Kroger alone boasts weekly shopper counts of 68 million people, according to *Media Week*. Wal-Mart, 150 million.

To put that into perspective, that means the audience at these stores is larger than all three major broadcast television networks combined.

Indeed, the Wal-Mart Smart Network is a massive in-store digital video network spanning nearly 2,700 stores that sells over $500 million in ad placements to brands hoping to connect with consumers close to the sale in what is known as "the last mile."

"Our role is to develop best practices across the shopper continuum, connecting what is in-store with what is out-of-store and to make sure all the media comes back to the shopper," Danielle Bottari, senior vice president and director of shopper marketing for MediaVest's new shopper unit, tells *Media Week*.[8]

Or, as Tonya Collins, customer planning for OgilvyAction, puts it: "Companies know the battle will be [won] or lost in-store."[9]

The problem: most in-store advertising is just that—advertising, and not just advertising, but advertising developed for television. To be most effective, digital needs to be optimized for the retail environment and bring something to the experience that helps influence behavior at the moment of decision.

To that end, experiences like those from Nike and Nanette Lepore will start to define what makes a successful digitally enabled in-store experience, as will far more easily implemented solutions that brands can use to wage that in-store battle.

HBO, for instance, recently created an in-store digital wall display that showed wrapped gifts on display screens as part of a holiday promotion. Shoppers could wave their hands to "unwrap" the gifts, which revealed HBO DVD releases of *The Sopranos*, *The Wire*, and others.

The technology for that solution, from Orlando-based Monster Media, also enabled Toyota to use retail window displays to show a Lexus RX sports utility vehicle seemingly crash and break into pieces—which passersby could then manipulate using body movements to undue the damage—as part of an effort to highlight fourteen different safety features in the vehicle.

These kinds of initiatives obviously require a new level of cooperation between individual brands and retailers. While retailers have been loath to give up floor space to individual brands, the costs associated with creating their own compelling digital experiences in-store may thaw those age-old convictions for some.

For others, shouldering the expense may become less a differentiator and more a reflection of the cost of doing business in the on-demand era.

Q&A

The Future of the In-Store Experience, from the Father of Social Retailing®

IF TOM NICHOLSON has his way, teenage girls will no longer wait until they're home from the mall to ask the eternal question, "Do these jeans make me look fat?"

Nicholson, CEO of digital agency LBi IconNicholson, has personally led a technological revolution in retailing, having spearheaded efforts to transform the shopping experience at Prada, Nanette Lepore, and Bloomingdale's by enabling shoppers to use touchscreen interfaces to connect with runway

Tom Nicholson, founder and CEO of LBi IconNicholson

video and information on cut, color, and accessories related to the clothing they carry into dressing rooms.

Now, Nicholson is taking fashion forward—mashing up social networking, in-store technologies, and youth shopping habits to delight customers as never before possible.

Rick Mathieson: What is "social retailing" and why do retail marketers need to know about it?

Tom Nicholson: Social retailing is leveraging a lot of the things that are happening online today in the marketing environment—the social applications, social networking, and all of the things that are driving desktop applications to migrate to mobile devices, iPhones, and such—and bringing them to the retail environment.

[Today, marketers are] using these social networking applications to drive people into the store, to drive brand awareness, and to build word of mouth. But once consumers get into the store, it's like it's 1900. They walk in and they are surrounded by the physicality of the objects—the things that you can't get in a virtual world and the online world. Nothing about the digital experience today really exists in the store, beyond the cash register itself, where you're networked in some fashion, or maybe the security system.

Social retailing really is nothing more than taking a lot of those features and activities that are happening online today, and finding a way to move them into the in-store environment where customers are actually doing their shopping.

This is no small equation because the stores themselves are not typically supportive of opportunities with devices and screens. You might have a kiosk in the corner, or something like that, but the stores themselves aren't set up or wired to figure out how to integrate the actual shopping experience with the digital assist or support experience that you get online.

With social retailing, there's continuity here from the Prada store; we started evolving it over the years and took it to one of our clients,

Nanette Lepore, the renowned fashion designer. She asked us to do something to help her reach out and connect with her audience. This is a client that doesn't traditionally spend a lot of money on advertising and marketing. Budgets are mostly focused on runway shows and other forms of merchandising—opening stores and putting money into bricks and mortar and selling to department stores.

She wanted to reach her audience, so we spent some time ethnographically going into the store, observing her customer base.

We realized that Nanette's brand is a super feminine, high-end fashion brand. It wasn't like the Prada store, where Prada was trying to make technology a front and center statement about the brand.

Nanette has a brand that really didn't lend itself to having monitors sitting around the store and televisions and interactive devices.

We did notice that she featured mirrors in the store quite a bit, where people could try on clothes and see what they looked like. That was the aesthetic of the store: very feminine, a lot of mirrors, a lot of things going on in the environment that were very minimal and lean and clean.

At one more point in the observation, we were noticing this thing that's happening in the world today where kids—I say "kids" because it's skewed toward the younger audience, though every year it gets older—use their mobile devices to network when they are out and about shopping. They are networking and calling their friends on their cell phones. [They're] snapping pictures of the things they are considering buying and sending it to their friends on the little screen.

And we said, "What if instead of trying to invent a new behavior, what if we take this behavior that is already happening with social networking and augment it. Let's build it into something that can actually give higher fidelity imagery, that can allow people to now conduct the same kind of chat session in the store, on a bit larger scale, so that it's not tied to a little screen that's two and a half inches wide."

We found the technology that could allow a plasma panel to be behind the mirror so that the mirror itself was pretty much untouched.

It didn't feel like a computer screen. And we enabled the customer to go up to the mirror and basically see what they'd look like.

I'm talking about the typical use of a mirror in the dressing area. The mirror itself then was connected through a video feed camera that would capture their image and send it out to a site on the Internet.

We then said, "Well, we need some interactive communication," and decided to enable some of the features that you get in text messaging and instant messaging right into the mirror itself, so that the people getting the image from the person in the store could then respond straight to the mirror. So the [shopper] was actually seeing themselves and seeing the text communication up on the same mirror, merged and blended with their image.

At the same time, we empowered the ability to have the person [outside the store, sending from] their cell phone or from their desktop computer to actually choose other garments from the Nanette Lepore inventory that they thought would be interesting for the shopper to try on. This created a real dynamic between the two—the in-store shopper and their online friends or family.

When you look at it, we've done nothing more than repeat what's already happening in the online world, but we allowed it to happen in the physical store. And I must say that the reactions we got were just really powerful.

It was a natural. People walked in. It felt comfortable. They knew exactly what to do, and it was something that came very naturally because they've been doing it now for several years online. The difference now was that they could actually do it in the store with the garment.

We added a few other features that would enhance it, more experimentally. The idea that the person, when they took the recommendation from their friend, could actually touch [an image of the garment] and blow it up into a larger [view] that would appear on the mirror screen—it's almost like holding it up in front of you, overlaid on your own reflection. It would appear on the mirror at full-sized scale to fit [your reflection] and they would be able to actually try on the garment virtually there in the store.

The term "social retailing" was coined because "social shopping" had been out there on the Internet to describe this idea of people doing the same thing strictly on the Internet between websites or between social sites. So we used it as a manifestation of this idea of merging the social sites and social applications with the in-store retail experience.

We did a pilot at Bloomingdale's that was really successful. We learned a lot from that, and we're now in the process of bringing that into some of the physical stores for Nanette Lepore.

RM: What were some of the things that you learned? Did social retailing capabilities increase purchase amounts?

TN: We did learn that it created a lot of interest in the store itself. Nanette has a boutique in Bloomingdale's, so it was able to be measured within that single boutique. [There] was something like a three times sales increase year-over-year. It stirred up a lot of interest.

More importantly, though, was that this thing was picked up pretty much worldwide, in something like eighty publications around the world. It was picked up by bloggers, and it was put all over the web, as things happen when there is something new and unique. It gets a lot of play and a lot of word of mouth.

Nanette's fashions inspire an emotional response from people. They are very recognizable as her brand. And this enables people now to talk more and share it with friends, and it taps into the whole word-of-mouth environment that's been going on online for several years now. That's nothing new.

But to be able to do that from the store, and to have people talking about it, and people meeting up in the store, this creates a broad-range fringe effect just from a straight marketing point of view that has no media cost involved in spreading that word. It's closer to public relations spending than it is for advertising, where you have to constantly replenish the media costs. Like many social applications today, once you create the network effect, it takes over and your actual costs of marketing or public relations go way down, and people now are talking about you. They are sharing things and you're getting all of that lift to your brand in a way that, in terms of efficiency, is almost unheard of.

At least for the next year or two, you get a real brand lift just from the fact that you're doing that and people are talking about it.

RM: And longer term?

TN: Eventually, I would say this concept of bringing the digital environment and connecting it into the physical store will become more commonplace. Something like this will be expected—almost the price of entry—to do retailing, because today people are doing it with their cell phones and, in some cases, having a little trouble getting connections in the stores.

The store is empowering [that connectivity], getting behind it, bringing the networking into the store. And even if it's on handheld devices, this is really going to be the future of in-store retailing.

People will learn how to capitalize on this, and really use it to their advantage and invest into the infrastructure; instead of taking advertising out in the *New York Times* at $100,000 for a Sunday ad, they can put that into the infrastructure costs in the store, and there's a recurring payback.

A few innovative ones are starting to do that, and we're going to see more of it. And the people who aren't doing it, will. If they are planning to be national brands, they are not going to be able to compete against it.

RM: There's an artful symmetry here—stores using digital technologies to lure consumers into stores, and then using digital technologies to enable them to connect with the outside world while they are in the store.

TN: I think you're at the heart of it. This is a phenomenon that certainly we've been recognizing now for a bit. The way that we focus on it is just simply by calling it "the empowered customer." The age of advertising as we know it is going by the boards.

The new marketing reality is about getting inside and understanding your customer and empowering that customer. Because people are empowered today. They can go out and find what they want, when they want it. They can see all the choices available to them, on demand. They can drive their purchase, or even the brands, that they choose to work with. They now not only can take care of their own needs, but now they can talk to everybody about that, and convey the good, the bad, and the ugly of the products and the services that they are getting from their retailers or from their merchandisers.

But the fact is, you have problems when you go into a store. You lose your cell phone connection, or you can't send those images very easily. Customers get frustrated. They are used to that kind of connectivity now, so retailers better start servicing that.

Retailers have a real leg up on the virtual world in that they have the physical products in the store. The products are there. You can touch them. You can feel them. You can try them on. And all they have to do now is tap into some of the features that are so readily available online.

Any company today that's not looking at how to use some of these new technologies to enhance the customer experience for their audience is going to lose market share.

RM: What do you say to retailers who might be thinking, "We spend this money getting consumers into stores. The last thing we want is to have them focusing their attentions outside of the store."

TN: That's a great point. But retailers who try to have the walled garden are going to be like the old AOL. It's trying to get the walls up higher, trying to keep people in, and not letting them get what they need and want, even if it means going somewhere else to get it. This idea of [mobile phone–enabled] price comparison while you're standing in the store, it scares the daylights out of retailers I'm sure, but it's here.

Using integrated databases, other retailers can communicate to you that down the street there's a better product, or the same product, for less. And the stores that don't recognize that their job is to give people what they need first and foremost, and then figure out how to make money with that, aren't going to make it in the coming years.

Today, you can fool people a little bit, still, with advertising and brand messaging telling people that you've got this great product that's really only mediocre, by having a great ad on the Super Bowl or what have you. But those days are waning.

People see through it. They know what they are working with. They can tell their friends, they can write reviews, read reviews—and people have to fess up and have great products now. And they also have to do some research, by the way, because the data that you get back from something like social retailing is worth its weight in gold to the retailer.

We showed it to one senior department store exec, who looked at it and said, "You mean I can know definitively what people took into the dressing room but didn't buy? Wow, that's big." The data is the thing sleeping underneath all of this, just like Google, who has this body of data that tells them a lot about their audience and their customer base. This is the hidden iceberg beneath social retailing.

When you have data being captured, and know what people are recommending to their friends in the store, you get a really good feel for the audience and the market that you couldn't have any other way, so it has myriad benefits.

RM: Higher-end luxury brands are embracing these technologies now, but how will social retailing play out as it goes to the Wal-Marts, the Sears, or the K-marts? Will the investments make sense, and will the technologies even make sense for their clientele?

TN: There are three different views on that. Let's take it from an infrastructure point of view first. Yes, today it's very expensive to do this. So certain retailers who get a brand lift from it can invest in [this technology] and put something in their stores. But that's not what you would call mass market because of the cost involved.

[But] the costs will definitely come down, like everything else. If there's something that takes root with early adopters, you have complete confidence that it's going to grow into a more mass market situation.

From a customer or product point of view, what we did with fashion was unique to the needs of someone trying on clothing in a department store or in a designer's boutique.

What do you do with a store selling cameras [or furniture or] other items? It's a different type of challenge; it will have a different manifestation in that kind of store. We are working with some clients right now to explore what kinds of scenarios work in other retail environments.

If you really want to generalize this to its highest level, the idea of putting networks together that formed the web-based Internet 15 years ago was nothing more than existing networks getting plugged into each other so that you could communicate across everything around the world.

Today, you extend that into the physical in-store experience and there's this idea of the "Internet of objects." The network now has tentacles reaching into physical environments through mobile devices, through RFID readers, through video cameras.

RM: What about individual product brands hoping to extend the brand experience into stores that carry their products?

TN: That's a good point. Can the supplier actually afford to bring this all in on their own for one product line? The answer is probably not. There's no efficiency of scale there.

The place where individual product brands can play [a role] is in creating experiences tied to the mobile device—services that consumers will want to access when they are in a physical store environment.

RM: What should brands be thinking about before getting started in something like social retailing?

TN: The first step is to see if you can free up some of your advertising money to learn more about your customers and their needs.

We are not selling a silver bullet here; we are not selling social retailing as a canned solution for all retailers. The first step is going in and trying to figure out what it is they are trying to do with their businesses, where the weak points are, where the opportunities lie, and how can some of these tools be put into play to meet them. Social retailing may or may not be the first thing they should look at right now.

RM: Looking out ten years, describe what you think the in-store experience might be like for the next generation.

TN: It's going to look a lot more like the online world looks today. The physical walls will still be there, but the virtual walls will be broken down. There will be an ecosystem of partners and suppliers who can refer customers to each other. The customer will feel completely connected with themselves, with the retailer, and with brands. [The physical and virtual] will start to blend and merge, and mobile devices will have a lot do with that, but so will in-store technologies.

This is why companies like us exist, to figure that out for clients who want to get one step ahead of their competition, like they did fifteen years ago when people wanted their first website. Now we're trying to go beyond the Internet itself into the physical environments as it expands.

So I can see our company engaging in another thirty years of innovation. And it's going to be fun.

Use Smart
Ads Wisely

A LOT OF ONLINE display advertising only seems dumb. In truth, it's getting smarter—and a bit scarier—by the day.

Advertising technologies like "interest-based advertising" and "behavioral targeting" that once targeted people based on rudimentary consumer profiles are rapidly giving way to a new generation of "smart advertising"—technologies that enable marketers to create a single Internet banner ad that every visitor to a website may see, but that will use a mind-boggling array of data mining capabilities to dynamically customize itself to fit each viewer's age, gender, location, profession, household income, personal interests, online activities, past purchase behavior, advertising response characteristics, and much more.

Thus far, we have not dealt extensively with display advertising in regard to search marketing and banner ads.

That's because in the on-demand era, there are so many more powerful ways to use digital media, as evidenced by the initiatives we've explored so far. And let's face it, display ads can be dullsville—we've all had banner blindness for quite some time.

But over the last few years, the technology behind text, display, and video-based online advertising has undergone a transmutation that can, and likely will, have a profound effect on the relationship between consumer and brand across just about all the strategies, tactics, and channels we've discussed in this book—to both positive and ill effect.

It will also spark a much-needed conversation about consumer privacy along the way. In fact, it already has.

HAVE WE GOT AN OFFER FOR YOU—AND ONLY YOU

On its face, smart advertising is a dream come true to marketers.

The response rates for banner ads have been cratering, and even text-based search engine advertising, the primary driver of Google's meteoric growth, has seemed to plateau. Today, only 25 percent of web surfers are likely to click on a text-based ad from a search, and only 12 percent will ever click on a top banner ad, according to a recent survey from iPerceptions.[1]

In fact, comScore now pegs the click-through rate for banner advertising at 0.01 percent. Video's not much better, with only 11 percent of Internet users saying they ever click on a video ad.

To be fair, the comScore research has shown that there may very well be brand lift from online ad campaigns that isn't readily captured. Apparently, even when people don't click on ad banners, exposure to them can lift online promotional sales up to 27 percent for two to three weeks, and offline sales up to 17 percent.[2]

It's unclear how that can be verified, or if such statistics are measured against coinciding marketing communications activities in other media. Either way, as part of an integrated campaign, all touch points are branding moments that can help or hinder consumer perceptions.

Not that marketers are buying it. Growth in spending on online advertising is slowing down, and online advertising networks are working feverishly to demonstrate that they can deliver effective and efficient ways to not only reach consumers, but also incite them to respond to commercial messages.

Google, for instance, will serve ads to you based on the words you enter in its search engine, the sites you visit, or the content of your Gmail messages. Others are going even further.

Yahoo!'s Apt platform uses behavioral targeting that tracks the sites a user has visited and then pitches products to them based on their interests. And its Smart Ads platform delivers this kind of relevance in a fascinating new way.

With Smart Ads, a single display ad template can be created with numerous variables so that it can dynamically change to offer the most relevant pitch possible.

For example, let's say an airline has placed an ad in the travel and destinations section of a popular news website. The version of the ad that you see might be presented with a special offer based on the last place you bought tickets to, or a place you visit often, or the destination websites you surf.

You might also get vacation offers based on your gender and your interests. If you live in New York and you're into volleyball, the ad you see on the home page of the site might pitch airline tickets to a beach volleyball excursion in the Bahamas.

A golfing aficionado in Chicago may see the same ad, dynamically rendered to her interests, and tied to a different price point because of her geographic location, the fact that she has a higher income, or has a tendency only to buy first-class tickets.

Alaska Airlines is just one of the companies said to be looking into this kind technology. And others are already using it to impressive effect.

In one campaign for HP, for instance, the Yahoo's Smart Ads platform resulted in over 20,000 different creative executions across 140 million U.S. consumers, and resulted in an ROI that was twenty times higher than its typical online campaigns. In 2009, the platform was extended to mobile, whereby one campaign for Travelocity could factor in elements such as demographics, location, time of day, even weather. The result was a click-through rate that was 600 percent higher than typical Travelocity display ad campaigns.[3]

"It starts to marry the concept of targeting . . . with the construction of the ad," Todd Teresi, former senior vice president of Yahoo's display marketplaces, tells Reuters. The aim, he says, is for "consumers to view advertising to be as relevant as the content they're looking at."[4]

For its part, global ad agency holding company Publicis wants to upstage Yahoo!—and all of Madison Avenue, for that matter—with its own smart ad network capabilities that will enable advertisers to display one of hundreds, maybe thousands of variations of an ad to individuals who fit into specific consumer profiles. Not so much to compete with search engines and web portals, but on a bet that Internet companies will want to work with ad agencies to enable these kinds of solutions, not supplant them.

The market is expected to be huge for such targeted ads—doubling from $1 billion today to well over $4.4 billion by 2012.[5] Indeed, the prospects do seem promising for marketers.

According to industry reports, these kinds of technologies might mean that an ad for the new GMC Arcadia would feature body copy that uses a superlative like "most accommodating third-row seats in the class," which would only be shown to consumers that data mining shows to conduct a lot of comparison shopping online, or to consumers with large families. Someone who doesn't fit those criteria would see more general copy, like "lots of interior space."[6]

The same ad would be changed if the person has already seen the ads.

"You're basically creating a templated ad," Carl Fremont, head of global media for Publicis shop Digitas, tells me. "This templated ad has many data components or copy content components. And that messaging is then tailored to that individual based on what we know about them."

Fremont says it's more than just a situation of matching ad to the site a person is visiting. "What we know about them could be beyond demographics," he tells me. "It could be behavioral—in terms of what they recently purchased, what their interest levels are—and [then assembled] based on what messages we want to serve to them."

MODEL BEHAVIOR

There are essentially two models of behavioral targeting:

1. Network targeting: Data is collected across the various sites a consumer visits in a specific network to build a basic profile, persona, or segment.

2. On-site targeting: Data is culled from user behavior at a specific site, very typical in e-commerce, and is used to enhance the user experience.

In regard to on-site behavioral targeting, eBay, for instance, uses algorithms to determine gender (based on your first name) and age (from the shopping categories you choose). Based on some basic profiling, ads will be served to anticipate the kinds of products you might be interested in. And the site itself will change: If you're deemed to be value-oriented, search results will be presented sorted by cost.

Netflix, Amazon, TiVo, and iTunes do much the same in their own unique ways. For instance, Apple's Just for You feature scans what songs, movies, and TV shows you've recently purchased, and your thumbs-up or -down responses to suggested content to refine offerings to you on a real-time basis. Amazon's Recommended for You feature offers a wide array of personalization options, including the ability to note when a purchased item was a gift—which can be useful, as a single Amazon account might cover purchases for an entire family—for themselves and for others. And Netflix's Cinematch recommendation engine is famous for scanning users' rental histories and their ratings of those films (ranked from one to five stars) to offer up fairly accurate suggestions for movies they might enjoy.

To date, we haven't heard any jokes about any of these brands thinking that someone is gay based on his or her movie purchases or rentals, the way TiVo has notoriously mislabeled some subscribers (or so they claim). But one too many art house films and who knows what you'll get pitched next.

Meanwhile, companies with names like ATG and 7 Billion People are working to analyze such things as click speed and other behavior to deliver even more customized experiences. For instance, an online shopper who lingers over product reviews might be presented with links to pages with more product information. Those who are more likely to be swayed by demonstrations may suddenly find videos to watch.[7]

"Now we have the ability to automate serendipity," is how Dave Morgan, founder of targeted television promotion company Simulmedia, likes to put it.[8]

Morgan was the founder of Tacoda Systems, the groundbreaking behavioral marketing firm he sold to AOL for $275 million in 2007. Using data samples from millions of Internet users, Tacoda made a name for itself by being able to pinpoint the exact ad to serve to the exact right person at the exact right time.

"We learned that you could deliver much more relevant commercial messaging to browsers if you understood a limited amount of anonymous browsing behavior—the kind and content [the user] had consumed before," he tells me. "Sometimes it was as simple and as intuitive as people that have looked at automobile sites respond well to automotive ads. But we also found out sometimes very nonintuitive things by understanding the kinds of content people would look at."

For instance, using predictive modeling techniques, Tacoda discovered people who look at certain travel opportunities are also predisposed to pitches for flat panel televisions.

"Without understanding all of the psychological or sociological reasons that it works, it just does," says Morgan. "You look to social sciences or normal commercial or business behavior to look for hypotheses for where you'll find connections. And sometimes [you] just run analysis and you find where the highest correlations are, and they can come together that way."

Today, Morgan is working to bring a new level of targeting to television screens. His startup, Simulmedia, uses predictive data modeling to help television broadcasters deliver program promotions—those commercials you see for upcoming TV programs—to the right segments, down to geographic targeting, audience profile (including average attention span), time of day, and the placement within commercial pods and more.

Others are taking different approaches on behalf of product advertisers.

Canoe Ventures is a technology consortium of cable television operators, including Comcast, Time Warner, Cox, Cablevision, and others; it has launched a solution called Community Addressable Messaging (CAM). This CAM solution combines cable zoning technologies and overlays it with data from Experian to allow advertisers to target campaigns down to specific zip codes based on the same income data.

Speaking before the Advertising Research Foundation, Canoe CEO David Verklin explains that with Canoe, an advertiser like American Express is able run advertising promoting its green card nationally, "and in the 370 cable zones where the average household income, according to Experian, the third-party database used by direct mailers all around the country, indexes above $100,000, the gold card creative will run."

"This will be the first time a national ad has ever been served to a demographic slice of the United States," he says.[9]

While in its early stages—at least one early test of CAM was deemed a failure, for instance—such solutions presage what is considered the holy grail of television advertising: the ability to target spots to individuals.

"The technology exists to make it happen. And the motivation exists to make it happen," David Graves, principle analyst at Forrester Research, Cambridge, Massachusetts, tells *Brandweek*. "[The industry] could agree or disagree on the timeline, but it's going to happen."[10]

As *Brandweek* reports it, the idea here is to target TV ads by household so that, say, a fifty-year-old man watching *Heroes* sees an ad for mutual funds while a sixteen-year-old girl watching the same show next door sees an ad for makeup.

It's hard to tell how it'll work—there are multiple people in most households, so targeting each individual could prove difficult. A spot aimed at me is going to be completely irrelevant to my wife, much less the kids. Same show. Widely disparate audiences.

But kinks aside (we'll get to some simple, more direct methods in just a bit), smart ad technologies like these and others suggest John Wanamaker's famous lament—"Half the money I spend on advertising is wasted; the trouble is I don't know which half"—may soon be as antiquated as Nielsen diaries, in part because we'll have a far greater understanding of which types of ads appeal to which audiences, and how and where to reach them.

On the one hand, all of this seems like the ultimate manifestation of Rule #1—Insight Comes Before Inspiration, and its corollary Know Thy Customer. In this case, insight comes from the digital breadcrumbs—our target audience leaves as it makes its way around the Internet or cable networks.

And why not? In poll after poll, consumers say they're more willing to put up with advertising if it's relevant to them. These solutions can ensure that. And to be clear, 65 percent of marketers say they plan on using these kinds of technologies, according to a recent survey from Datran Media.[11]

Who doesn't want the specific sites they visit to be uniquely tailored to them—and for any advertising they do need to suffer through to actually be relevant to their needs and desires?

Really, that's exactly what this technology represents. At long last, the merely promotional becomes personally useful. Except when it doesn't.

By actually attaining this level of knowledge in the name of service, some argue, we also stand perilously close to invasion of privacy.

The potential for problems begins because this knowledge is not always given freely by consumers. They come from a form of what heretofore has been seen by some as an accepted form of spying.

On the Internet, much of this is accomplished through cookies—those little trackers that sites drop onto your computer when you visit, or more typically, register with a site. Follow the trail from all the cookies placed on your computer, and you start to get a pretty good picture of who's on the other side of the computer screen.

Many argue that people can and frequently do delete cookies from their machines. But newer technologies can "recapture" previous information if you revisit a site after deleting the cookie it laid on your computer. And once we consumers beat that, there will be some newer form of technology to watch our every step on the web.

A Little Too Much Face Time

Facebook, for one, faced user outrage when it famously announced its ill-fated Beacon program, which ties into data from external websites— even tracking purchases at third-party sites. The idea was to enable Facebook users to share their other web interests with friends—which would be notified through user profile pages.

But as some saw it, the real value of Beacon was to enable advertisers to send exquisitely targeted advertising to users based on their web surfing behavior.

Fortunately, Facebook changed its policies after over 70,000 users petitioned the company to add better opt-out mechanisms, and CEO Mark Zuckerberg apologized on his blog for the debacle.

However, that didn't prevent later controversies over Facebook Connect, ostensibly designed to enable users to log onto many partner sites using their Facebook password (again meaning surfing habits could be tracked, though Facebook says such data will not be used).

Even today, the company is enabling solutions such as a recent "Meet the Volkswagens" Facebook campaign that features an app that purports to help you find the right VW based on data from your Facebook profile. Think date of birth and educational history, for instance. It is a rudimentary example at best—the recommendations have been ridiculed for being wildly off base. But it illustrates that your data can and will be used to serve you in ways you might not expect—and may come to regret.

Indeed, using only basic user-provided information on Facebook and MySpace profile pages—name, birthdates, and so on—a recent study published in *The Proceedings of the National Academy of Sciences* reports that identity thieves could compare the data with voter registration lists and pinpoint a person's Social Security number in as few as ten tries.[12]

As Paul Stevens, a director of policy and advocacy with the Privacy Rights Clearinghouse, puts it: "People don't realize when they go online that there are bits and pieces of information that they're giving out, which may seem innocuous at the time," he says, adding, "but when you look at them in the aggregate, it paints a very complete, comprehensive picture of the individual—and that information can tell a marketer or anyone else for that matter, a great deal about that person."

Not to be outdone, Google has faced some complaints about its Gmail email system for trolling through email conversations in order to deliver targeted ads. And then there's Google's Android.

ANDROID INVASION

Android, Google's operating system for mobile devices, and Chrome, Google's web browser (and now, operating system), are designed to make search easier. But they could also become powerful advertising delivery mechanisms.

In Android's case, cookies or other mechanisms could potentially track users' web surfing behavior. Factor in geo-location capabilities, and suddenly Google could know a lot more about you—what you do online, what sites you visit, where you shop, where you roam in the real world, when, and even, conceivably, with whom.

For that matter, Google even has a mapping app called Google Latitude that lets you track the physical location of the other people in your network. Apps like Loopt from Loopt Inc, and Where, from uLocate, bring the capability to other mobile devices.

Advocacy groups such as the Center for Digital Democracy and the U.S. Public Interest Research Group are so alarmed by these kinds of advancements that they petitioned the Federal Trade Commission to launch an investigation into the privacy implications of marketing practices targeted to mobile phone users. At this writing, the FTC is considering steps to regulate online ads that target consumers based on their Internet activity.

And Google's not alone. Yahoo, Microsoft, and thirty other companies have formally received inquiries from the House Energy and Commerce Committee about their ad-targeting technologies. "Once data is shared, it cannot simply be recalled or deleted—which magnifies the cumulative consequences for consumers, whether they realize it or not," FTC commissioner Pamela Jones Harbour writes in an memorandum explaining her concerns about the data collection and sharing that facilitates smart ad targeting.[13]

All of these companies insist they're adamant about protecting user privacy. In most cases, data collection happens when people register for sites and opt to have the site personalized to their tastes. Even then, the data is usually aggregated to build profiles of consumer segments, as is the case with most targeted advertising solutions.

For example, Google recently teamed up with Boston-based data analysis firm Compete to enable ads to target you based on your credit, or FICO, score.

On its face, it seemed like a great way to sell luxury goods to rich folks, and garbage to everyone else. And on its face, it also sounds terrifying—a company pitching products to you based on some of your most private information. But it's not really quite so sinister.

Rather, the companies used a database of about 2 million web users who agreed to give out their credit scores when they applied for new credit cards, and who agreed to have their web surfing habits tracked whenever they visited sites with the Google Content Network (GCN), the world's largest network of websites, reaching 80 percent of global Internet users.

According to Sandra Heikkinen of Google's Global Communications & Public Affairs group, by analyzing anonymous data based on the users' clickstreams (i.e., which sites the users visited), Google was able to build profiles of the kinds of people who enter certain search terms and visit certain sites.

It then knew that if you visit a certain site, you probably fall within a certain credit score, among other characteristics, including income, geographic location, basic surfing behaviors, and so on. In other words, no one is being targeted using their specific, individual credit score, but rather by a demographic profile based on aggregate data from other people who visit the same sites they do. This data in hand, Google can match its clients' ads to sites (and search words) used by certain consumer segments—a notion that most of the ad-targeting models in this chapter embody, and a notion that is in complete keeping with our tenet Know Thy Customer.

Indeed, even when consumers give companies explicit approval to track their behavior, it is usually applied in the aggregate, meaning it is anonymized, then analyzed based on segmented demographic data, to build user profiles. Ads are then aimed at the profile, not the individual person.

What's more, Google, Yahoo, and Facebook, as well as solutions like Digitas's ad-serving systems, all have opt-out features, and all say they don't track anyone's behavior without permission.

Still, while some industry observers point to an anonymization and the ability to opt out as catchall answers—escape hatches for ensuring user privacy—others feel this may not go far enough to address the fear that our clickstreams may still be tracked—and perhaps accessed—even when the data is not collected by a single entity, much less analyzed or applied in the form of targeted advertising.

Indeed, as a society, we will have conversations over the next few years about the kinds of information that can and cannot be collected about us, and who can and cannot have control of the digital tracks we leave scattered across the Net.

That's because given the amount of personal information these technologies access and apply, some fear the term "targeted" may take on unintended meaning.

After all, an on-demand era of anytime, everywhere access seems to mean that you and your personal information are also on demand—anytime, everywhere. And that is one of the challenges our society must wrestle with.

Then there are data breaches. Even when brands are diligent about respecting our privacy, some fear it doesn't mean personal data won't somehow be appropriated by others. Who's to say that data won't be stolen by identity thieves or misapplied by government operatives conducting broad, and, in more unfortunate scenarios, illegal, wiretaps?

For all the nightmares these possibilities may hold, what may be more alarming is that these "advances" in advertising technologies are not happening in a vacuum.

RADAR LOVE?

Those same radio frequency identification (RFID)–based technologies that Prada and Bloomingdale's use to bring excitement to the retail store and that billboards from MINI USA use to do shout-outs to passing drivers, are rapidly being deployed in some amazing new consumer goods innovations.

Think frozen foods that tell the microwave how to cook them, coffee makers that brew up the perfect cup of coffee based on the type of bean being used, family refrigerators that alert owners when supplies are running low, and mobile technology that sends you a shopping list via text message.

All very cool. But to some, also kind of creepy.

Already, groups such as Consumers Against Supermarket Privacy Invasion and Numbering (CASPIAN) have petitioned the industry to provide "kill switches" on items with RFID tags. Why? The group fears connectivity with other wireless or mobile networks means it is within the realm of possibility to use the technology to track your whereabouts and behavior. The group's cofounder, Katherine Albrecht, author of *Spychips: How Major Corporations and Government Plan to Track Your Every Move with RFID*, seems to fear Big Brother scenarios that, as she posits in a companion book aimed at religious audiences, could presage the prophecies many believe are foretold in the book of Revelation. Such beliefs aside, Albrecht's concerns over the tracking capabilities of the technology are shared by others.

The European Union's Parliament's technology assessment task force, for instance, recently completed a study on the considerable threats to privacy posed by radio frequency identification technology.

The study, titled "RFID and Identity Management in Everyday Life," finds that plans to embed RFID technology in customer loyalty cards, such as those used by Metro Group's Future Store project, could potentially result in the disclosure of shoppers' personal data, or be used to track customer movements in a store.[14]

Add that to things like the RFID-based Speedpass-style badges affixed to our cars to pay for toll roads, public transport cards, the biometric passport, and new micro-payment systems, and possible threats proliferate.

Here in the United States, industry vendors are telling Congress the same thing when it comes to new ID cards being proposed by the Department of Homeland Security.

"We have a situation where the government is issuing [identity] cards to themselves that are more secure than what they are about to issue to the citizens. There is something significantly wrong with the situation," says Neville Pattinson, vice president of government affairs and standards at Gemalto, a digital security company based in Amsterdam."[15]

Factor these technologies with new "neuromarketing" technologies and the expression "you can run, but you can't hide" takes on new meaning.

BRANDING BY BRAIN SCAN

You know the old joke: If Henry Ford had asked people whether they'd be interested in an automobile, they'd have told him no, they really just wanted a faster horse.

For all the targeting capabilities new ad tech is bringing to bear, it leverages only the behavioral manifestations of our digital lives. The information may not, however, reflect what products we really prefer, or what we really want from a brand.

The fact is, people may not (in fact, usually don't) really know what they prefer, or they may censor their real preferences when asked about them. Social desirability (the urge to seek approval) may shade their responses. Or they may just want to pick "the right answer" in surveys and focus groups.

Which brings in the whole field of neuromarketing and the use of functional magnetic resonance imaging (fMRI), or "brain scans," to quite quickly and accurately reveal how you really feel about something.

Scientists at Baylor University, for instance, have used fMRI to determine true preference for Coke or Pepsi, and scientists at UCLA can tell whether you're really a Republican or a Democrat.

Chrysler, meanwhile, has been using fMRI technology to gauge consumer interest in different makes of cars.

The *New York Times* recently revealed some of the particulars of at least one Chrysler study, which was called "Cultural Objects Modulate Reward Circuitry."

In the study, twelve men, whose average age was thirty-one, underwent brain scans while they looked at different kinds of cars— small cars, limos, and sports cars. According to the *Times*, the hypothesis was that since sports cars are social status symbols, they would be perceived as the most rewarding and would produce the greatest activation of the brain's "reward" circuitry.

Sure enough, that's what happened. The cultural message that a sports car is sexy has literally been encoded in the average male brain. As the *Times* put it, "If our culture had deemed things like fuel economy, safety or more passenger room as sexy, there's little doubt that the average male reward pathway would follow suit."[16]

Alas, despite what men say, they can't convince their inner Steve McQueen that it's cool to be Larry David—no matter what they say in focus groups.

But the whole notion of neuromarketing raises serious questions. What happens when guesswork is taken out of advertising? What happens when the same technologies that track our behavior can also scan our brains as we drive past billboards or walk into stores, to send us just the right pitch—nearly guaranteed to work—right at the most opportune moment?

What responsibility do marketers bear in protecting consumer privacy and, for lack of a better term, mental sovereignty? What do we, as a society, need to do to make sure that happens?

It all comes down to two simple tenets that embody Rule #10.

OPT OUT IS NOT ENOUGH

Throughout this book, we've talked about the all-important ability for consumers to choose, shape, and share interactions as they see fit, at their initiation. Yet anyone who's ever tried to opt out of a marketer's unsolicited email promotions, keep magazine publishers from selling their names or addresses, or asked their financial institutions not to share personal information with other divisions or partner companies, knows that's almost laughably naive.

And there may be better, less invasive models.

TAG Networks is a cable television channel that enables you to play games using your TV remote control. If you like, you can set up a player profile to save your high scores and play with other viewers around the nation. Along the way, you can also opt in to have the channel's advertising tailored to you based on some basic demographic info: your gender, age, and zip code, and soon, some basic "this, not that" kind of information. Once the player profile is in place, advertisers are able to send highly relevant ads to users on a very targeted basis.

According to TAG Networks CEO Sangita Verma, once they see how the information will be used, 99 percent of those who build player profiles supply it.

"Currently, when people are talking about targeting advertising on TV, it's being targeted to the household," she says. "We're targeting right down to that user."

Indeed, such solutions already deliver a limited version of Canoe Venture's quest for individually targeted television advertising today—but with explicit viewer permission. As with the best online customization offerings, the level of personalization is designed and activated by the users themselves.

Beyond fMRI brain scan research, Chrysler has been especially innovative in mining user data and mashing it with syndicated data to dramatically boost the effectiveness of its advertising in ways that render personally identifiable information nearly irrelevant.

Hit hard by economic conditions that pushed it into bankruptcy, the carmaker turned to agency partner Organic to assemble a team of statisticians, economists, software engineers, and media planners to create a "media modeling" system that is unprecedented in its ability to calculate the best ways to allocate marketing dollars, and how to craft and target messaging.

Not only did the team discover that television ads generated more website traffic if they tripled the amount of time the URL is seen onscreen, but they could determine in real time which kinds of offers spurred more traffic through online ad buys. They even determined that if you use the "build your car" configurator on the brand's website, you were much less likely to be ready to buy a car than someone who entered a zip code to locate a dealer.

So sophisticated was the solution that they were able to predict sales of Jeep vehicles generated by one campaign within one percentage point of actual sales figures.[17] While data is obviously collected, it appears thus far to be based on specific interactions with the brand, and driven by creative content and offerings rather by accessing personal information beyond the aggregate.

Far too often, however, industry reaction to questions about consumer privacy in direct appeals to specific consumers or consumer segments is to build in an opt-out feature. And it's perfectly logical: If a consumer doesn't like some new service, feature, or capability that coincidentally creates privacy concerns, he or she can always decline it by finding the mechanism to shut it off.

Many product RFID tags, for instance, do indeed have kill switches that enable consumers to shut off privacy-compromising features before they leave the store. And operating systems like Android have similar features, as do many websites.

But in my view, "activation switches" are more appropriate—meaning such targeting features should be shut off as a default mode, leaving it up to the consumer to turn them on and off as they desire, with all user data deleted from the system entirely, and reapplied only when and as the user wishes. This is true of smart advertising, as well.

To my way of thinking, if they're called "smart," such technologies ought to be smart enough to work when consumers want them to, and not when they don't, using only the information consumers want to offer, when and how they want to offer it. In the upcoming interview with Peter Schwartz, founder and CEO of the Global Business Network, you'll see I'm not alone in my contention—and why consumers may soon gain an upper hand.

Yet even when pressed, Facebook and others have been seen by some as hedging. When confronted with outrage over its Beacon ad targeting program, CEO Mark Zuckerberg wrote in his blog, "If you select that you don't want to share some Beacon actions or if you turn off Beacon, then Facebook won't store those actions even when partners send them to Facebook."

That's not the same as saying your web usage won't be tracked by Facebook's partner sites without your explicit approval, and that the information will not be accepted or used even if it is gathered without approval.

"Essentially he's saying the information transmitted won't be stored but will perhaps be interpreted," industry analyst Om Malik pointed out at the time.[18]

I have no doubt Facebook, Google, Yahoo, and every other player is working to advance business goals while protecting user privacy—and there's really no indication they haven't been completely successful in doing that so far. In fact, with many if not most models, the companies don't even house personally identifiable information internally.

But put simply, instead of targeted ads that dynamically present me with relevant offers, I'd like to propose a different model. A model in which, should I decide I would like offers targeted to me, I would press a button to let the brands I select know I am now accepting offers based on certain information I would like to share with them at that moment—the type of product I'm looking for, or a price range, or location and contact information, for instance—and having so shared, I instantly receive an appropriate response.

Now that's what I call "smart" advertising.

Which leads me to the most important tenet in this book.

FOLLOW THE GOLDEN RULE

Consumer control is built into the very nature of the phrase "the on-demand brand," and for good reason.

Harking back to the Burger King Syndrome introduced at the start of this book, to be successful in the digital era, brands and their adherent brand experiences must be available to consumers when, where, and how consumers want them.

To be clear—we exist to service our customers, not the other way around. While technology will increasingly enable the ability to market down to granular levels of consumer profiling—even to the proverbial "niche of one"—society at large has a responsibility to make the decision to use the technology very carefully, as do we as marketers. This is not a philosophical debate about speculative scenarios. It's here, it's now, and it's happening today.

Consumer backlash will no doubt pressure companies to course-correct in some instances, though regrettably, government regulation may be required to stem more insidious practices.

As we've discussed throughout this book, digital technologies can offer tremendously powerful ways to enhance the brand experience—forever transforming the way consumers interact and transact with the brands they know and trust.

As consumers ourselves, we know the pull and appeal of the Burger King Syndrome in our own lives.

In the digital era, it's "Have it your way."

Or no way at all.

The Social Net— Privacy 2.0

Peter Schwartz, founder and CEO of the Global Business Network

IN PETER SCHWARTZ'S view, the end of privacy isn't just a distinct possibility— it's already here.

Not just because business and government work so hard to undermine our privacy, but because we seem so intent on giving it away.

Those seemingly innocuous buddy lists, location-aware friend finders, and social networking sites make it easier than ever to stay connected with our friends' every musing and every move. And since these capabilities make our lives more efficient and pleasurable, we not only fail to recognize the encroachment on our personal information, we embrace it.

But at what price?

Schwartz, founder of think tank Global Business Network, and a world-renowned "scenario planner" for government and business, gets paid to think about matters of such importance.

It was Schwartz, for instance, who authored the Pentagon's "An Abrupt Climate Change and Its Implications for United States National Security," and who has perennially served as Hollywood's go-to futurist for prescient films like *War Games*, *Deep Impact*, and *Minority Report*.

At the World Economic Forum in Davos, Switzerland, Schwartz recently moderated a session titled "The Impact of Web 2.0 and Emerging Social Network Models." In his view, social networking and other technologies raise alarming questions about the balancing act we as business people, and as a society, must do to keep the digital world safe for both commerce and personal liberty.

The thing is, Schwartz says, some people want to give up their privacy—as long as they have control over it, and it gives them access to the information, products, services, and experiences they want, on demand.

But marketers be warned: Those who don't want your marketing messages—smart ads or otherwise—may soon have new ways of tuning you out.

Rick Mathieson: You recently moderated a session at the Davos Economic Forum on the impact of social media on economic development. Spill the beans: What's your view?

Peter Schwartz: The honest truth is I think I was even too modest there—I think it is more profound than I had realized. I think what is happening is something quite new in the ways in which communities are formed.

Just to tell an anecdote, my wife and I were recently at the *Fortune Magazine* High Tech Conference in Half Moon Bay [California], and one of the founders of Facebook, Mark Zuckerberg, was up on stage and he got into a conversation with the audience. Now this is an audience of very high-tech people, [venture capitalists], etcetera.

And the question was asked, "How many had a Facebook page?" And all but a dozen—myself included in the dozen—hands went up out of about maybe 400 people in the room. I was astonished, and so as an experiment, I went on and put myself on Facebook, and of course I now see the consequences.

The point is that in a network economy, network connections make all the difference. One is establishing a whole new fabric of interconnection that was never possible before, even in the most mundane sorts of ways.

My son is a freshman in college. There's a Facebook section for freshmen, a Facebook section for his dorm. He met all the kids who live around him [on Facebook], and formed his community before even arriving on campus.

So what has happened is a radical transformation of the community formation process that I think at a scale that we've never seen before.

RM: How does this network economy change our notions of what others (including businesses) should know about us, and what we should know about each other?

PS: It's about understanding the network topology of community formation. And by that I mean that once upon a time, you could say there were model train lovers, and they would show up at a meeting of the Model Train Society.

And if you were in the business, like Lionel, of selling model trains, why, that was a natural place for you to put ads and have booths and so on, and you understood what the natural community of your customers was, because I self-identified in a very obvious and self-labeled way: I like model trains, I'm a gardener. I'm a sports buff. Whatever it is you are.

What we now have are new self-organizing communities whose a priori identification doesn't exist, they emerge. Something binds them together. Something creates that set of connections. Something creates that pattern of a network's evolution and elaboration.

If you understand that, you understand something significant about the people and their relationships and what will be important to them and what will not. And that has to be discovered because it is emergent not identified a priori. Now, what should we allow businesses to know about us in this or any other community? I think as a general rule, as much as we want.

In other words, everybody needs to have the right to, in a sense, opt out. No, better yet, opt in. That is, one needs positive permission to obtain information about you. I think that should be a general principle, except in the most mundane, unidentifiable ways, such as a transit agency collecting data on how many passengers are going through the turnstiles without identifying who's who. That kind of information clearly is banal. I'm talking about requiring permission to get information that could be identified with you and determine your characteristics in some meaningful way. And everybody has different thresholds of what they want to be known, because they want various degrees of service.

Some people wish to remain essentially anonymous and other people could care less. That said, there is something important happening, however—I'm astonished by it—which is the self-revelation of young people. I know much more about my seventeen-year-old son by reading his Facebook page than talking to him directly. Anybody whose got an adolescent knows that you've got to read their Facebook page if you want to see what's really going on. I'm astonished they would put things online they wouldn't tell their parents.

There's something else going on here that I don't fully understand, in all candor, because, of course, my generation would do precisely the opposite. I'm sixty-two. [My generation] wouldn't dream of putting some of this stuff, including pictures and stories and what's going on in our lives, etcetera, etcetera, online. We strove to keep all of that confidential. And here these kids are just revealing everything. I'm amazed. The purpose at one level is clear, i.e., kids want to socialize. They want to be accepted. And this is the new norm, so if they don't do this, they're not "in."

In part, this is simply a function of this is what kids do.

RM: Beyond the socializing, these channels are increasingly becoming venues for highly targeted, data mining–enabled "smart advertising." As a longtime scenario planner, how do you see these kinds of technologies evolving over the next decade?

PS: I see a reversal of polarity. I touched on it briefly in an article I wrote for *Fortune* a few years ago on the top ten companies in 2054. Right now, in a sense, all of us are passive recipients of "information offers" of various sorts that come at us, and we have to find some mechanism for filtering it, and we make certain decisions based on our interest. We sit in a small bubble surrounded by this increasing torrent of efforts to attract our attention, to have our channel focus on them for the moment.

I think that's going to reverse in much the same way it once was the media that were passive and the consumer was active. You had the newspaper, the broadcast television screen that we all sat around and watched together, and so on, turning the channels.

We played a different role. Now they're coming at us and finding us without us having to find them. I think ultimately that breaks down, simply out of the inability to adequately make choices in the face of what will be an overwhelming clutter of information that becomes ever less useful.

What will happen instead is that we will create a kind of electronic envelope around us that has an active set of receptors, not passive receptors on the surface.

There is a kind of radar called "phased array." Imagine if you were completely surrounded by phased array radar. And you have intentions and desires either for information, or action, or communication, or transactions, and that phased array radar around you seeks out in that information environment the interconnections and information and a localized information that you need at that time, and creates the connections and transactions and operates in your behalf.

I call it a "transaction envelope." And rather than you being the passive recipient, the environment now awaits you reaching out to it, in one way or another, based on your intentions. But it is a whole set of electronic interactions mediated by this new interface between you and the world.

RM: How should brand marketers evolve themselves to accommodate this new electronic transaction envelope?

PS: There are two elements of it. One is just simply in the capacity to articulate your value proposition in a way that is both articulate and is well tuned to that process of search. In other words, as I search out what I want, is your offer well suited not simply in terms of its content, but in the way in which I want to engage with what it is you have to offer.

Let me just take two contradictory examples. There are some people who react very well to animated interfaces and all kinds of cool stuff happening on the screen. And other people, it makes them crazy and they want to just leave a page. So I'm talking about the most banal level of things—the ability to adapt to my information styles, just to take a real example of the most modest sort. So there are all kinds of things that will be universal and will customize the experience to the individual coming to them.

The second piece, and more difficult to achieve is this: Think about it as reverse sponsorship. Right now it's superstars who get sponsored, right? Tiger Woods and the like.

Well, I could have a lot of my transactions and interactions sponsored by brands and companies and services that I like. And they could attract value from that sponsorship. So they can get closer to me.

Just to take a real example. I love BMW. I'm a BMW junkie. I'm an Apple junkie. I just switched to Apple from Windows. I'm ecstatic. I used to be a Mac guy, but I went to the dark side. And now my life is liberated again. I'm three or four times more productive.

But having said that, I'm clearly an Apple and BMW guy. They ought to sponsor me somehow. In fact, in the last issue of the BMW company magazine that they send out to all their customers, there's an article on the next generation diesel that they brought for me to test drive and I'm interviewed in it.

There ought to be ways of doing that kind of thing, in effect, for brands hoping to capture loyalties. It's essentially the scenario today where cell phone service is offered to you free because the operator can connect the brands that make sense for you. Which is a perfect example because the truth is the cell phone within twenty years may well be an implant.

RM: Really? How will we use them? Will we just say "call home"? Or just think it?

PS: You'll think it. They may actually be—and this will be shocking to people—bio tattoos. Basically they could be printed on the back of your hand. They would be invisible. You won't see them. They'll be just subcutaneous organic material forming an organic circuit that is a cell phone.

RM: Given all the access points that would be able to extract information from that mobile phone, parties will want to exploit this capability. How do we protect individual privacy?

PS: I'm afraid we passed that point already. Look, even your tires identify where you are now. They're Bluetooth-enabled and are designed to send a signal to your car if there's something wrong with your tire. That very same signal is unique to every single tire. It is a unique identifier. Devices already exist to read the passing tire signals. I know what tire you bought; I know where you are. I mean, game over.

Unfortunately, that point has been passed. We no longer have the option of not revealing our location or identity. There are too many forms that will exist of unique identification. Credit cards, ATMs, there are just so many, I think this a game that we have already passed.

RM: A few years ago, we learned that AT&T had secretly cooperated with the government to help eavesdrop on U.S. citizens without warrants. What can be done to disincentivize this kind of abhorrent activity by brands we entrust with personal information?

PS: I think we can come up with all the disincentives and incentives we wish and it will still happen for two reasons: error and intention.

There will be errors. People will lose laptops with big databases on them. How many times has this happened in the last few years? So accidents will happen no matter what incentives you construct, so that's number one, things will get out by accident.

But second, there will be those who intend for one reason or other, for good or ill—I'm doing this in the nation's interest, or I'm doing this in my own personal interest—who will attempt to, and will successfully, subvert any controls that you impose.

That is not to say one shouldn't impose controls. One should make it hard to screw up and hard to steal, but it will happen. So therefore you can't trust anything. You have to assume that anything that can be known will be known.

RM: That's a scary thought.

PS: Unfortunately, I think that is the fact of reality and that there's no getting around it.

RM: What happens when we factor in new fMRI technologies that can tell how you really feel about Coke or Pepsi, whether you're really a Republican or Democrat, or whether you'll respond to offer A or offer B?

PS: That is going to happen without a doubt. One thing that has just continued to happen over time and that will continue to develop—

and this is not a particularly radical idea, but I think it will be true—is our understanding of human psychology, behavior, motivation, communication, etcetera, which just continues to move ahead rather deeply.

To some extent it'll always be an art coming up with the great ad or the great marketing strategy that touches people deeply. But having said that, the scientific and intellectual foundations upon which our understanding of all of that is based will be ever more profound.

And therefore, our ability to do what we want to do in a kind of conscious, systematic, and somewhat less random way will be enormously increased. Someone will be able to say these types of people, or this particular demographic group, definitely prefers Pepsi or Coca-Cola—and more. They like Cherry Coke with cinnamon.

You will create exactly the right offer that will attract the attention of the transaction envelope when I'm looking for a drink. You will no longer be guessing about the right offer, you will know exactly what offer to make.

The difference is, in the comfort of my transaction envelope, that offer will come at the point of my intention, not yours.

THIS BOOK IS JUST THE BEGINNING

Listen to expanded audio casts of many of the Q&A interviews featured in this book, as well as exclusive interviews with many of the other top marketers and thought leaders featured in this book, including:

Tom Bedecarré, CEO, AKQA

Andy Bateman, CEO, Interbrand

Julie Bornstein, Sr. VP, Sephora Direct

Courteney Monroe, EVP, Consumer Marketing, HBO

Prinz Pinakatt, Coca-Cola Europe

Tina Sharkey, Chairwoman, BabyCenter

—And many, many more.

Plus, get the latest news, insights, and commentary on the ever-changing world of marketing in the on-demand era.

www.OnDemandBrand.com

NOTES

INTRODUCTION

1. Lenhart, Amanda, "Adults and Social Network Websites," Pew Internet & American Life Project, January 14, 2009.

2. *comScore*, "Social Networking Explodes Worldwide as Sites Increase Their Focus on Cultural Relevance," August 12, 2008, http://www.comscore.com/Press_Events/Press_Releases/2008/08/Social_Networking_World_Wide.

3. Based on projections extrapolated from Stefan Swanepoel, Inman News, "Micro Blogging Twitter Participation Rises Sharply," December 29, 2008, http://www.inman.com/community/groups/real-estate-bloggers/2008/12/29/micro-blogging-twitter-participation-rises-sharply.

4. Statistics from Nielsen Online, per Reuters, "Twitter Users Don't Stick Around," April 29, 2009, http://www.stuff.co.nz/technology/2372601/Twitter-users-don-t-stick-around.

5. John Horrian, "Mobile Access to Data and Information, Pew Internet & American Life Project, March 5, 2008, http://www.pewinternet.org/Reports/2008/Mobile-Access-to-Data-and-Information.aspx.

6. Miller, Claire Cain, "Who's Driving Twitter's Popularity? Not Teens," *New York Times*, August 25, 2009, http://www.nytimes.com/2009/08/26/technology/internet/26twitter.html.

7. Nielsen.com, "How Teens Use Media," June 2009, http://blog.nielsen.com/nielsenwire/reports/nielsen_howteensusemedia_june09.pdf.

8. Mary Madden, "Online Video," Pew Internet & American Life Project, July 25, 2007, http://www.pewinternet.org/~/media/Files/Reports/2007/PIP_Online_Video_2007.pdf.

9. Sydney Jones, Susannah Fox, "Generations Online," Pew Internet & American Life Project, January 28, 2009, http://www.pewinternet.org/~/media//Files/Reports/2009/PIP_Generations_2009.pdf.

10. Dean Takahashi, "PC Gaming Hits $10.7 Billion in Revenues Worldwide," VentureBeat, August 19, 2008, http://venturebeat.com/2008/08/19/pc-gaming-hits-107-billion-in-revenues-worldwide/.

11. Projections from Forrester Research, http://www.forrester.com/Research/Document/Excerpt/0,7211,42463,00.html.

RULE #1

1. Lenhart, Amanda, Madden, Mary, Rankin Macgill, Alexandra, Smith, Aaron, "Teens and Social Media," Pew Internet & American Life Project, December 19, 2007, http://www.pewinternet.org/Reports/2007/Teens-and-Social-Media.aspx?r=1.

2. Guthrie, Marisa, "Redefining Beauty," *Broadcasting & Cable*, January 21, 2008, http://www.broadcastingcable.com/article/112070-Redefining_Beauty.php.

3. Guthrie, Marisa, "Redefining Beauty," *Broadcasting & Cable*, January 21, 2008, http://www.broadcastingcable.com/article/112070-Redefining_Beauty.php.

4. Waldron, Alex, "A Case Study in Integration: The Dove Campaign for Real Beauty," *Marketing+MyMarketing*, March 5, 2009, http://www.marketingmag.com.au/case_studies/view/a-case-study-in-integration-the-dove-campaign-for-real-beauty-1098.

5. UNEP DTIE SCP Branch: Communications, "Creative Gallery on Sustainability Communications," http://www.unep.fr/scp/communications/ad/details.asp?id=51901&cat=9.

6. Guthrie, Marisa, "Redefining Beauty," *Broadcasting & Cable*, January 21, 2008, http://www.broadcastingcable.com/article/112070-Redefining_Beauty.php.

7. Captured in video at the Cable Television and Marketing (CTAM) conference and shown by Antonio Neves, in "Scion's Marketing Story: As You've Never Heard It Before," on *3 Minute Ad Age*, November 20, 2008, http://adage.com/video/article?article_id=132729.

8. Sullivan, Laurie, "Toyota Expands Scion Lineup in Gaia Online," *Marketing Daily*, January 28, 2008, http://www.mediapost.com/publications/index.cfm?fa=Articles. showArticle&art_aid=75140.

9. *BlogHer Advertising Information*, http://www.blogher.com/files/BlogHerAdvertisingInformation.pdf.

10. Byron, Ellen, "The New Odd Couple: Google, P&G Swap Workers to Spur Innovation," *Wall Street Journal*, November 28, 2008, http://online.wsj.com/article/SB122705787917439625.html.

11. Itzkoff, Dave, "Every Network That Rises Must Converge," *New York Times*, August 28, 2005, http://www.nytimes.com/2005/08/28/arts/television/28itzk.html?pagewanted=all.

12. Nielsen figures cited by Randall Stross in "Why Television Still Shines in a World of Screens," *New York Times*, February 3, 2009, http://www.nytimes.com/2009/02/08/business/worldbusiness/08iht-08digi.20007725.html.

13. Car, David, "As TV Dwindles, It Still Leads," *New York Times*, May 25, 2009, http://www.nytimes.com/2009/05/25/business/media/25carr.html.

14. Wentz, Laurel, "Forsman & Bodenfors Snares Media Grand Prix," *Advertising Age*, June 17, 2008, http://adage.com/cannes08/ article?article_id=127803 (login required).

15. *Advertising Age*, "Forget Buzz and Focus on the Biz, Says Pontiac Exec," February 12, 2007, http://goliath.ecnext.com/coms2/gi_0199-6288547/Forget-buzz-and-focus-on.html.

16. Nick Brian, shown on video by Antonio Neves in "Brand Building Must Give Way to Hard Sell During Recession," *3 Minute Ad Age,* November 26, 2008, http://www.youtube.com/watch?v=KraUsY4WzHY.

RULE #2

1. CreativityWorks08, "HBO Voyeur," http://www.dandad.org/inspiration/creativity-works/08/hbo.html.

2. *USA Today,* "Interactive Campaigns Build Buzz with Fun," January 18, 2007, and CareerBuilder.com, January 23, 2007, http://www.mushygushy.com/factsheet.

3. Sachoff, Mike, "CareerBuilder takes Monk-E-Mail Mobile, *Web Pro News,* October 24, 2007, http://www.webpronews.com/topnews/2007/10/24/careerbuilder-takes-monk-e-mail-mobile.

4. *Campaign Brief,* "Saatchi & Saatchi Sydney Mobilises United Nations 'Voices' Campaign," March 10, 2008, http://www.campaignbrief.com/2008/03/saatchi-saatchi-sydney-mobilis.html.

5. *Communication Arts,* "Advertising Annual 2008," http://www.commarts.com/SearchOn.aspx?page=1&col=683&inum=365&pj=14830&m=27872 (login required); and YouTube figures, http://www.youtube.com/watch?v=mMOPj6-4nDU&feature=related.

6. Morrissey, Brian, "R/GA: Digital AOY 2008," *ADWEEK,* February 16, 2009, http://www.adweek.com/aw/content_display/news/agency/e3i4e22c70790e72ba29f89bbd5a5739866?pn=1.

7. Morrissey, Brian, "Apps: The Newest Brand Graveyard," *ADWEEK,* December 8, 2008, http://www.adweek.com/aw/content_display/news/digital/e3ie8946cda1b3f6da290f925a3e6422b93.

8. eMarketer, "US Web Widget and Application Advertising Spending, 2007 & 2008," http://www.marketingcharts.com/interactive/widgets-to-wiggle-into-budgets-40mm-worth-in-2008-3877/emarketer-widget-app-ad-spend-2007-2008jpg/.

9. Morrissey, Brian, "Apps: The Newest Brand Graveyard," *ADWEEK,* December 8, 2008, http://www.adweek.com/aw/content_display/news/digital/e3ie8946cda1b3f6da290f925a3e6422b93.

RULE #3

1. Stross, Randall, "Advertisers Face Hurdles on Social Networking Sites," *New York Times,* December 13, 2008, http://www.nytimes.com/2008/12/14/business/media/14digi.html.

2. *eMarketer,* "US Social Network Ad Spending Growth Lowered," December 10, 2008, http://www.emarketer.com/Article.aspx?id=1006799.

3. The Luxury Institute, "Six in 10 Wealthy Consumers Online Use Social Networks," April 3, 2007, http://www.marketingcharts.com/interactive/six-in-10-wealthy-consumers-online-use-social-networks-3810/.

4. Hall, Emma, "How to Get the Most out of Social Networks and Not Annoy Users," *Advertising Age,* April 27, 2009, http://adage.com/digital/article?article_id=136233 (login required).

5. Stross, Randall, "Advertisers Face Hurdles on Social Networking Sites," *New York Times*, December 13, 2008,
http://www.nytimes.com/2008/12/14/business/media/14digi.html.

6. Leahul, Dan, "P&G marketing chief questions value of Facebook," *Brand Republic*, November 18, 2008, http://www.brandrepublic.com/News/862767/P-G-marketing-chief-questions-value-Facebook/.

7. Morrissey, Brian, "Jeep Seeks Friends on Social Networks," *ADWEEK*, August 16, 2006, http://www.adweek.com/aw/iq_interactive/article_display.jsp?vnu_content_id=1003018561.

8. Stross, Randall, "Advertisers Face Hurdles on Social Networking Sites," *New York Times*, December 13, 2008.

9. Roush, Wade, "Second Earth," *Technology Review*, July/August 2007,
http://www.technologyreview.com/printer_friendly_article.aspx?id=18911.

10. Siklos, Richard, "A Virtual World but Real Money," *New York Times*, October 19, 2006, http://www.nytimes.com/2006/10/19/technology/19virtual.html.

11. Semuels, Alana, "Virtual Marketers Have Second Thoughts About Second Life," *Los Angeles Times*, July 14, 2007, http://articles.latimes.com/2007/jul/14/business/fi-secondlife14.

12. Morrisey, Brian, "Brands Take Social Media Into Real Life," *ADWEEK*, April 20, 2009, http://www.adweek.com/aw/content_display/news/digital/e3if46ca983d59bcb8f2368f341974b749f.

13. Morrissey, Brian, "Apps: The Newest Brand Graveyard," *ADWEEK*, December 8, 2008, http://www.adweek.com/aw/content_display/news/digital/e3ie8946cda1b3f6da290f925a3e6422b93.

14. York, Emily Bryson, "Ordering Pizza Hut from Your Facebook Page? It's On the Way," *Advertising Age*, November 10, 2008,
http://www.crainsdetroit.com/article/20081110/EMAIL01/811100290/1092.

15. Story, Louise, "Promoting a Thirst for Sprite in Teenage Cellphone Users," *New York Times*, June 7, 2007,
http://www.nytimes.com/2007/06/07/technology/07sprite.html.

16. Zmuda, Natalie, "Dealing with Negative Blog Posts," *3 Minute Ad Age*, May 21, 2009, http://adage.com/brightcove/lineup.php?lineup=1266084202.

17. Johnson, Carolyn Y., "Hurry Up, the Customer Has a Complaint," *Boston Globe*, July 7, 2008,
http://www.boston.com/business/technology/articles/2008/07/07/hurry_up_the_customer_has_a_complaint/.

18. Klaassen, Abbey, "Using Social Media to Listen to Consumers," *Advertising Age*, March 30, 2009, http://adage.com/digital/article?article_id=135605 (login required).

RULE #4

1. Hampp, Andrew, "Diet Coke Launches 'Style Series' in Unusual Places," *Advertising Age*, December 10, 2008, http://www.commercialalert.org/news/archive/2008/12/diet-coke-launches-style-series-in-unusual-places.

2. Olson, Elizabeth, "Practicing the Subtle Sell of Placing Products on Webisodes," *New York Times*, January 3, 2008, http://www.nytimes.com/2008/01/03/business/media/03adco.html.

3. Graser, Marc, "Coppola Drives Scion's Web Series," *Variety*, October 1, 2008, http://www.variety.com/article/VR1117993231.html?categoryid=1009&cs=1.

4. Furrier, John, "Social Media Is the New Standard for Emerging Online Advertising," *Furrier.org*, http://furrier.org/2008/03/27/social-media-is-the-new-standard-for-emerging-online-advertising/.

5. Elliott, Stuart, "For the Honda Brand, a Cinematic Stroke," *New York Times*, January 11, 2009, http://www.nytimes.com/2009/01/12/business/media/12adcol.html.

6. Fong, Mei, "Clinique, Sony Star in Web Sitcom," *Wall Street Journal*, March 27, 2009, http://online.wsj.com/article/SB123810039778551339.html#mod=rss_media_marketing.

7. Bosman, Julie, "Commercials Find New Life on Web," *New York Times*, September 14, 2006, http://www.nytimes.com/2006/09/14/business/media/14adco.html.

8. Mullman, Jeremy, "Anheuser-Busch Pulls the Plug on Bud.TV," *Advertising Age*, February 18, 2009, http://adage.com/madisonandvine/article?article_id=134701.

9. Chattman, Jon, "Branded Entertainment Deals Seek Proactive Metrics," *Media Daily News*, November 28, 2008, http://www.mediapost.com/publications/index.cfm?fa=Articles.showArticle&art_aid=95206.

10. Schofield, Jack, "World PC Market Keeps Growing, Despite Recession," *Guardian.co.uk Technology Blog*, http://www.guardian.co.uk/technology/blog/2008/jul/17/worldpcmarketkeepsgrowing.

RULE #5

1. Extrapolating from stats cited by Mary Madden, "Online Video," Pew Internet & American Life Project, July 25, 2007, http://www.pewinternet.org/Reports/2007/Online-Video.aspx.

2. Proffitt, Steve, "User-Generated Ads Hit the Super Bowl," National Public Radio, January 31, 2007, http://www.npr.org/templates/story/story.php?storyId=7096491.

3. Bosman, Julie, "Chevy Tries a Write-Your-Own-Ad Approach, and the Potshots Fly," *New York Times*, April 4, 2006, http://www.nytimes.com/2006/04/04/business/media/04adco.html?scp=1&sq=Chevy%20Tries%20A%20Write-Your-Own-Ad%20Approach,%20and%20the%20Potshots%20Fly&st=cse.

4. FritoLay (corporate release), "Doritos Challenges Fans to Crash the Broadcast with Their Own Consumer-Created Super Bowl Commercial," *PRNewsire*, September 14, 2006, http://www.redorbit.com/news/technology/656486/doritos_challenges_fans_to_crash_the_broadcast_with_their_own/index.html.

5. Horovitz, Bruce, "Two Nobodies from Nowhere Craft Winning Super Bowl Ad," *USA Today*, February 2, 2009, http://www.usatoday.com/money/advertising/admeter/2009admeter.htm.

6. *Business Week*, "Keep Up with the Jones, Dude!," October 26, 2005, http://www.businessweek.com/innovate/content/oct2005/id20051026_869180.htm?chan=sb.

7. Heinz Corporation (corporate release), "Heinz Invites America to Vote for the Next Great Ketchup Commercial," EON, August 27, 2007, http://eon.businesswire.com/portal/site/eon/permalink/?ndmViewId=news_view&newsId=20070827105569&newsLang=en,

RULE #6

1. La Monica, Paul R., "Commercials Get 'Lost,'" *CNNMoney.com*, http://money.cnn.com/2006/05/25/news/companies/commercials/index.htm.

2. Arc Worldwide (corporate release), "Arc Worldwide, Whirlpool and Nestlé Purina PetCare Discuss Emerging Media and Consumer Engagement at ad:tech," July 27, 2006, http://www.marketwire.com/press-release/Arc-Worldwide-696838.html.

3. King, Rachael, "Building a Brand with Widgets," *Business Week*, March 3, 2008, http://www.businessweek.com/technology/content/feb2008/tc20080303_000743.htm?chan=technology_ceo+guide+to+tech_green+computing.

4. Ibid., http://www.businessweek.com/technology/content/feb2008/tc20080303_000743.htm.

5. Smith, Steve, "Look Who's Gaming Now," *OMMA: The Magazine of Online Media*, marketing & Advertising, January 1, 2006, http://www.mediapost.com/publications/index.cfm?fuseaction=Articles.showArticle&art_aid=37933.

6. Clifford, Stephanie, "Dairy Queen, the Video Game," *New York Times*, December 23, 2008, http://www.nytimes.com/2008/12/24/business/media/24adco.htm.

7. *Gamer's Game*, citing comScore research in "Study Finds Average Gamer is Forty-One," http://www.gamersgame.com/statistics/.

8. Extrapolating from stats cited by Gavin O'Malley in "Yankee: In-Game Ads to Reach nearly $1 Billion in 2011," *Online Media Daily*, July 9, 2007, http://www.mediapost.com/publications/index.cfm?fa=Articles.showArticle&art_aid=63668.

9. Alhadeff, Eliane, "Serious Games as Customer Touchpoints," December 14, 2007, http://www.futurelab.net/blogs/marketing-strategy-innovation/2007/12/serious_games_as_customer_touc.html.

10. PopCap Games (corporate release), "Survey: Tens of Millions of 'White Collar' Workers Play 'Casual' Video Games—One in Four Play at Work, and Senior Execs Play Even More," September 4, 2007, http://www.popcap.com/press/release.php?pid=227.

RULE #7

1. Morrissey, Brian, "Nike Plus Starts to Open Up To Web," *ADWEEK*, July 20, 2009, http://www.adweek.com/aw/content_display/news/e3ibdf529f18374f6c9e0916614874bf862.

2. Wacksman, Barry, "Mother of Invention," *ADWEEK*, May 19, 2008, http://www.rga.com/assets/attachments/May19_MotherofInvention_Barry.pdf.

3. Steinberg, Brian, "TiVo, Domino's Team to Offer Pizza Ordering by DVR," *Advertising Age*, November 17, 2008, http://www.highbeam.com/doc/1G1-189551119.html.

4. Reuters, "CBS Offers Mashup for Web Couch Potatoes," October 21, 2008, http://economictimes.indiatimes.com/Infotech/Internet_/CBS_offers_mashup_for_Web_couch_potatoes/rssarticleshow/3622089.cms.

5. Hansell, Saul, "The iTunes Store: Profit Machine," *New York Times Bits*, August 11, 2008, http://bits.blogs.nytimes.com/2008/08/11/steve-jobs-tries-to-downplay-the-itunes-stores-profit/.

6. Estimated, based on revenue reports from Apple, January 21, 2009, http://www.apple.com/pr/library/2009/01/21results.html.

RULE #8

1. Cellular News, "Ladies Lingerie by SMS," May 8, 2007, http://www.cellular-news.com/story/23613.php.

2. Howard, Theresa, "USA Lags on Cellphones' Marketing Potential," *USA Today*, June 18, 2008, http://www.usatoday.com/money/advertising/2008-06-18-cannes-mobile-marketing_N.htm.

3. Extrapolation from Alice Z. Cuneo's article, "Advertisers Target iPhone," in *RCR Wireless*, December 5, 2007, http://www.rcrwireless.com/apps/pbcs.dll/article?AID=/20071205/FREE/71204013/1015/ and Duncan Riley's "AdMob + iPhone + LandRover = Good Results," *Tech Crunch*, December 3, 2007, http://www.techcrunch.com/2007/12/03/admob-iphone-landrover-good-results/.

4. Hendery, Simon, "Advertiser Clicks on to Mobile Market," *New Zealand Herald*, July 24, 2008, http://www.nzherald.co.nz/simon-hendery/news/article.cfm?a_id=264&objectid=10523136.

5. Chang, Rita, "Mobile Effort Gets More to Say 'I Can' Purchase a Porsche," *Advertising Age*, February 9, 2009, http://adage.com/digital/article?article_id=134360 (login required).

6. *MediaBuyerPlanner*, "Gartner: Mobile Ad Spending to Top 13B by 2013," August 31, 2009, http://www.mediabuyerplanner.com/entry/44880/gartner-mobile-ad-spending-to-top-13b-by-2013/.

7. *Phonecontent.com*, "Calvin Klein uses SMS with Digital Billboards to Launch the CK IN2U Fragrance," March 28, 2007, http://www.phonecontent.com/bm/news/1747.shtml.

8. *MobiAD News*, "Calvin Klein Uses Mobile to Attract Perfume Buyers," December 10, 2007, http://www.mobiadnews.com/?p=1243.

9. York, Emily Bryson, "Kraft iPhone App—iFood Assistant," *Advertising Age*, January 19, 2009, http://www.everythingloonoofus.com/no_way_back_from_here/1-lay-of-the-land/case-studies/kraftiphoneapp-ifoodassistant.

10. Morrisey, Brian, "Pepsi Brand App Comes With NC-17 Rating," *ADWEEK*, October 9, 2009, http://www.adweek.com/aw/content_display/news/digital/e3i763b9b978b250321c6f755654592e2d6.

11. Paul, Ian, "Mobile Apps: What's in Your Future?," *PC Magazine*, July 20, 2009, http://www.pcworld.com/article/168686/mobile_apps_whats_in_your_future.html.

12. Morrissey, Brian, "Marketers Enlist Mobile Phones as Utility Vehicles," *ADWEEK*, November 27, 2007, http://www.dynamiclogic.com/na/pressroom/coverage/?id=573.

RULE #9

1. *Media Buyer Planner,* "Mall Advertising Booms, Has Room to Grow," October 19, 2006, http://www.mediabuyerplanner.com/entry/38775/mall-advertising-booms-has/.

2. Ho, David, "Interactive display redefines window shopping," *Atlanta Journal-Constitution,* August 23, 2006, http://www.highbeam.com/doc/1G1-150014751.html.

3. *Wine Spectator.com,* "Wine Spectator Announces New Mobile Platform," October 6, 2008, http://www.reuters.com/article/pressRelease/idUS156439+06-Oct-2008+BW20081006.

4. IconNicholson, "Facebook Meets The Mall," January 14, 2007, http://docs.google.com/gview?a=v&q=cache:WMyu8fNCTLUJ:www.iconnicholson.com/news/press_releases/doc/nrf011407.pdf+Iconnicholson+%22facebook+meets+the+mall%22&hl=en&gl=us&sig=AFQjCNGCE5c-7FVTG7bfenChhQ4YkvRx_w.

5. IconNicholson, "Social Retailing(SM) Meets Bloomingdale's," *PRNewswire,* March 15, 2007, http://www2.prnewswire.com/cgi-bin/stories.pl?ACCT=109&STORY=/www/story/03-15-2007/0004546997&EDATE=.

6. Gartner Research, "The Store of the Future 2012–15 Report Findings," April 2008, p. 3, http://www.visaeurope.com/documents/pressandmedia/RetailWorldCongress_summary.pdf.

7. *BusinessWire,* "Bazaarvoice Introduces MobileVoice, Bringing Product Reviews to the Mobile Device and Into the Retail Store," January 20, 2009, http://www.businesswire.com/portal/site/google/?ndmViewId=news_view&newsId=20090120005440&newsLang=en.

8. Bachman, Katy, "Suit Your Shelf," *Media Week,* January 20, 2009, http://www.mediaweek.com/mw/content_display/esearch/e3ie53ceefa152782efaacb9d7b938be63c.

9. Ibid.

RULE #10.

1. *iPerceptions,* "iPerceptions Study Uncovers Consumers Real Online Ad Preferences," October 6, 2008, http://www.iperceptions.com/en/news/iperceptions-study-uncovers-consumers-real-online-.

2. *comScore,* "Whither the Click? comScore Brand Metrix Norms Prove 'View Thru' Value of Online Advertising," November 17, 2008, http://www.smartbrief.com/news/aaaa/industryPR-detail.jsp?id=BD7D575A-7B36-48C1-82E1-2CC5D071FE1F.

3. *Marketing Vox,* "Yahoo to Bring Behavioral Targeting to Mobile," May 21, 2009, http://www.marketingvox.com/yahoo-to-bring-behavioral-targeting-to-mobile-044141/?utm_campaign=rssfeed&utm_source=mv&utm_medium=textlink.

4. Gershberg, Michele, "Yahoo Beefs Up Target Advertising Tools," Reuters, July 2, 2007, http://www.reuters.com/article/industryNews/idUSSP25867220070702.

5. *Marketing Vox,* "Behavioral Targeting Ad Spend Poised to Grow, with Help from Online Video," June 23, 2008, http://www.marketingvox.com/behavioral-targeting-ad-spend-poised-for-growth-with-help-from-online-video-039399/.

6. As illustrated in an info graphic accompanying story by Louise Story, "It's an Ad, Ad, Ad, Ad World," which appeared in the *New York Times,* August 6, 2007, http://www.nytimes.com/2007/08/06/business/media/06digitas.html?_r=5&ref=business.

7. Baker, Stephen, "The Web Knows What You Want," *Business Week,* July 16, 2009, http://www.businessweek.com/magazine/content/09_30/b4140048486880.htm?chan=technology_technology+index+page_top+stories.

8. Garfield, Bob, "Your Data with Destiny," *Advertising Age,* September 15, 2008, http://adage.com/digital/article?article_id=130969 (login required).

9. Ives, Nat, "How Canoe's CAAS Will Change Cable TV Advertising," *3 Minute Ad Age,* April 2, 2009, http://adage.com/video/article?article_id=135727.

10. Cummings, Betsy, "Addressable Advertising Gets Closer to Reality," *Brandweek,* May 5, 2008, http://www.brandweek.com/bw/magazine/current/article_display.jsp?vnu_content_id=1003798282.

11. Karpinski, Rich, "Will Using Behavioral Data Lead to Smarter Ad Buys," *Advertising Age,* April 20, 2009, http://adage.com/adnetworkexchangeguide09/article?article_id=136003.

12. Fetini, Alyssa, "Is Your Facebook Account a Gold Mine for Identity Thieves?" *Time Magazine,* July 8, 2009, http://www.time.com/time/nation/article/0,8599,1909133,00.html.

13. *Internet Retailer,* "Feds Give Online Marketers One More Chance on Behavioral Marketing," February 19, 2009, http://www.internetretailer.com/dailyNews.asp?id=29480.

14. *European Parliament,* "RFID and Identity Management in Everyday Life," June 2007, http://www.europarl.europa.eu/stoa/publications/studies/stoa182_en.pdf.

15. O'Conner, Mary Catherine, "RFID Vendors Brief Congress on PASS Card Security," *RFID Journal,* July 20, 2007, http://www.rfidjournal.com/article/articleview/3495/1/1/.

16. Friedman, Richard A., "What's the Ultimate? Scan a Male Brain," *New York Times,* October 25, 2007, http://www.nytimes.com/2006/10/25/automobiles/autospecial/25neuro.html.

17. Steel, Emily, "Modeling Tools Stretch Ad Dollars," *Wall Street Journal,* May 18, 2009, http://online.wsj.com/article/SB124259801821028103.html?mg=com-wsj.

18. Malik, Om, "Zuckerberg's Mea Culpa, Not Enough," *Gigaom,* December 5, 2007, http://gigaom.com/2007/12/05/mark-zuckerberg-on-beacon-we-made-mistakes-not-enough/.

ACKNOWLEDGMENTS

This book would not have been possible without the generous time and insights of many people, including, but not limited to, the following: Tabor Ames, PQ Media; Jeff Arbour, The Hyperfactory; Whitney Ashley, The Rose Group; Andy Bates, Interbrand; Suzanne Bedau, Disney/ABC Television Group; Tom Bedecarré, AKQA; Mike Benson, ABC Entertainment; Allyson Bentley, Goodby, Silverstein & Partners; Josh Bernoff, Forrester Research; Jordan Bitterman, Digitas; Alex Bogusky, Crispin, Porter + Bogusky; Julie Bornstein, Sephora; Katie Boylan, Edelman; John Butler, Butler, Shine, Stern & Partners; Joe Case, Nationwide Mutual Insurance Company; Katie Cerruti, Goodby, Silverstein & Partners; Jennifer Conway, Dotted Line Communications; Dennis Crowley, Foursquare; Roy Elvove, BBDO; Beata Fagring, Forsman & Bodenfors; Lauren Farmer, HBO; Steven Feldman, Cielo Group; Alexis Frank, Interbrand; Carl Fremont, Digitas; Yvonne Fulchiron, TiVo; Christine Haker, Monitor; Jeff Hasen, HipCricket; Dave Herbert, Transit Films; Joe Herbert, Transit Films; Mandy Holder, IconNicholson; Jon Howell, TiVo; Linda Hymer, Forsman & Bodenfors; Alex Johnson, Alex Johnson Photography; Tristan Jordan, MasterCard Worldwide; Gabriella Kallay, PQ Media; Susan Kappes, BBDO; Steve Keyes, Volkswagen Group of America; Laura Klauberg, Unilever; Melissa Klein, Launch Squad; Anita Larsen, Unilever; Belle Lenz, DiGennaro Communications; Mira Leytes, IconNicholson; Caitlin Looney, Mozes; Dean Macri, Cielo Group; John Mastrojohn, Unilever; Tim

McIntyre, Domino's Pizza; Jason Mirvis, The Electric Sheep Company; Courteney Monroe, HBO; Dave Morgan, Simulmedia; Molly Morse, Kekst & Company; Tom Nicholson, IconNicholson; Dominick O'Brien, Glue London; Kim O'Brien, Burger King Corporation; Christine O'Donnell, Goodby, Silverstein & Partners; Bridget O'Malley, Edelman; Molly Parsons, AKQA; Coral Petretti, The Disney/ABC Television Group; Prinz Pinakatt, Coca-Cola Europe; Dorrian Porter, Mozes; Patrick Quinn, PQ Media; Ben Relles, Barely Political/Digital; Derek Robson, Goodby, Silverstein & Partners; Steve Sapka, Crispin, Porter + Bogusky; Chuka Schneider, Crispin, Porter + Bogusky; Peter Schwartz, Global Business Network; Doug Scott, OgilvyEntertainment; Tina Sharkey, BabyCenter; Linda Shaw, Unilever; Maria Shterew, Medicis Pharmaceutical Corporation; Adrian Si, Toyota Motor Corporation; George Simpson, George H. Simpson Communications; Joddy Sloan, Domino's; Paul Stevens, Privacy Rights Clearinghouse; Mike Switzer, Nationwide Mutual Insurance Company; Allison Takahashi, Toyota Motor Corporation; Angela Thompson, Makena; Kevin Townsend, Science + Fiction; Sibley Verbeck, The Electric Sheep Company; Sansita Verma's TAG Networks, Jocelyn Weiss, BBDO; Victoria Weld, Kekst & Company; Stephanie Wendelin, OgilvyEntertainment; Michael Wilson, Makena; Rick Wootten, SonicWALL; Tim Zuckert, Shift Control Media; and many others.

A special thanks to Ellen Kadin, William Helms, Cathleen Ouderkirk, Debbie Posner, Mike Sivilli, Jenny Wesselmann, and the rest of the talented team at AMACOM Books. It is always a pleasure to work with you.

And to J & K—you make it all worthwhile.

INDEX

ABC Entertainment, 91, 132, 135–138, 151
activation mechanisms, 184–186
Adidas, 104, 109
advergames, xxii, *see also* branded games
advertising
    customer insights as basis for, 5–8
    display, 231–232
    in-game, 141–143
    mobile, 200
    in mobile platforms, 182–184
    within social networking sites, 60–62
    traditional, 15–18, 43–45
    see also smart advertising
AE, *see* American Eagle
A&E Television Network, 38, 140–141
Ahmad, Nussar, on user-generated content, 187
AKQA (company), 43, 44
Albrecht, Katherine, 244
alternative (alternate) reality games (ARGs), xxii, 136, 152
Amato, Steven, 92, 105, 115
Amazon.com, xii, xiv, 79, 80, 86, 167, 210, 235
American Apparel, 64, 65
American Eagle (AE), 93, 94, 102–103, 109
AMF Pension, 15–17
Amp (brand), 194–196
Android (program), 240–241, 248
Anheuser-Busch InBev, 71, 103–104, 119
AOL, 85, 227, 236
Apple, 51, 167, 171, 235, 257
applications
    for smart phones, xv, 45–48, 74, 76, 191–196
    for social networking sites, 45–48, 74–75
AR, *see* augmented reality
Arbour, Jeff, xxi–xxii, 148, 196, 197
ARGs, *see* alternative (alternate) reality games
audio, targeted, 38
augmented reality (AR), xxii, 38–40, 212
AXE, 2, 11, 21, 25, 26, 139, 163, 164

BabyCenter (website), 66–68, 70, 75
Backus, Dale, 121

Baked In (Alex Bogusky), 52
banking, xii
Barely Digital (website), 130–131
Barely Political.com, 128–131
Barrett, Jamie, on Goodby, Silverstein & Partners, 170
Bartley, Simone, on "Voices" campaign, 36
Bateman, Andy, 46, 165, 184, 261
Baylis, Nick, on mobile platforms, 182
BBDO (company), 33, 34, 145
Beacon (program), 239, 249
Beattie, Alistair, on social networks, 61
Bedecarré, Tom, xvii, 43, 44, 48, 261
behavioral targeting, 232–239
behavior tracking technologies, 240–243
Benson, Mike, xxi, 135, 137, 149, 151–156
Berlin, Andy, 175
Bernbach, Bill, 45
Bernoff, Josh, on feedback, 78, 79
Best Buy, 65, 78, 80
BlackBerrys, xii, 193
Bloomingdale's, 211–213, 221, 225, 243
Bluetooth, 197, 257
BMW, 39, 188, 189, 201–203, 257
Bogusky, Alex, xxi, 51–57, 102
Bornstein, Julie, 216, 217, 261
Bottari, Danielle, on in-store experiences, 218
branded apps, xxii
branded entertainment, xxii, 89–112
    brand's story in, 97–99
    content of, 105–106
    guidelines for, 96–97
    POS of, 99–101
    and product placement, 92–96
    Adrian Si on, 107–112
    and television series, 89–91
    and viral videos, 102–104
branded games, xxii, 135–156
    at ABC Entertainment, 135–138
    Mike Benson on, 151–156
    calls to action in, 145–147
    engaging consumers with, 138–141
    and in-game advertising, 141–143

branded games (*continued*)
  on sensitive topics, 143–144
  sharing of, 148–149
  value propositions in, 144–145
branded online entertainment, xxii
brands
  control of, 116–117
  on-demand, xvii–xix
  on social networking sites, 62–64
  stories of, 97–99
Bravissimo, 179–180, 184
Brien, Nick, on recession, 19
Budweiser, 40, 56, 71, 103–104, 109
Burger King, xi, xii, 40–43, 49, 52–56, 139, 140
Burger King Syndrome, xiii, 180, 250
business, on-demand revolution and, xiii
Business Network, 68–69
Butler, John, xvii, 13, 45
Butterball, 165

Cadillac, 139, 140
calls to action, in branded games, 145–147
Calvin Klein (brand), 187–188
CAM (Community Addressable Messaging),
  237–239
"Campaign for Real Beauty," 1, 3–5, 7–8, 11,
  21, 23–24
Canoe Ventures, 237, 247
CareerBuilder.com, 35–36, 49
Carmen Has a Crush on You (website), 37–38
CASPIAN (Consumers Against Supermarket
  Privacy Invasion and Numbering), 244
CBS, 70, 82, 84, 161
Chantix, 157
Chevrolet, 116–117
Chrysler, 61, 245–248
Cielo Group, 188, 199–200
Ciesinski, David, on "Top This" contest, 125
Clinique (brand), 98–100
Coca-Cola, 44, 84
  Design the World a Coke website of,
    117–118
  and Diet Coke Style Series, 92–93
  "Essence of Coke" campaign of, 117
  Facebook page of, 12–13, 63
  Fanta brand of, 148–149, 194
  Green Eyed World series of, 100
  "Happiness" campaign of, 139
  and QR codes, 185–186
  and Sprite Yard, 75–76
Collins, Tonya, on in-store experiences, 218
Comcast, 67, 78–79
communication, xxiii
communities, online, 65–66
Community Addressable Messaging (CAM),
  237–239
Conrad, Lauren, 186
consumer control, in smart advertising,
  249–250

consumer-created content, xxiii, *see also* user-
  generated content (UGC)
consumers
  anticipating wants of, 214–215
  engaging, with branded games, 138–141
  see also customers
Consumers Against Supermarket Privacy
  Invasion and Numbering (CASPIAN),
  244
content
  branded, 91–96
  of branded entertainment, 105–106
  user-personalized, 123–125
  video, 40–43
  see also user-generated content (UGC)
control
  of brand, 116–117
  consumer, 249–250
Coors Light, 157
CoverGirl, 203, 209
Cozza, Matt, 125
Crest Whitestrips, 62–63
Crispin Porter + Bogusky, 41, 42, 51, 56, 170,
  171, 174, 175
crowd sourcing, xxiii, 117
Crowley, Dennis, 76, 77
CSI: New York (television series), 70–71, 82, 84,
  86
customer insights, 1–30
  advertising based on, 5–8
  and experimentation with digital initiatives,
    15–18
  innovation based on, 8–11
  Laura Klauberg on, 1–2, 21–30
  from multiple platforms, 11–14
  and relevance of digital marketing, 2–5
  and traditional advertising, 15–18
customers
  empowered, 227
  relationships with, 59–60, 162–164
  see also consumers
customer service, 80

Dairy Queen, 141
Daisy Maids, 188, 189
Degree (product), 25, 27, 93, 97
Dehnert, Kristin, 121
Dell, 65, 78
Department of Homeland Security, 244
Diet Coke (brand), 92–93
differentiation, product, 157–158
digital age, in-store experiences in, 207–208
digital marketing
  experimentation with, 15–18
  relevance of, 2–5
digital media, 31–57
  Alex Bogusky on, 51–57
  at CareerBuilder.com, 35–36
  at HBO, 32–35

and making it yours, 49
with mobile applications, 45–48
at Pepsi-Cola, 31–32
with personalizable video, 37–40
and traditional advertising, 43–45
at United Nations, 36–37
video content for, 40–43
digital signage, 217–219
digital video recorders, see DVRs
Discovery Channel, 144–145
Disney, Walt, 212
display advertising, 231–232
Domino's Pizza, 52, 79, 80, 160, 161, 174
Doritos, 39, 100, 101, 118–121, 145, 146, 174
Doroff, Frank, on social retailing at Bloomingdale's, 212
Dove, 1, 3–8, 11, 21, 23–25, 28, 92, 95, 118
Drum, Carly, on video games, 147
DVRs (digital video recorders), 92, 160–162

eBay, 52, 235
Electra, Carmen, 37–38
Electric Sheep Company, 80, 82
endorsements, paid, 72–74
entertainment, branded, see branded entertainment
The Entertainment Economy (Michael J. Wolf), 92
ESPN, 87, 102, 192
Ettinger, Amber Lee, 128, 130, 132
events-based social networking sites, 70–72
Everything's Miscellaneous (David Weinberger), 86
Evolution (video), 5–6, 23, 25, 28, 95

Facebook, 2, 157, 159, 160, 192, 215, 242, 253
    apps for, 74–75
    Blue Nile and, 167
    Burger King and, 42
    Coca-Cola and, 12–13
    controversies surrounding, 239–240, 249
    FedEx and, 46
    Laura Klauberg on, 28, 29
    Lynx Effect and, 163–164
    and network effect, 60–62
    Procter & Gamble and, 62–63
    and reason for being, 66–69
Facebook Connect (program), 239–240
Fanta, 148, 149, 194
Federal Trade Commission (FTC), 73, 241
FedEx, 46, 47, 56, 192
feedback, on social networking sites, 77–80
Flickr, 33, 63, 137
42Below (brand), 196–197
Fremont, Carl, 196, 234, 235
Friedrich, Rick, 128, 130
Frito-Lay, 39, 119–120

FTC, see Federal Trade Commission

games, branded, see branded games
Gap, 215
General Electric (GE), 38–39, 174
General Mills, 67, 68, 84
GENERATION WOW (blog), xviii
Goodby, Jeff, 171, 175
Goodby, Silverstein & Partners, 169–177
Google, 9–11, 228, 232, 233, 240–242, 249
Graves, David, on CAM, 238
Greatrex, Mark J., on social networking, 75, 76
Greenberg, Bob, on on-demand content, 160
Groundswell (Josh Bernoff), 78

Harbour, Pamela Jones, on ad-targeting technologies, 241
Hayshar, Norman, on user-generated content, 115
HBO, 32–35, 49, 218
Heikkinen, Sandra, on ad-targeting at Google, 242
Heinz, 113–115, 125
Herbert, Dave, 119–121
Herbert, Joe, 119, 120
Hodder, Kent, 90, 91, 106
House Energy and Commerce Committee, 241
HP, 105, 163, 233–234
Huber, Chet, on local searches, 181
Hulu, xvi, 105
Hyperfactory, 148, 196–197
hyper-targeting, xxiii

IconNicholson, 211, 214
in-game advertising, xxiii, 141–143
innovation, customer insights and, 8–11
insights, of customers, see customer insights
in-store experiences, 207–230
    anticipating consumers wants in, 214–215
    in digital age, 207–208
    digital /signage in, 217–219
    Tom Nicholson on, 221–230
    and on-demand revolution, 208–210
    as services, 215–217
    and social retailing, 211–214
integrated marketing campaigns, 180–181
In the Motherhood (television series), 1, 21, 25, 92, 93, 100–102
iPhones, xii, 27, 46, 48, 74, 181, 191–194, 201, 210, 215
iPod, 158, 167, 171
iTunes, xiv, 167, 235
I've Got a Crush on Obama (video), 128, 129, 131

Jeep, 61, 70, 136, 248
Johnson & Johnson (J&J), 66–67, 70, 79
Jones Soda, 124–125

Kaczmarek, Ed, on applications at Kraft, 193
Kauffman, Leah, 128–130, 132
Keller, Michael, on games at Dairy Queen, 141
Kimball, Charlie, 73–74
Klauberg, Laura, xxi, 2, 21–30
Klein, Russ, 55
Klump, Bill, on "Turkey Talk-Line," 165
Kraft, 193

L.A. Candy (Lauren Conrad), 186
Land Rover, 71, 72, 182
Larrigan, Chris, 113, 114, 121, 125
Lauren, David, on Polo Ralph Lauren, 209
Laurs, Ilja, 196
Lee, Jo, on Bravissimo, 180
Levy, Doug, on mobile applications, 196
Levy, Keith, on Bud.tv, 104
Linden Labs, 65, 80
Lost (television series), 90–91, 135–138, 151–
    154, 156
The Lost Experience, 91, 92, 136, 137, 152–
    154, 156

Macri, Dean, on mobile platforms, 199–205
Madison, Holly, 72
Madison & Vine (publication), 19
Major League Baseball (MLB), 87–88, 192,
    204
Malik, Om, on Beacon program, 249
marketing
    digital, 2–5, 15–18
    integrated, 180–181
    mobile, xxiii, 180–181
    neuro-, 245–246
    proximity, 196–198
    and recession, 19
Markie, Biz, 94, 95
Mars Inc., 63–64
MasterCard, 117, 123
Mayo-Smith, John, on software in advertising,
    44
mBranding, 184
McBrearty, Rachel, on social retailing, 211
McCleary, Bryan, on communication, 10
McConnell, Ted, on social networks, 60, 61
McGuinness, Brian, on Second Life, 65
media, digital, *see* digital media
MET | Hodder (company), 89, 136
Microsoft, 51, 144, 147, 148, 241
MINI USA, 13–14, 45, 243
mixed reality, xxii, *see also* augmented reality
MLB, *see* Major League Baseball
mobile marketing, xxiii, 180–181
mobile platforms, 179–205
    as activation mechanism, 184–186
    advertising in, 182–184
    applications for smart phones in, 191–196
    at Bravissimo, 179–180
    in integrated marketing campaigns, 180–181

Dean Macri on, 199–205
    and proximity marketing, 196–198
    social networking sites for, 75–77
    text messaging in, 186–191
mobs, 190, 191
Monroe, Courtney, 33, 34–35, 261
Monster.com, 35, 136
Morgan, Dave, on behavioral targeting, 236–237
Motrin (brand), 79
Mozes Inc., 190, 191
MTV, 11–12, 62, 69, 82–83, 102, 105, 118
Mukherjee, Ann, on interactions with brands,
    119
multiplatform communication, xxiii
Murphy, Ted, on paid endorsements, 72, 73
Murrow, Noam, 34
MySpace, 60–62, 157, 212, 240

Nanette Lepore (company), 213–214, 218,
    221, 223–225
Nationwide Insurance, 46, 49
Nelson, Chris, 33
Netflix, 235–236
network targeting, 236–239
neuromarketing, 245–246
New Kids on the Block, 190
new media, xiii–xviii
New York Times, 64, 226
Next New Networks, 128, 130, 131, 133
Nicholson, Tom, 211, 212, 221–230
Nigro, Lisa, 100
Nike, 43, 74, 116, 158–160, 174, 194, 195,
    208, 218
Nokia, 44, 159, 203–204
Novo-Nordisk, 73–74

Obama, Barack, 63, 127, 129, 132, 141
O'Brien, Dominick, on personalized content,
    124
on-demand brands, xvii–xix
on-demand revolution
    and banking, xii
    and business, xiii
    and in-store experiences, 208–210
    and television, xi–xii
    terms for, xxii–xxiv
online communities, creating, 65–66
on-site targeting, 235–236
opting out, of smart advertising, 246–249
Organic (company), 61, 247
Ouellette, Nicole, 80

paid endorsements, 72–74
Papa John's, 39, 186
Pattinson, Neville, on RFID technology, 245
PepsiCo, 60, 71
Pepsi-Cola, 31–32, 82, 83, 194
personalizability, ownability, and sharability
    (POS), of branded entertainment, 99–101

personalizable video, 37–40
Peterzell, Lori, on branded games, 141
Pew Internet & American Life Project, 4–5, 114
P&G, *see* Procter & Gamble
Philips, 97–98
Phillips, Wes, 121
PhotoID (application), 194, 195, 208
Pinakatt, Prinz, 148, 185, 261
platforms, 11–14, *see also* mobile platforms
PlayStation 3, 67, 141
PlayStation Home, 67, 69
Polo Ralph Lauren, 192, 209
Ponce, Barbara, on Dream the Impossible website, 98
Porsche, 182–183
Porter, Dorrian, on text messaging by fans, 190, 191
POS (personalizability, ownability, and sharability), of branded entertainment, 99–101
Prada, 211, 221, 222, 243
privacy, smart advertising and, 239–240
Procter & Gamble (P&G), 9–11, 59–60, 62–63, 77, 96, 196, 209
product differentiation, 157–158
product placement, 55, 92–96
products as services, 157–177
  adding value with, 164–166
  as central components of offerings, 166–168
  for DVRs, 160–162
  Nike+ as, 158–160
  and product differentiation, 157–158
  in relationships with customers, 162–164
  Derek Robson on, 169–177
professionals, user-generated content by, 120–123
proximity marketing, 196–198
Prudential Health, 143–144
Pryor, David, on mobile marketing at Porsche, 183

Quick Response (QR) codes, xxiv, 185–186
Quinn, Patrick, on digital media, xvii

Rascal Flatts, 190, 191
Rash, John, on network television, 15
Ray-Ban, 40
Rayport, Jeffrey, on Scion's target audience, 8
reality, augmented, *see* augmented reality
recap specials, 89–90
Reebok, 65, 70
relationships, with customers, 59–60, 162–164
Relles, Ben, on user-generated content, 127–134
retailing, social, 211–212
Reuters, 64, 65
RFID technologies, 14, 45, 211–213, 243–245, 248
R/GA (company), 44, 159–160, 174

Richer, Mark-Hans, on marketing trends, 19
risks, of user-generated content, 117–120
Robson, Derek, xxi, 163, 166, 169–177
The Rookie (initiative), 93, 97, 102
Rosedale, Phillip, 80
"Routan Babymaker 3000" (application), 17, 18
Rubin, Henry Alex, 41

Scheppach, Tracey, on advertising, 136, 137
Schnatter, John, 39
Schwartz, Peter, 248, 251–259
Science + Fiction (company), 93, 99
Scion (brand), 8–9, 94–95, 107–112
Scott, Doug, 96, 105
Scott, Jake, 33
Second Life, 9, 12, 64–65, 70–71, 76, 81–88
sensitive topics, branded games for, 143–144
Sephora, 216–217
services, 215–217, *see also* products as services
Shanken, Marvin R., on Spectator Mobile, 210
sharing, of branded games, 148–149
Sharkey, Tina, 66, 67, 75, 261
short code, xxiv
short message service (SMS), 179–180
Si, Adrian, xxi, 94, 95, 107–112
signage, digital, 217–219
Silverstein, Rich, 170, 175
Simulmedia, 236, 237
Skittles, 63–64
Small Pieces Loosely Joined (David Weinberger), 86
smart advertising, 231–259
  and behavioral targeting, 232–239
  behavior tracking technologies for, 240–243
  consumer control in, 249–250
  display advertising as, 231–232
  and network vs. on-site targeting, 235–239
  and neuromarketing, 245–246
  opting out of, 246–249
  and privacy, 239–240
  RFID technologies in, 243–245
  Peter Schwartz on, 251–259
smart code, xxiv
smart phones, xv, 45–48, 74, 76, 181, 191–196
SMS (short message service), 179–180
Snack Strong Productions, 100, 101
social networking sites, xiv, 59–88
  advertising within, 60–62
  creating online communities with, 65–66
  and customer service, 80
  definition of, xxiv
  events-based, 70–72
  failure of brands on, 62–64
  feedback on, 77–80
  keeping people coming back to, 69–70
  mobile applications for, 74–75
  on mobile phones, 75–77
  paid endorsements on, 72–74
  and personal relationships with brands, 59–60

social networking sites *(continued)*
   and reason for being, 66–69
   Sibley Verbeck on, 80–88
   and virtual worlds, 64–65
social retailing, xxiv, 211–214, 222–225
Solano, Mariana, on advertising at Land Rover, 182
SonicWALL, 146, 147
Sony, 64, 67, 69, 84, 95–96, 98–99, 141
Soohoo, Andrew, on social viewing, 162
Spectator Mobile, 209–210
Spencer, Christophe, on marketing at Calvin Klein, 188
Sprint, 93, 101, 166, 167
Sprite, 75–76, 136, 186
Spychips (Katherine Albrecht), 244
Starbucks, 62, 63, 193
Starwood Hotels, 64, 65
STA Travel, 69, 70, 164
Stevens, Paul, on privacy, 240
Stop and Shop, 214
story of brand, 97–99
"Story Until Now" recap specials, 89–90
Stribling, Susan, on Diet Coke Brand, 93
Suave (brand), 1, 92, 93, 101
Subservient Chicken (website), 42, 52–54, 56, 102
Sullivan, Chuck, on advertising at Jeep, 61

targeted audio, 38
television
   and branded entertainment, 89–91
   and on-demand revolution, xi–xii
   recap specials on, 89–91
Teresi, Todd, on behavioral targeting, 234
text messaging, xv, 179–180, 186–191
Tezanos, Melisa, on control of brand, 116
360-degree programming, xii
TiVo, 52, 92, 160, 161, 235, 236
Toffler, Van, on multiple platforms for MTV, 11, 12
Townsend, Kevin, 93, 97, 99, 101, 104, 106
Toyota, 8–9, 94, 107, 139, 218–219
transaction envelopes, 256
transmedia communication, xxiii
24 (television series), 25, 27, 93, 97, 102
Twitter, xiv–xv, 62, 63, 70–73, 78, 159, 162

UGC, *see* user-generated content
UN (United Nations), 36–37
Unilever, 1, 3, 6, 8, 10, 11, 21, 22, 26, 97, 100, 163
Uniqlo (brand), 47, 49
United Nations (UN), 36–37

upfronts, 22, 26
U.S. Public Interest Research Group, 241
USA Today, 119, 120
user-generated content (UGC), xvi, xxiii, 113–134
   and control of brand, 116–117
   at Heinz, 113–115, 125
   from professionals, 120–123
   Ben Relles on, 127–134
   risks and rewards of, 117–120
   and user-personalized content, 123–125
user-personalized content, 123–125

value, adding, 164–166
value propositions, in branded games, 144–145
van Stolk, Peter, on Jones Soda labels, 125
Ventimiglia, Milo, 93
Verbeck, Sibley, on social networking sites, 80–88
Verklin, David, on CAM, 237
Verma, Sangita, on targeted advertising, 247
video games, xxiii, *see also* branded games
video(s)
   content for, 40–43
   online, xv–xvi
   personalizable, 37–40
viral, 95–96, 102–104
viral videos, xxiv, 95–96, 102–104
virtual worlds, xxiv, 64–65, 67, 68, 70–71
Visa, 68–69, 209
Vogel, Katie, 100
"Voices" campaign, 36–37
Volkswagen, 17–18, 240
"Voyeur" campaign, 32–33, 35

Wacksman, Barry, on technology, 160
Wanamaker, John, on advertising, 238
"weenies," 212
Weinberger, David, 86–87
Weisberg, Rob, on interactive television, 160
"Whopper Freakout" campaign, 41, 55
"Whopper Virgins" (campaign), 41, 52
widgets, xxii
Wine Spectator, 209–210
Wolf, Michael J., 92
Wootten, Rick, 147

Yahoo!, 181, 233–234, 241, 242, 249
YouTube, 6, 32, 41, 78, 114–116, 128, 132, 133, 137, 166, 174

Zuckerberg, Mark, 239, 249, 253
Zuckert, Tim, 138–139, 146–148

ABOUT THE AUTHOR

Over the last few years, Rick Mathieson has emerged as one of the leading voices on marketing in the digital age. An award-winning writer, author, speaker, and frequent media commentator, Mathieson helps brands understand and capitalize on new digital platforms as part of integrated communications initiatives.

His insights on postmodern marketing have been featured in *ADWEEK, Advertising Age, Wired, Broadcasting & Cable, Madison & Vine* and on MSNBC, CBS Radio, and NPR. His research into next-generation business models has earned praise from *USA Today* and Dow Jones Interactive. His first book, *Branding Unbound*, was hailed as "one of the best marketing books of the year" for its "visionary and grounded" perspective on mobile as an emerging marketing and media channel.

Mathieson has also been a featured speaker at industry events such as Digital Hollywood, the Microsoft Leadership Forum, Yahoo's "Branducation" lecture series, the Global Retail Executive Council, and the American Management Association's "Corporate Branding" series, among others.

Over the last few years, he has briefed executives from FedEx, Virgin America, Bloomingdale's, Yahoo, MasterCard, Hard Rock Café, Accenture, Novartis, Franklin Templeton, and many others, on trends in digital marketing and emerging media platforms.

As Harvard Business School's Working Knowledge puts it, Mathieson is "a strategic marketing expert" whose work "demystifies successful practices in a way that should encourage and inspire other marketers."

A veteran of the advertising industry, Mathieson also serves as vice president and creative director for one of Silicon Valley's most prominent advertising agencies. Over the course of his career, he has produced award-winning creative work for a Who's Who of global brand names, including HP, Palm, T-Mobile, Ferrari Club of America/West, and Specialized Bicycles.

Mathieson can be reached via his website at RickMathieson.com.